Mediterr[anean]

Alexandria

Port Said

Lower Egypt

Giza
Saqqara

Cairo
Memphis
Dahshur

*Sinai
Peninsula*

Tell el-Amarna
(*Akhetaten*)

*Red
Sea*

Abydos

Dendera

Valley of
the Kings

Luxor
(*Thebes*)

Upper Egypt

Aswan

OMM SETY'S EGYPT

OMM SETY'S
EGYPT

A Story of Ancient Mysteries, Secret Lives,
and the Lost History of the Pharaohs

Hanny el Zeini & Catherine Dees

PITTSBURGH

Omm Sety's Egypt
A Story of Ancient Mysteries, Secret Lives, and
the Lost History of the Pharaohs

Copyright © 2007 by Hanny el Zeini and Catherine Dees

ISBN-13: 978-0-9767631-3-0
ISBN-10: 0-9767631-3-3

Library of Congress Control Number: 2006927425
CIP information available upon request

First Edition, 2007

St. Lynn's Press • POB 18680 • Pittsburgh, PA 15236
412.466.0790 • www.stlynnspress.com

Grateful acknowledgment is given to the following: to Jonathan Cott for
permission to quote from the poems of Omm Sety; to Dr. Nicholas Reeves
for permission to quote from copyrighted material posted on
valleyofthekings.org; to Mark Stone for the maps and diagrams and other
original artwork that appear in this book. Unless otherwise stated,
all photographs are copyrighted by Hanny el Zeini. Every effort has
been made to trace and contact copyright holders. If an omission is
brought to our notice we will be pleased to correct the situation
in future editions of the book.

Cover Design – Jeff Nicoll
Book Design – Holly Wensel, NPS
Editor – Abby Dees

Printed in the United States of America
on recycled paper ♲

This title and all of St. Lynn's Press books may be purchased for educational,
business, or sales promotional use. For information please write:
Special Markets Department, St. Lynn's Press, POB 18680,
Pittsburgh, PA 15236

10 9 8 7 6 5 4 3 2 1

to

Omm Sety
True-of-Voice
Maat-Kheru

that her name may be remembered

Table of Contents

I wake in the dark to the stirring of birds,
a murmur in the trees, a flutter of wings.
It is the morning of my birth, the first of many.
The past lies knotted in its sheets asleep.

from *Awakening Osiris: the Egyptian Book of the Dead*
trans. by Normandi Ellis

What if, one day, you fell down and lost consciousness, and when
you woke up you found strange memories in your head? And
what if you pursued those memories, only to discover that they
had instead been pursuing *you*?

PROLOGUE

Egypt

Giza – March 23, 1956

Just before midnight, a sun-bronzed Englishwoman climbed unnoticed to the top of the Great Pyramid and stayed through the long, cold night. She was 52, an accomplished student of ancient Egypt, and a woman with a complicated inner life.

She hugged herself against the chill and watched the dazzling bowl of stars turn slowly overhead.

In a few hours she would board a train with a one-way ticket in her hand – her destination, Abydos, a remote village with a ruined temple where she had left her heart more than 3000 years before. She knew that once she returned to the place where the memories began she would never leave. There wasn't a doubt in her mind. She had made a promise.

At dawn she picked her way carefully down the great, uneven stones at the northeast corner of the pyramid, said goodnight to a surprised guard, and returned to her apartment to gather up her few possessions.

Abydos was the ancient name of the place she remembered, but in 1956 Abydos did not appear on most Egyptian maps. Instead, about 350 miles south of Cairo there was a barely visible dot labeled *el Araba el Madfouna* – The Buried Hamlet.

When the woman presented herself at the ticket counter of the Cairo central station the clerk assumed she would purchase a round-trip ticket, but she said no. He tried to explain in English the economy of buying a two-way ticket. Again she said no, but he persisted. To put an end to this futile discussion she told him she was going to el Araba el Madfouna and nowhere else.

"And where the devil is this Araba?" he said.

She informed him it was quite simply the most important place in Egypt.

"Believe me, Madame, I have never heard of it. Is it one of the villages – a dependency of el Baliana?"

"Yes," she said with perverse pleasure, "and to satisfy your curiosity, I am going to *live* there, too."

The poor man, incredulous, turned to the senior clerk on the bench behind and whispered in Arabic: *This blue-eyed khawagaya* is going to live in a place called el Araba el Madfouna. She must be suffering from the sun.* She laughed to herself and pretended she hadn't understood a word of it, but of course she had. "So it is a one-way ticket to Baliana," he said, handing her the change. "May God protect you, Madame!"

As the train pulled away from the station heading south, she piled her things around her in the compartment and watched the sprawling old city recede from her sight. She would miss Cairo and the people in it, her friends of many adventures. And she would miss the old museum with its dusty, busy rooms where she had prowled so freely these past twenty years.

Now, all the farewell cups of tea had been drunk, the teary hugs dispensed with, and she had taken her last nostalgic walk through the museum's cluttered corridors. Goodbyes were hard, but there were no regrets. Her thoughts were on Abydos.

Through the grimy veil of her train car window the modern world was soon left behind and a far older one began moving slowly across the passenger's field of vision. She had purposely taken a seat on the right side of the train where she could see the silhouettes of the many pyramids that stood in a 40-mile chain along the edge of the Western Desert – first Khufu's, Menkhaure's, and Khafra's, and then Zoser's Step Pyramid, glimpsed through thick groves of palms, with the crumbling pyramids of

---

*European woman

Abusir beyond. And then the pyramids of Dahshur – the ones she knew intimately from her years with the great archaeologist Dr. Ahmed Fakhri. Of all the people she had worked with since she came to Egypt, Dr. Fakhri had been the kindest to her. It was because of him she was on her way to Abydos today.

Her train sped south, a noisy iron creature disturbing the quiet of the scattered mud-brick villages, causing sudden eruptions of white egrets from the lush green fields and earthen canals as it passed. After a while the patchworks of village cultivation began to change, and now there were monochromatic tracts of tall sugarcane that extended all the way to the sheer limestone cliffs to the west.

Three hundred and forty miles from Cairo, at the provincial town of el Baliana, the woman left the train and took a taxi the final miles to her destination.

It was late afternoon when the car made its dusty, bumpy entry into the dun-colored settlement, with dogs and children chasing after. Foreigners were a rarity here, except for the ones who sometimes came for a while to work in the ruins of the Sety Temple, but they never stayed. Tourist amenities – let alone electricity and running water – had yet to come to this God-forsaken village in the middle of nowhere. That day, nobody in the village of el Araba el Madfouna could have guessed that the khawagaya was coming to stay for good.

She told the driver to leave her at the outskirts of the Sety Temple precincts. As she stepped out she was greeted with curious stares, but that didn't concern her; there was something she needed to do before anything else. Immediately, she set down her modest belongings and entered a small cafeteria where she paid the proprietor for some bread and beer. Outside again, she pulled a handful of wildflowers from the banks of the irrigation canal – and with this collection of beer, bread and flowers she walked with determined steps towards the temple.

It was the rule then to close the main gate before sunset, which the guards were only too happy to do. In the Buried

Hamlet one didn't linger near the haunted ruins after sundown. There were many things to fear here, not the least being the distant escarpment called Pega that each night cast its ominous shadow over miles of ancient burial grounds and engulfed the temple, gathering up the souls of the dead.

With the sun still well above Pega, the stranger calmly removed her shoes, entered the temple through the first court, walked until she came to the small chapel of Osiris, and there laid out her humble offering.

To this woman who remembered – who had known it when it was newly built – it was still beautiful beyond words. No matter that the temple's roof was missing and that the outer courts were a shambles, or that her glorious gardens were nowhere to be seen. She was home.

Her name was Dorothy Eady, but the world would know her as Omm Sety.

From the BBC announcement of its 1981 film, "Omm Sety and her Egypt":

> *Omm Sety has become one of the most famous characters in Egypt. Tourists go to Abydos not just to see the monuments, but to see Omm Sety herself.*

Of all the adventuring Englishwomen of the 20th century, none ever ventured into the exotic realms of past and present in quite the way Dorothy Eady did.

Dorothy was the name she was given at her birth in 1904. When she died in the Egyptian village of Abydos she had long been known as Omm Sety, the intriguing, unconventional, out-

spoken woman who was devoted to the worship of Isis and
Osiris. She had another name as well, an ancient one that had
once belonged to a young, blue-eyed priestess of Isis: Bentreshyt
– *Harp-of-Joy*.

She was all of these.

Not to be confused with the many born-again Nefertitis,
Hatshepsuts and Cleopatras among us, Omm Sety had her feet
planted firmly on sensible ground, scholarly ground. She was a
largely self-taught Egyptologist who had worked under some of
the greatest archaeologists of her time. Omm Sety's resourceful, original mind won her respect and regard in the community
of Egyptologists. Though she had a cautious disdain for other
people's paranormal claims, especially when they involved past
lives in ancient Egypt, the inescapable truth was this: All the
while she was working in the temples and pyramids of Egypt she
was living a secret double life as the beloved of a 3300-year-old
pharaoh who could materialize at will from the Beyond.

During her long career with the Egyptian Antiquities
Department she was responsible for a number of significant
finds. However, almost no one knew that her uncanny gift for
analysis and discovery was at times aided by something, and
someone, "extra" – and by her own vivid memories of a life in
19th Dynasty Egypt.

Ever since she was a child growing up in England she had
had uninvited paranormal experiences – visitations, visions,
unnerving premonitions. She was reluctant to speak of them,
knowing what people would think. It was her business and no
one else's what went on inside her private world. And for much
of her life she was happy to keep it that way, until she found a
confidant to whom she could finally tell everything. Even after
years of our knowing one another, she was reluctant to call me
by my first name alone, preferring to call me Dr. Hani.

Omm Sety was my friend. I use that word to the fullest
extent of its meaning. To an outsider, our friendship must have
seemed an unlikely one. She was the eccentric, the outrageously

frank, the impenetrable – while I was the scientist, the practical one with heavy responsibilities in the world of industry. Nevertheless, we became friends almost immediately upon our first meeting in 1956.

It was really very odd, the way our paths converged. There is a Turkish word, *kismet* – in Arabic we say *kesma* – the unknowable workings of destiny.

Within a few months of Omm Sety's arrival in Abydos I was realizing my own long-held dream. I was 38 and had just been named chairman of the Egyptian Sugar and Distillery Company. My family and I had taken up residence in the company's main compound at Nag-Hamadi, only a short drive from Abydos. Because I had always had a keen interest in archaeology and personally knew many of the working archaeologists and their projects, I was eager to explore the latest excavations at Abydos. But it wasn't until the end of that year that I could take time away from my new job.

By then I had already heard of Omm Sety. News travels fast in the Egyptian countryside. This was during the troubling period of the Suez Canal Crisis, when there was a great deal of anti-British sentiment. One of the drivers for our company, who lived in a village close to Abydos, came to me with the story that a khawagaya from England had joined a demonstration of young students who were shouting anti-British slogans. This sounded quite incredible. I assumed the woman must be one of those cranks who sometimes get an infatuation with Egypt and vent their feelings in the most bizarre style; although it did intrigue me to learn that this woman had recently left the comforts and good life of Cairo to come and settle in such an isolated and lonely place.

What I encountered on my first visit to Abydos that December was hardly a crank, but a sharp-witted, vital woman with blue eyes and light blond hair. And wonderfully funny. The day I arrived she lost no time giving me her opinion about the British, which included some choice and very earthy Arabic swear words. I had never met anyone quite like her.

She had a makeshift office inside the Sety Temple where her job was sorting and fitting together thousands of inscribed stone fragments and making accurate drawings of them all. As I looked at the colossal heap of fragments I didn't envy her the task, but she seemed quite happy. At that time the Sety Temple was in a sorry state of disrepair, as was the adjacent ruin known as the Osirion, an underground structure of austere beauty and mysterious origin. To anyone who understood the history and significance of Abydos, the condition of its principal monuments was heartbreaking. The Sety Temple contained some of the most sublimely beautiful incised wall art found anywhere in Egypt, and here it sat, roofless and open to the elements. It was all but forgotten. In time, Omm Sety would single-handedly change all that.

Our early meetings were brief and far apart, but eventually I was able to go to Abydos once or twice a month. Because of Omm Sety's presence and encyclopedic knowledge of the Sety Temple I always came away knowing more than when I arrived.

Our common point of interest was our fascination with Egypt's lost past. It was a past to which she seemed to have unusual access – something I did not understand about her at first, since she was not a university-trained Egyptologist. I did not yet know that some of her easy familiarity with New Kingdom history and details of the original temple architecture were a result of her relationship with the very man who had built the temple – Sety I, the great 19th Dynasty pharaoh.

It was many years into our friendship before she told me about the secret side of her life, knowing how peculiar I would find it. For a long time I was the only other person who knew. At first I couldn't let myself believe it, even though I considered Omm Sety to be the most transparently truthful person I had ever known. Reincarnation was not a new concept to me, but her situation was so unusual that I had to think about it for quite some time.

In many ways she appeared to be living more in the past than the present – completely naturally and without affectation. I saw that she always removed her shoes upon entering the temple, and that she never missed a day of placing offerings in the shrines of Isis and Osiris, even when she was quite ill. She had made a religious calendar for herself that gave the proper prayers and offerings for each day of the ancient Egyptian year. She knew the time-honored folk practices – some would call it magic – for assisting women in childbirth and for protecting the village children from scorpions. All of this I saw and respected.

As the years passed, I grew concerned that much of what she knew would be lost. Even though bits and pieces of her story were known to some of her closer friends, no one knew it all. I encouraged her to begin keeping a personal diary of Sety's nighttime visits and their wide-ranging conversations – which included revelations about some of the most recognizable royal names in Egyptian history: Nefertiti, Akhenaten, Hatshepsut, Sneferu, Ramesses II, Queen Tiy; and of course, Sety himself. I also began bringing my tape recorder with me when I dropped in. I felt it was important to capture this living archive of knowledge about Egypt's past, not only for my own curiosity, but for posterity and for a new generation of Egyptologists to consider.

She developed the habit of sending me her diaries and extensive notes at the end of each year. After her heart attack in 1972 she had become reluctant to leave her personal writings in her home, should anything happen to her. If I was abroad or in Cairo she would send them through my driver or a trusted friend.

The tapes and diaries preserved the record of an extraordinary life, but beyond that, they gave important clues to some of the puzzling unknowns of Egyptian history. In the 25 years since her death, new discoveries have validated many of her insights. I am not surprised; I expect that more will come.

By the end of her life she had a worldwide roster of friends and admirers, and tourists were streaming to Abydos. Sadly, she died just a few days before the BBC aired its documentary about her, *Omm Sety and Her Egypt*. Her passing was noted in the *Times* of London and in other newspapers around the world.

Today, when I listen to the tapes of our many conversations, her vivid personality fills the room and I see us sitting again at the edge of the Osirion on a warm Egyptian afternoon, speaking of ancient things. We are in a timeless state. I hear her clear voice describing what she believes to be the location of a great Hall of Records at Luxor. I hear us engaged in one of our heated debates about the pharaoh Akhenaten, a man she thoroughly disdained for throwing over the old religion and weakening the empire. And then I hear her in a calmer mood saying matter-of-factly, "I know where the tomb of Nefertiti exists."

When I open the pages of her diaries, I find evidence of a love that is beyond our normal definition of it: *His Majesty came again last night. I was asleep and he woke me with many kisses....* Here was Sety, apparently flesh and blood, visiting his lover in her tiny garden, coming to her from his abode in Amenti, the strange interpenetrating world beyond that somehow allowed them to touch. And here was Omm Sety, a woman well past middle age, whom Sety still saw as the young girl he loved and lost and found again.

A number of years ago I had the privilege of collaborating with journalist and author Jonathan Cott on a book about Omm Sety's life.* But, as always with a life so complex and layered, there is more to be told. In Omm Sety's case, I feel I owe it to her and to history to tell the rest of her story, especially as it relates to the unsolved mysteries of Egypt's past. I am joined in this present book by Catherine Dees, a friend and writer who shares my deep love of Egypt.

Our own friendship extends back nearly twenty years to a dinner party in Cairo where we were seated next to each other at a table with several Egyptologists, whom I knew very well. Catherine had been to Egypt twice before and was doing research for a historical novel. As she jokingly told my wife and me that

---

*Jonathan Cott, *The Search for Omm Sety*, Doubleday, 1987, Warner, 1989

evening, she was looking for an excuse to stay in Egypt and not have to return home to the "real world."

At one point the conversation around us turned to the frustrating problems of archaeological exploration and the usefulness of some of the modern non-invasive techniques. A Japanese team had just been in Cairo to scan the Great Pyramid with a sophisticated sensing device, looking for hidden chambers.

One of the Egyptologists, an Englishman, made a doubting face. "If Omm Sety were still here I'd take her word for where things can be found, any day, over the most state-of-the-art equipment out there." Others nodded.

It was a private opinion given in a private setting. Such blasphemy would never be uttered in public, no matter how much these scholarly men might have admired the mysterious ways of Omm Sety's mind. Much of her knowledge had come from decidedly unscientific sources and could not be acknowledged as anything but intriguing speculation. But after a little wine around a convivial table they had to admit that Omm Sety knew things that no one could possibly know.

She had been gone seven years by then, but she had left a vivid imprint on many people's lives, including mine. For the rest of the evening we took turns recalling some of her exploits and achievements. "I wish I could have known her," Catherine said with obvious regret.

The following year I invited Catherine and two friends to join me on a driving trip to Abydos. She and I had been enjoying a brisk correspondence about Egyptian history and I had a feeling that my new friend could use some first-hand exposure to many of the things we had been talking about in our letters. We traveled south from modern Cairo into the heart of old Egypt, observing a way of life little changed from pharaonic days. We visited the site of Akhenaten's sacred city of the sun at Amarna and lingered in the haunted ruins.

When we reached Abydos all of us could feel the looming presence of the distant escarpment called Pega. Entering the Sety Temple, we removed our shoes – out of respect, as

Omm Sety always did. We took our time visiting every hall and court of the temple, admiring the beautiful sculptured figures of the gods to whom Omm Sety made her offerings on feast days, including "My Lady Isis." This was a tour like the countless tours Omm Sety had given to anyone who wanted to understand the wonders of the temple.

At the end of one passage we faced the exterior wall of the Hall of the Sacred Barques – the room that once contained the ceremonial boats used in sacred processions for carrying the statues of the gods. The hall was closed. We peered through the iron grating in the heavy metal door. This was the domain of Omm Sety, her "office." I asked one of the watchmen to ask the chief *ghaffir** to bring the key and open the door for us to go inside. The ghaffir came in a hurry, apologizing earnestly for not having the key. "Omm Sety always had the key in a small hand-bag that she kept fixed around her waist," he explained. "I think it must have been buried along with her." We had no choice but to continue looking through the bars. There was the bench at which she used to sit to make her drawings of the temple frag-ments, with paper still on it and two unfinished colored scenes, the last things she had been working on.

We left the temple and came out into the open air. A few yards to the west, deep inside an enormous depression, is one of the most imposing, majestically serene monuments of ancient Egypt: the Osirion. We stood at the top looking down at the architectural wonder. Peace and a sense of the holy infused this place. I could imagine the frail form I had last seen eight years earlier, a few months before her death. Her presence was always powerful, even at the end. Omm Sety was with us here. As we left Abydos, Catherine said, "Now I feel that I've met her."

When I decided to write this book, the memory of that visit came vividly to my mind. I asked Catherine to be my co-author and she graciously accepted. In this book there will be two identifiable voices, Omm Sety's and my own. This is only

---

*watchman

part of the truth. My co-author's contribution has been substantial and invaluable.

I pray that Omm Sety is pleased with our efforts and is living in great joy with His Majesty in the heavenly halls of Amenti.

ONE

The Way It Was

*"If you could only imagine how beautiful it was.
How can I tell you...?" OS*

It is said that the Nile resembles a lotus plant, with its roots
buried deep in the African continent and its flower opening
into the broad delta far to the north. If you look at a map,
it is very easy to make that small leap into symbolism. The
ancients would have seen that and more, because for them the
lotus had layers of meaning beyond simply its beautiful form.
Modern culture is not always comfortable with blurring the lines
between what we call "reality" and wishful thinking. But if you
were living in the Egypt of 1300 BC, everything was more than
it appeared. Every place you set your foot was filled with the
energy of the *neteru*, the gods.

That was then, you could say, but even today there are signs
of the old gods lingering among the ruined temples and shrines
that lie along the river's banks. When you leave the cities and go
out into the countryside, if you know how to listen and observe,
you find echoes of that distant past in the villages, though less
and less now. Newer forms of religious devotions may have
swept away the old, but the folk practices speak of an elder time
– like women still leaving offerings before images of the goddess Hathor, praying for a son, and married couples reverently
touching an ancient statue of Sekhmet for help with infertility.

Omm Sety knew only too well how the past can haunt the
present.

Sometime in the early 1970s Omm Sety and I were sitting together in the small cafeteria near the Sety Temple when a group of French tourists arrived, filling all the empty tables. Someone turned on a cassette recorder and we heard the famous Franco-Egyptian singer Dalida crooning a melancholy Gypsy song in which a girl asks a handsome man,

> *And you, beautiful Gypsy prince –*
> *From what country do you come?*

and he replies sadly,

> *I come from a homeland*
> *That does not exist anymore.*

I translated the French words for Omm Sety and she fell into one of those long spells of silence with which I was already familiar. I let her have her reverie. After a while she said in a distant, dreamy voice, "And me, I come from a homeland that is living in my heart – now, and as it was before." She finished in a whisper, "If you could only imagine how beautiful it was. How can I tell you…?"

1300 BC

What was it like, this homeland of her heart? This was the Black Land, whose people greeted the sun each day with gratitude and prayers under the watchful gaze of the gods. The dark soil beneath their feet was rich and fertile because each year the river god Hapi brought them the Inundation; and at night when they cast their eyes upward they saw the body of the sky goddess, Nut, arched against the canopy of the heavens. Each night she swallowed the sun and gave it forth again by day.

Theirs was a world of beauty and symmetry, gods and magic. Chief among the gods was Amun of Thebes, who contained within himself aspects of all the other neteru.

No people loved earthly life more, yet death was not to be feared. They knew that eternal life awaited them in the land of the West, which they called Amenti. If they feared anything, it was the moment when the acts of their hearts would be weighed before the Lord Osiris in the hall of judgment, and all secrets would be known.

In this blessed world the highest duty of its king was to preserve the perfectly balanced Order-of-Things set into place in the beginning by the unknowable One-Beyond-All, the giver of life. To violate this trust was to invite Chaos to the Black Land. And so the people looked to their king to protect them from the terrors of Chaos, and they did their part by observing the daily rituals and offerings that told the gods all was well in the Black Land.

But all had not always been well. Fifty years before this time, a new kind of king had come to the throne in Thebes – a religious visionary with his own concept of the Order-of-Things, and a zealous devotion to a single, exclusive god: the Aten, the Disc-of-the-Sun. In a stunning decree he abolished the worship of the old gods. There would be no more Amun, no Lord Osiris to judge the deeds of the heart, no compassionate Lady Isis, no Horus to battle evil, no Hathor to protect women and children. No god but the Aten, remote and unknowable.

The Amun priesthood and temples held vast estates, with huge bureaucracies to run them. Now the temples were closed and their revenues used to pay for construction of the king's splendid new city of the sun, Akhetaten.* Everything was suddenly in disarray. Corruption among public servants grew rampant. Abroad, Egypt's far-flung empire fell prey to enemies because of the king's inattention. He was not a warrior like some of the great kings before him, he was a poet who seemed to spend much of his time in ecstatic contemplation of his unique god.

The king was Akhenaten; his queen was Nefertiti. Later pages will speak more about this complex man and his reign, and

---

*modern Tell el-Amarna

3

about the mysterious, powerful Nefertiti. After he died, his successors referred to him only as *the criminal* or *the heretic*, and they lost no time undoing the effects of his religious revolution.

Into this moment in Egypt's history came a king named Sety, a brilliant man of restless energy. His cartouche name was *Men-Maat-Ra*, meaning Enduring-is-the-Truth-of-Ra. By nature and by heritage he was a military man, following in the steps of his father, Ramesses I, and before that, the kingship of the admirable general, Horemheb. Sety's reign had one overarching theme: to put right what had been disturbed, by securing the outposts of empire and restoring equilibrium to Egyptian life at home. He understood very well the psychological necessity of religious tradition in the lives of his people, and so he sponsored magnificent additions to Amun's great temple at Thebes, and built other striking monuments and temples, all to give honor to the old gods. The most beautiful of these would be in Abydos – and for good reason.

Abydos

When Omm Sety tried to explain to the incredulous clerk at the Cairo train station that Abydos was the most important place in Egypt, it was a true statement – except that it was a few thousand years late.

No one really knows when this piece of fertile land at the desert's edge became the spiritual heart of ancient Egypt. To someone living in those times it seemed as if it had always been so. Lying on the western side of the Nile 90 miles north of Luxor (ancient Thebes), Abydos is held within the curved embrace of a high limestone mountain. Its two jutting projections still bear the old names *Lord of Offerings* and *Lady of Life*. Since pre-dynastic times there had been burials here, and by the earliest dynasties kings and nobles were building their tombs and monuments in the shadow of the holy mountain. Why did they choose this place over other sacred locations in Egypt? It may have been because of the deep notch in the mountain's silhouette

– Pega, the gateway to the West, the land of the dead. But more than anything, they chose Abydos because the tomb of their savior-god Osiris was here.

Every Egyptian child knew the story: Osiris had once lived on earth as a man, born of Earth and Sky. He brought civilization to the people of the Nile and taught them agriculture, writing, the great laws of life and the worship of the gods. He was their beloved king and he was everything that was good and compassionate, as was his beautiful sister-wife Isis, mistress of healing and magic. There was another sister, the protective goddess Nephthys.

But in the Black Land such goodness could not exist without the challenge of the forces of darkness. Osiris had a brother, Set, who out of anger and jealousy arranged to have him killed on the banks of the Nile at Abydos. His body was cut up into many parts and strewn over the length of the land, and the triumphant Set took his brother's throne. Meanwhile, the grieving Isis was working a great magic to bring her husband back to life. Yet even with the most powerful magic Osiris could only stay on earth long enough for his son Horus to be conceived. With the final death of his body, Osiris went on to become lord of the Underworld and judge of souls, but his essence would be held within his tomb at Abydos (one version of the story says that only the head of Osiris was entombed there). Horus-the-Son was to live forever to avenge his father's death and continue the battle against Set's forces of chaos.

This allegory of good and evil, death and resurrection and the salvation of souls was carried deep in the psyche of the Egyptian people. Every year, pilgrims from every part of Egypt streamed into Abydos for the Feast of Osiris to witness a sacred seven-day mystery pageant, a re-enactment of the life, death and resurrection of the god. It climaxed with a great battle between Horus and Set, which Horus always won, to the wild cheers of those who participated and watched.

At the end of the pageant, as Omm Sety described it, there was loud rejoicing, with songs of triumph. "The actual death and resurrection of Osiris took place inside," she explained from her own remembrance, "and only the priests and priestesses were present. The part of Osiris was never played by a person, but a life-sized wooden statue. Then the god was carried outside, upright, as a living god rather than as a dead mummy. There came the words, *Osiris, our hope, Osiris, Osiris!* as the people greeted their risen god."

The parts of the other gods were played by priests and priestesses specially trained for their privileged roles in the mystery play. A priestess playing Isis, for instance, might apprentice for years to perfect the gestures and song of the *Lament for Osiris*, in which she grieves for her murdered husband and entreats him to return to her. With her in grief is her faithful sister Nephthys, and together they cry out for Osiris to return.

Each year began with this highly ritualized celebration of the mystery of the Holy Family of Egypt, and each year Osiris died and rose again as a promise to all who witnessed that they too could overcome death and be as gods.

A pilgrimage to Abydos was a chance to present one's soul to Osiris and be washed clean again. If you had the good fortune to die at that moment, you were doubly blessed. People left instructions in their wills that their hearts were to be buried at Abydos, and if that were not possible then a stone monument, a cenotaph, would be erected instead. Down through the ages, the sacred burial grounds of Abydos became filled with cenotaphs of kings and nobles and ordinary people wishing for an eternity with their beloved god.

It was natural that Sety would want to add to the monuments in such a holy place, especially after the years of Akhenaten's great heresy. Whenever Sety was not occupied on the eastern frontiers, he visited his new temple to oversee its progress. Nearby, he erected a small palace retreat for himself, which he named *Heartsease*, a poignant choice for someone whose personal life had seen its full measure of heartache and betrayal.

He was a man of greatness and valor, but he was also a man of sorrows whose rash heart led him one fateful day to disturb the Order-of-Things – not in the grave manner of the Heretic, but a disturbance nonetheless. He knew that for the sin of entering into a forbidden love he had brought down upon himself the punishment of the gods.

Sety's sin is not to be found in history books, it probably never will – but it plays an important part in our story, for it was the cause of his 3300-year search for a young temple priestess named Bentreshyt, and for atonement in the holy city of Abydos.

This is a story about Egypt – about a particular moment in its long history, and how that moment cast its shadow forward across time.*

---

*Note: Throughout the book, Omm Sety's quoted words are taken from conversations I and others had with her, from her personal notes and diaries, and from articles she wrote.

TWO

Dorothy

"'But when I grow up,' I told him,
'I'm going to live in Egypt.'" OS

Nothing about Omm Sety was ever ordinary – not her exuberant laugh, her questing mind, or her larger-than-life presence. Even if she had had no psychic connection at all with the far past, her intellect alone would have left a memorable legacy. That legacy will feature prominently in our book. But there are certain things about her life that should be spoken of first.

In the early years of our friendship I knew very little about Omm Sety's life before Egypt. I knew that her father, Reuben Eady, had been a tailor and that the family had lived in a flat in a London suburb and that she was an only child. In time, she began telling me about her early life, starting with an incident in 1907 when she was three.

When the family doctor answered the urgent call to the Eady residence he arrived to find Dorothy Louise unconscious at the bottom of a steep staircase. The doctor carefully examined the girl and could find no pulse or other signs of life. He sadly informed the parents that their child had died, then went back to his office to prepare the death certificate.

On his return an hour later, the doctor was dumbfounded to find that the dead had apparently come back to life, and was at that moment playing on her bed, fully alert, her plump cheeks stuffed with candy, while her parents hovered anxiously.

Most peculiar of all, Dorothy began talking about going home, even though, of course, she *was* home.

But that wasn't what she meant. There were new thoughts in her mind now, new images – new memories. Soon after the accident Dorothy began having dreams of a beautiful building with huge columns and the loveliest garden extending far off to one side. In that garden she saw pools, stone paths and tall trees.

Being only three, she didn't have words to describe the magnificent temple she was seeing because she had never seen anything like it in her short life. But she knew this place was *home*. Sometimes she would cry bitterly, begging her parents to let her return there. Reuben and Caroline Eady didn't take the matter seriously at first; such childhood fantasies were transient things, their friends assured them.

"All I can remember about the fall," Omm Sety once told me, "is that when I regained consciousness I felt, well, sort of funny. It was as though I not only changed my skin, which was black and blue with bumps all over, but I also felt that something in my head had changed its orientation. I was not the same after that."

A few years ago, I met a woman who was a distant relative of Omm Sety's on her father's side. She had come to Egypt with a group of British tourists. In our conversation about Dorothy I asked what she knew about the fall down the stairs. She said that the family believed the whole affair about her "dying" had really been a case of an elderly doctor's poor eyesight and malfunctioning stethoscope. It was a bad concussion, nothing more. If that was so, I asked, then how do we explain the sudden change that came over her when she woke again? The dear woman had no answer. Whatever the explanation, the child appeared to have awakened from her fall with an overlay of images and memory quite apart from anything she had encountered in her first three years as Dorothy Eady.

I recently came across an interesting passage from Omm Sety's diaries, dated August 20, 1972. She and Sety had been speaking about someone from His Majesty's past, and Sety mentioned that the person was living again on earth. Omm Sety then asks if the person had been reborn as a baby, and Sety replies,

> *"I do not think so. People are sent back to earth for two reasons, usually to pay for some sin; more rarely, to fulfill some important work in the world. For the first reason they are usually sent into a body very closely resembling their original one. They enter the new body at the very moment of its death, or at a time when it is deeply unconscious. This is what happened to you, and though you were only a little child, you became different."*

> *I said, "Some people believe that everyone returns to earth, over and over again, until at last they become perfect and sinless and become part of the being of the Great God."*

> *He said, "If they believe this, perhaps it happens so for them. But for us, it is not so."*

When Dorothy was four, the family went on an outing to the British Museum. It was going to be a boring place, she thought, because she was expected to be quiet and walk slowly. As they entered the Egyptian Galleries she was suddenly transfixed by all the statues and animal-headed gods. She gazed intently at them, then began to run about and kiss the feet of each one, oblivious to the laughter around her. Her parents were embarrassed to be part of this scene, and it only got worse. When it came time to leave, Dorothy refused, screaming that these were her people and she wanted to stay with them. Prying their hysterical child from the feet of the Egyptian statues, the Eadys hurried her from the museum.

Some time later her father brought home an exploration magazine with a series of Egyptian photographs. One showed the half-buried Sety Temple at Abydos. It was roofless and the courts were full of sand. In front of the building was a sort of lake with two fishermen who held strange-looking nets. Dorothy recognized the temple at once. This was the home of her dreams, except that in her dreams it was always perfect and now it wasn't. And there was a picture of the well-preserved mummy of Sety I, which she recognized as well. She *knew* him.

She pestered her parents anew with her fantastic tale, this time saying that the Sety Temple was her home. They were vexed and at a loss, even a bit frightened. They could only hope that she would outgrow whatever the problem was. Her father didn't judge her too harshly, for reasons of his own. Although he was a fine, established master tailor with a devoted clientele, he had unfulfilled dreams of his own, dreams of a life in show business. Like his daughter, he was restless and unpredictable and given to drama. Reuben Eady had Irish blood in his veins, Omm Sety liked to say, explaining the family eccentricities.

When Dorothy was six or seven there was an incident at school. Her teacher had discovered her unusual talent for art and drawing and had asked her to draw a cat and a fox for display in the classroom. Which she did, except that the perfectly drawn cat's head had the body of a human female, and the fox had the body of a man – both looking vaguely Egyptian.

"Why would you do such a thing?" the teacher demanded.

"Because they look more beautiful this way," Dorothy said. The pictures were never displayed.

Dorothy couldn't help creating incidents. She had a pronounced sense of justice and an affinity for underdogs, which often put her in the way of trouble. On the way home from school one day she saw two men engaged in a street fight – Cockneys, she recalled. One was a big hulk of a man and the other was younger and much smaller, and being beaten to a pulp while a crowd egged them both on. It was unbearable to watch. Counting on her way with words, she convinced a passerby to lend her his hockey stick – just so that she could feel the weight of it, she said sweetly – then she ran into the middle of the melee and struck the big man hard on his back with her weapon. The sight of the small girl and the large stick stopped the bully in his tracks. He shouted obscenities at her as the owner of the hockey stick ran to reclaim it and pull the girl to safety.

This was a child who did not consider the consequences of her actions if she believed she was in the right. It was a trait that was to leave a considerable amount of disturbance in her wake, even up to the last days of her life. But with her engaging smile and explosive laugh she was usually forgiven her well-intentioned excesses.

In her family and among close relatives there were no children her age, and the children she knew from school didn't understand her at all. She had no use for toys or dolls. She would rather be alone reading books about Egypt. Her other consuming passion was for animals. She would pick up anything that came her way that had no obvious home: frogs, snakes, lizards, wild rabbits. Her harried mother never knew what was about to join the rag-tag menagerie, but the poor child had few friends, she reasoned, so what was the harm in it?

In London, Dorothy's youngest aunt, only a few years older, was her closest friend and confidant. She had accompanied the family on that outing to the museum and she was fascinated by Dorothy's strange ideas about things. They delighted in their time together, talking and giggling late into the night when they were supposed to be asleep. From beneath the covers they would chant their rebellious anthem:

Early to rise, early to bed
Makes you healthy, wealthy and dead!

When they talked about what they would do when they were grown, one of them, at least, knew exactly what her plans were, and her final destination – and that one was Dorothy.

I remember asking Omm Sety if she thought that her bizarre childhood behavior had to do with that fall, and she answered with her charming sense of humor, "Well, it *is* quite possible that my chute down the staircase could have knocked some screws loose in my head."

Whatever it was, her father's tolerance had finally been worn away. His only hope was that a proper and sober schooling would fill her mind with more normal ideas. He enrolled her in a good school and hoped for the best, but Reuben Eady was no match for his daughter's stubborn determination. Every chance she got she would sneak out of school, a truant, and go to the British Museum.

the famous Dr. Budge

By the age of ten she had become something of a fixture in the Egyptian Galleries, and Sir E. A. Wallis Budge, the renowned Egyptologist and director of the collection, had noticed her. He wondered what on earth the child could be doing, staring at the hieroglyphic inscriptions with such intensity.

One day he asked her why she wasn't in school. She replied that she was not particularly interested in what she was taught there. "And what is it you wish to learn?"

She answered with a single, emphatic word: "Hieroglyphs!" And so it was that Dorothy Eady became the youngest and most unusual student of the great Dr. Budge. He immediately recognized her talent for copying the complex hieroglyphic figures and gave her some chapters of *The Book of the Dead* to copy and translate, rewarding her with bars of chocolate for work done properly. He was at a loss to explain such early aptitude and passion for an extremely difficult subject. And why would a girl from a good Christian family care to learn about a pagan religion that had been dead for 2000 years? As far as his new student was concerned, Dr. Budge knew everything she felt urgent to know about: the language, the gods and goddesses, especially Isis and Osiris – in whom she now fervently believed – and the *magic*. Dr. Budge was the keeper of mysterious and powerful secrets.

Omm Sety would recall Dr. Budge with great warmth. "He was my first and most earnest tutor. He adopted the ancient religion and deftly used Egyptian magic for benevolent ends. In fact, he wrote books on both subjects. He once said to me, 'My child, Egypt taught us everything. I follow all the Egyptian teachings, and when you go there one day I am sure you will do the same.'"

She once asked him to teach her about magic and he asked her why. "Well," she said, "I have an uncle who says awful things to me about Egypt and I want to get rid of him."

He drew back in pretend horror. "Oh, no, no, no – you're not the one to learn magic!" But magic – *heka* – was something that continued to fascinate her.

That same year, 1914, the Great War broke out. For two more years Dorothy continued her studies with her doting mentor at the museum, immersing herself in a wondrous world that was far more vivid to her than this one. But in 1916 when the air raids began over London, many families sent their children away to safer havens for the duration of the war. The Eadys made arrangements to send their daughter to the countryside, to her grandmother's farm in Sussex, where she had spent many summer holidays among the horses, cows and chickens.

Near the day of departure, just as the government was preparing to shut down the museum as a precaution, Dorothy paid a call on her tutor to bid him farewell. Budge was touched. He apologized for not having a bar of chocolate to offer her. "Will you study your hieroglyphs when you are with your granny?"

"Every day," she replied.

"What makes you so keen to continue, my child?"

"Because I used to know, and now I must remember it all again."

The old man regarded her silently. He was probably the first person besides her skeptical parents to become aware of her peculiar relationship with the far past. A diminutive man, he got down from his chair and held her affectionately at arm's length, saying sternly, "Don't you do anything foolish when you are in Sussex, and I don't want to hear about any problems you make for your granny. Now run along, child, and God bless you!"

She reluctantly said her goodbye and kissed the old man on both cheeks.

Sussex

From the first day, life in the countryside was uneventful and often tiresome for the city child. There was school with the village children and there were chores, which put her in contact with more animals. And there was the white horse. Whatever its original English name, it now had a new Egyptian name, *Mut Hotep*, after the favorite horse of Ramesses II.

"It was as if he smelled a friend," she said of their first meeting. The horse, who had been grazing, saw her and walked towards her until his head touched her arm and stayed there.

Mut Hotep was her ticket to a certain degree of freedom. A few miles from the village was the seaside town of Eastbourne with a well stocked public library. Every week or two she rode the obliging Mut Hotep to the library, where she would borrow all the books on Egyptology she could carry back with her. Fortunately, there were many, written by the prominent Egyptologists of the time – Sir William Flinders Petrie, a prolific scholar who regularly published his great discoveries in the Fayyum, Thebes, Memphis and, most important for Dorothy, Abydos; and Dr. Budge, whose long list of books was an absolute must for beginners and scholars alike. Of course she had already devoured some of Budge's books.

Still, despite the comfort of her books and the large country house, her loneliness was sometimes acute. She longed to see her young aunt and have more nights of laughter and story-telling. No one here in the country, not even her dear granny, could know the thoughts that occupied her mind. Her affinity for animals would always be a solace to her, even if it was not always wise or prudent. There was one particular instance she recalled from that time:

"One day on the farm," she said, "a man saw an adder, a very poisonous snake. It was close to the house and he wanted to kill it, so I snatched up the snake and ran off with it. The man pursued me but I could run faster and I got right away. When I was far out of sight of the house I sat down with the snake in my lap and was patting it and petting it when a voice behind me said, 'What are you doing with that snake, Miss?' I looked up and there was a Gypsy man. 'Do leave my snake alone,' I said.

" 'I won't hurt it,' he promised. 'What are you doing with it?'

"I told him that they were trying to kill it and I'd run away with it. 'But aren't you afraid of it?' he said, and I replied, 'No – not at all.'

" 'Don't you ever want to kill snakes?' he said. 'No,' I said firmly.

" 'Well, kiss it on its head and swear that you will never harm any snake, and no snake will ever harm you.' So I promptly kissed the snake and swore on its head that I would never harm any of its friends and relatives. 'Now let it go,' he said. I let the snake go and it went away.

" 'But when I grow up,' I told him, 'I'm going to live in Egypt, and there are poisonous snakes there, too.'

" 'So long as you don't break the truce they will never harm you.'

" 'But how can a snake in England give news to snakes in Egypt?'

" 'I don't know,' he said, 'but they can – and you will find it so.'

"And it *has* been so."

A band of Gypsies had made their encampment on the outskirts of the village, just a few families living in rather casual tents surrounded by their carts and shabby horses. Dorothy decided one morning to visit them, but knew enough not to tell her grandmother. Gypsies were not welcome company anywhere. People in the English countryside kept their distance from them and were suspicious of their strange ways and reputed lack of cleanliness. The Gypsy camp did have a very peculiar smell about it, she recalled, but not nearly as awful as she had been told.

Dorothy approached the camp with some caution; Gypsies were known to resent intrusions on their privacy. The first thing that drew her attention was a handsome, dark-haired young man who was bent over, holding the right front hoof of his horse as if something were wrong. Dorothy watched from a safe distance as the man pulled something from the hoof, a nail or sharp piece of splintered wood.

"Is the horse badly hurt?" she called out and went closer. Drops of blood were trickling from the ailing hoof.

The man looked up at her. "It needs treatment. Can you keep him steady for me?"

While the man went to his tent to get something Dorothy held the horse with great concentration. The man returned with a thick ointment and a piece of clean linen to bind the foot.

"Can I come again tomorrow and see how he is doing?"

The man nodded and turned away, saying under his breath, "Thank you, Miss."

That was the first of many visits to the Gypsy camp. Now another horse had become a good friend, always offering his head for a kiss. He was a beautiful beast, deep bronze with a white triangle on his face. She discovered that its owner was also a skillful juggler and Dorothy watched, captivated, as he performed his tricks for her. He tried to teach her some of them but she could never do them well.

She envied this clan of outsiders for the freedom they enjoyed and for the warmth of their feeling towards each other

– which gradually came to include the lonely girl with the bright gold hair. She loved them, every one of them, even though she could never pronounce any of their names. She didn't really know why she loved them. It certainly wasn't for the juggling tricks – she had given up hope of learning them anyway. But she *had* heard the stories that they had come from Egypt long ago.

Her granny, a reasonably observant woman, was beginning to wonder where the child was disappearing to on horseback for hours on end. When she learned about the visitations to the Gypsy camp she was horrified and told her never to go there again. Dorothy simply ignored the order. Early the next morning she set out from her house to pay a visit to the camp. Nearly there, she stopped short, her heart beating wildly. Her eyes strained to make out familiar forms in the mist, but there were none to be seen. The entire camp had just vanished. She ran around the site, frantically looking for any trace of her friends, and then she collapsed onto the wet ground, sobbing.

Not long after, news ran through the Sussex village that an unexploded German bomb had fallen close to the main road outside of town and was lying half-buried in the ground. German planes rarely ventured that far from their London raids, but somehow a bomb had landed here with its head three feet into the earth at a sharp angle.

Learning about it from one of the workers on the farm, Dorothy went straightaway to find a friend, an older boy of 17. Together they rode their horses to have a look at the bomb. On their way they met a man on horseback who was galloping furiously in the opposite direction. "There's a big bomb close to this road up ahead!" he yelled as he passed. "It could go off any moment. Turn round and go back!"

The young riders kept on going. When they got to within a hundred yards of the bomb site they spotted it sticking out of the ground, quite visible. Dorothy dismounted, but the boy was not so sure. Her mind was set on one thing: rendering the bomb harmless by doing whatever it was that people did to troublesome bombs. As for the boy, he suddenly became aware of the terrible danger they were in. A lengthy argument ensued before help finally arrived: A truck full of civil defense men and explosives experts pulled up next to them. "What the hell do you think you are doing here?" shouted the officer in charge. "Off with you both!"

Dorothy remounted her horse and followed her companion, already well down the road ahead of her. If she could have found a way to stay and join the fun she would have.

On their way home they passed several carts belonging to Gypsies about to settle in for the night. Dorothy eagerly asked their leader if they had seen her vanished friends, but the answer was no. Gypsies have learned through the centuries never to tell about each other to strangers. They couldn't have known that they could trust the young girl with their secrets. Even years later she couldn't explain why the Gypsy clan near her grandmother's farm should have left such an indelible mark on her life.

Dorothy received an unexpected letter from Dr. Budge. There were only a few lines, the old man asking his student prodigy how she was doing in the village and encouraging her to keep up her studies. It showed a grandfatherly regard for his perplexing and amusing child-scholar. Since the British Museum was closed for the duration of the war and Dr. Budge's letter had no return address, she knew it was futile to try to escape from the farm and go to London. But it was certainly in her mind to do it if she could have.

During the war, Sussex suffered almost nothing from the incessant air raids over the British Isles. The comparative peace gave Dorothy a unique opportunity to read and to explore the depths of her thoughts and perceptions. It was a time also when she became increasingly aware of her inexplicable power to "see" events taking place hundreds of miles away.

"My real problem," she said later, "was those horrible dreams in which I could clearly see pictures of what was going on at the Western Front. It was as though some part of me left my body and traveled far away to become a sort of war correspondent. Oh, Lord, how I hated those dreams, because they never failed to come true."

Twenty young men from the village had been recruited to serve in the army. Dorothy knew many of them from years of summer holidays there with her family. Some of the soldiers she saw in her terrifying dreams were boys she knew from those summers.

Once in a dream she watched a boy named Ralph being blown to pieces in the Somme Valley. He never came back. In her sleep she was helpless as she saw another young man, Robert, lose his left leg. A few weeks later a military ambulance arrived in the village and there was Robert, with one leg, struggling to walk with his crutches.

Another night she woke up screaming, "Leave the ship! Leave the ship!! Where are the lifeboats!" The housekeeper woke to the noise and ran to Dorothy's room to find the girl crying hysterically. Whether the cause of the nightmare was psychic sight or sheer coincidence, on that same night a British battleship had been sunk by the notorious German ship *Graf Spee*. There were other dreams, so disturbing that she dreaded going to sleep at night for fear of the awful knowledge that awaited her.

When she described her dreams for me many years later, I believed her. I thought that she was among those few who are destined from childhood to be sensitive, and maybe privileged by a certain gift which we in Egypt call "seeing ahead of one's time."

The war dragged on, and then it was over. During the long stay on the farm Dorothy had grown into a healthy, but rather plump young lady. Back home again in London her parents teased her about her size. Her mother thought she could benefit from dancing school, which Dorothy detested. She had quite different plans for herself anyway, plans that had had years to grow and ferment in her mind.

Strongly influenced by her readings in Egyptology and the esoteric and spiritual sciences, she searched out her old teacher at the British Museum. Their first encounter, a year after the end of the war, was an emotional one. She was wildly enthusiastic about resuming her lessons, and Dr. Budge gave her as much time as he could, but he was immersed in studying the results of several reports on field research that had recently come to his desk. The latest excavations in Egypt were providing great entertainment for a war-weary world ready to be dazzled by new discoveries.

Dorothy worked hard to advance her knowledge of hieroglyphs, but at school she was an indifferent student. Her mind was completely focused on Egyptology and the dream of returning to her heart's home. At 16, having barely finished her secondary schooling, she simply discarded any ambition to go on to university. The one question in her mind was how and when she would get to Egypt. An event two years earlier had only cemented her determination. It was something she could not tell a soul about, because nobody would have believed it.

the visitor

One night she had been roused from sleep, feeling a weight on her chest. She opened her eyes to see the figure of a man, bending over her silently, staring fiercely at her. There was no doubt who it was; she had never forgotten that photo of Sety I's mummy. This man at her bedside was in mummy wrappings, with only his face and arms free. His face was a dead man's but his eyes were alive and filled with the most terrible torment. Omm Sety described the visitation to me years later: "You could only say that the eyes had the look of somebody in hell who had suddenly found a way out."* She wasn't frightened, she recalled; it was a shock and a joy, all at the same time. When he reached down and tore at her nightdress she cried out, which brought her mother running to her room. The startling visitor was gone, and Dorothy told her mother that it was a nightmare and that

---

*as quoted in *The Search for Omm Sety*, by Jonathan Cott

she had torn her nightdress herself. But she knew exactly who had done it.

"After that," she told me, "I was always longing for him to come again. As I got a bit older I used to go to spiritualists, trying to get in touch with him. This went on and on and on, until I must have been 26 or 27 – always searching, always hoping he would come again. People in these spiritualist societies with whom I spoke about it said it's not a king, it's an evil spirit, and things like that – but I knew it wasn't. I was never persuaded that it was an evil spirit, but I *did* begin to think maybe it was just to be that one occurrence.

"I did know I'd always been attracted to Sety, and I'd always been attracted to this place, to Abydos, since I was a very, very small child, before I even knew who built it. I mean, I was *drawn* to this temple. And that's why, when men came to ask to marry me and asked my father, I would never accept. I was always looking for this one man. I never fell in love – I thought, oh, they don't make them like that any more!"

Without a doubt Dorothy loved this man, but why? And why had he come to her that one night and not again? The answers would elude her for a while yet, until after she had left England. For the moment she would have to be content with what was written in her scholarly books, which she scoured for clues among the scattered facts of Sety's life.

23

THREE

Sety

"He appears not so much preserved as sleeping –
but sleeping in the way that a leopard might..."

How Sety became a pharaoh of Egypt is a tale of the ebb and flow of dynastic fortunes. He was born towards the end of the 18th Dynasty, a golden age of expansion and empire lasting from 1550 – 1319 BC. In the beginning it was a dynasty of extraordinary exploration, temple building and high art, presided over by kings named Ahmose, Thutmosis and Amenhotep, and the female pharaoh Hatshepsut. A seemingly endless tide of tribute flowed into the royal coffers from Egypt's vassal states, which stretched from Nubia in the south to the Euphrates in the east.

And then, two hundred years into this brilliant age, around the time that Sety was born, the vital energy of the empire suddenly made a dramatic shift with the rise of Amenhotep III's son, Akhenaten. Whatever Akhenaten was – religious zealot or visionary – he was responsible for one of the most puzzling and misunderstood periods of Egypt's long history. Within a few years of his ascension to the throne, he had upended the traditional priesthoods and worship and set himself up as the only son of the only supreme god, from whom all life emanated. But the old gods and centuries of tradition could not be wiped out in a stroke. Many voices privately decried what they saw as the wholesale destruction of the Order-of-Things – an interesting irony, since Akhenaten liked to refer to himself as

25

Living-in-Truth, meaning that he was the very embodiment of the Order-of-Things.

Soon the edges of the delicately balanced empire began to fray. Vassal states sent desperate but futile pleas to Akhenaten's court for help to fend off invaders at their walls. Meanwhile, the enigmatic, seemingly indifferent pharaoh was overseeing splendid ceremonies to the one god, the Aten, in his newly-built holy city far from the ancient Theban center. His artists and sculptors were kept busy creating works in a new, naturalistic style, which may have been a reflection of Akhenaten's understanding of Living-in-Truth. He was living out a dream of paradise on earth with his beautiful wife Nefertiti and their six daughters.

By the time of his death – possibly at the hands of others – irreparable damage had been done to the stability of the kingdom.

Akhenaten's dream died with him. His immediate successor, Tutankhamun, was just a boy (possibly Akhenaten's younger brother or his son by his secondary wife Kiya). Tutankhamun's short reign was dominated by his elderly vizier, Ay, and the powerful general Horemheb, who lost no time reestablishing the old gods and tearing down all reminders of Akhenaten's existence. The name Akhenaten was expunged from the stones. If people referred to him at all it was as *the criminal*, or *the heretic*.

No full account of his life and times has yet been discovered. Except for the imploring letters from the besieged vassal kings, and Akhenaten's own lyrical hymns to the Aten, we have almost nothing that would explain who he was and why he made his religious revolution. Some writers have even suggested that he had a connection with Moses. If we look to the art of the period we find some clues, but not enough to show a deeper meaning. The story of Akhenaten's reign is an intriguing missing piece of Egypt's history.

Following Tutankhamun's early death Ay took the throne briefly, bringing the great 18th Dynasty to a sad and troubled end.

Whether Horemheb unseated Ay or became king after Ay's death, no one really knows, but Horemheb was immensely popular and he possessed the qualities and determination to bring order back to Egypt. With his reign the 19th Dynasty began. It was now the year 1319 BC.

To give his claim to the throne legitimacy the aging Horemheb married a sister of Nefertiti who was not young herself. Since they had no children, he hand-picked his own successor, his vizier and general of the armies, Ramesses. Both men shared a driving ambition to rebuild what many believed had been so recklessly dismantled. At Horemheb's death the double crown of Egypt passed to his trusted vizier.

Ramesses had come from an old military family in a part of the eastern Delta that worshipped the god Set as the warrior god. When Ramesses' first son was born it was only natural that he would give the child the auspicious name of Sety – Set's man.*

The boy Sety grew up in his father's footsteps, becoming known as a gifted military officer and leader, as befitted his bloodline. Sety was probably in his late 30s when his father became pharaoh. Ramesses, by then a man of advanced age, promptly appointed Sety co-regent to assure a smooth succession. The reign, and life, of Ramesses would last only two more years.

It was 1306, and Sety was now king. He was also a man with a family. As a youth he had married a non-royal woman who had borne him a son, Pa-Ramessu, but by the time Sety came to the throne he was a widower. With his second wife, a noblewoman named Tuy, he had a second son, Ramesses.

Both boys were brought up in the family military tradition. There are records that in the early part of Sety's reign Pa-Ramessu accompanied his father into battle. However close the relationship between father and older son might have been,

---

*Set was not always a symbol of evil. While it was Set who slew his brother Osiris, Set was also the god of the desert and was called the Great-of-Strength. As such, he was the patron of the military.

one thing was inescapable: Pa-Ramessu could never succeed his father to the throne because his mother was not of royal blood. At some point the younger boy, Ramesses, was named co-regent instead. This period is described in *Abydos: Holy City of Ancient Egypt.**

> Now we can sense a tragedy in Sety's personal and public life. His elder son apparently committed some great crime; perhaps he plotted against the lives of his father and little brother; probably we shall never know what he did. But whatever it was, it was punishable by death and disgrace in this world and the next. His body was found at the bottom of a deep pit at Medinet el Gurob in the Fayoum region. It lay in a fine stone sarcophagus from which the inscriptions had all been hammered out. But when photographed by infra-red light, the word "King's son of Men-Maat-Ra, Pa-Ramessu" could be seen. The body... had never been mummified and was wrapped in a sheep-skin; a disgrace accorded only to the worst type of criminal. Some forensic doctors have suggested that the man may have been buried alive....We have little doubt that this early tragedy in the reign of Sety must have left its mark.

Sety ruled Egypt for 16 years, during which time he laid to rest any possible questions of his right to the throne of Egypt. Nothing could contain his driving energy. Early in his reign he led successful military campaigns to recover parts of the eastern empire; he oversaw the restoration of temples and monuments defaced by Akhenaten and employed the finest architects and artists in the kingdom to proclaim in stone the names and images of the old gods.

---

*by Omm Sety and Hanny el Zeini, LL Company, 1981

28

Sety died in 1290, probably in middle age, leaving the care of the newly vitalized kingdom to the irrepressible energies of his son, Ramesses II. After his death, Sety was laid to rest in a magnificent tomb in the Valley of the Kings, but within 300 years the tomb was looted of its treasures; even the wrappings around his mummified body were rudely stripped of their gold and precious jewels. It was an unfortunate fact that few royal tombs escaped ransacking by thieves acting either on their own behalf or as agents of later kings strapped for funds.

Soon after the plunder of Sety's tomb his mummy was re-wrapped by the mortuary priest of the Valley of the Kings, who identified it with his seal and transferred it to a safer haven, the cliff tomb of Queen Ahmose-Inhapi near Deir el Bahri, not far from the Valley of the Kings. In that isolated tomb Sety's body (along with other royal mummies whose Houses of Eternity had earlier been plundered) became part of the famous royal cache of 50 mummies opened by Emile Brugsch in 1881. The cache's rock-cut chambers contained the remains of many of the greatest pharaohs of ancient Egypt, and their discovery caused a sensation all over the world, but in no place more than Egypt.

When the time came for the royal mummies to be trans-ported by boat down the Nile to Cairo, a very strange thing hap-pened: Throngs of Egyptians began streaming from their fields and houses to stand in solemn tribute along the riverbanks, the men firing guns into the air, the black-robed women calling out their shrill, timeless cries of mourning for the passing of their ancient kings.

At the Cairo Museum each of the mummies was tagged and given a catalog number. Sety became no. 61077.

For much of the 20th century his body was on display in Room 52 of the museum, along with his son Ramesses II and others from the royal cache, until President Sadat ordered the room closed to the public. He considered it a desecration that these noble ancestors of the Egyptian people should be objects of casual curiosity. Now, the Mummy Room has been reopened and visitors can walk among the sealed glass cases thinking their own thoughts about the silent figures within who had once lived in majesty as gods on earth. To look at some of them, it is hard to imagine their ever having lived and loved or that they once had warm blood coursing through their veins. And then there is Sety.

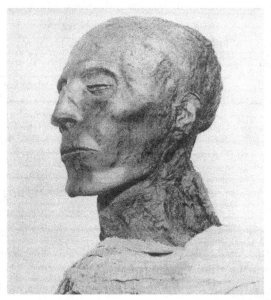

Head of the mummy of Sety I. (LL Company)

The face of Sety is an arresting one, handsome, elegant, his shaven head finely shaped. Of all the royal mummies, his seems closest to drawing breath at any moment. He appears not so much preserved as sleeping – but sleeping in the way that a leopard might, with a mysterious, vital tension. Sir G. Elliot Smith, the famous anatomist, took special note of Sety's appearance in his 1912 book, *The Royal Mummies*. It was, he wrote, "one of the most perfect examples of manly dignity displayed in a mummy that has come from ancient Egypt."

It was that face that Dorothy Eady held in her heart. The rest of the memories hadn't begun to unfold yet, but they would.

FOUR

Signs of Egypt Everywhere

*"We were — King Sety and I — on the verge of starting
an odyssey of some sort." OS*

L*ondon, 1920.* Ever since Sety's appearance to her two years
earlier, Dorothy had been having a recurring dream. It
excited her and disturbed her deeply, and she knew it was true.
She was an Egyptian girl and she was lying on a woven mat in a
very large room with other women and girls. It was night. Then
the dream would shift to another room, this one underground,
with a channel of water flowing around the perimeter. It was a
very sacred place, she knew, but she had not been brought here
to take part in a ritual. She was being confronted by an austere
man in high priest's garb, and there were others in the room
too, looking at her as if in judgment. The man was beating her
because she would not tell him what he demanded. Nothing
could make her say what he wanted her to say, and the beating
continued. When she woke she would be drenched in sweat and
screaming, and the family would know that Dorothy had had
another of "those dreams."

Dorothy was now 16, pursuing her independent studies and
living at home. England was not where she wanted to be, but
for the time being it would have to do.

The war had taken an awful toll on the country in every
way. For Dorothy's father, a master tailor, it meant a drastic

falling-off of his previously well-heeled clientele. But Reuben Eady saw it as a chance to re-invent himself and do something he had always dreamed of. Off and on through the years he had performed on stage as a juggler and magician; not that he had been able to make a living at it, but he knew a thing or two about music halls and theaters, and he loved them. His wife, Caroline, had already put up with a lot from her eccentric little family, so when Reuben came home one day and announced that he had just closed his shop for good she could only look at him and sigh, "What next?"

He didn't really know, exactly. He had ideas in his head, something to do with the newly emerging cinema industry. He could imagine having his own theater. But before he decided on anything he had to give himself some breathing space, take the family on a trip, look around the British Isles to see where the opportunities lay. If Caroline initially resisted the plan, Dorothy didn't; she didn't need convincing to set off on an adventure into the unknown.

Early in the Eady family's exploratory tour, as they were driving west through the Wiltshire countryside, they stopped at Stonehenge. Of course Dorothy had seen pictures of it before, but to be standing right *there*, with the morning light casting eerie shadows over the great towering stones – there was something so *Egyptian* about it all, she thought. To her eyes the roughly shaped obelisks had been arranged into a temple for worshipping the sun, like the obelisks of Egypt. She was sure there must have been an "Egyptian intervention" here.

While her parents strolled, Dorothy's curiosity led her to a nearby group of Bronze Age barrows and graves. Catching a glint of color at her feet, she bent down and picked up a handful of earth that contained a number of blue and green particles, and she shouted for her mother and father to come quickly to see what she had found. When the Eadys looked at her discovery they were not impressed, but Dorothy knew what she had: Egyptian mummy beads, and she was right. She was not the first person to have found mummy beads in the area of Stonehenge, or even scarabs. At the very least they were proof of ancient trade between the Mediterranean and the British Isles, not to mention even more intriguing possibilities.

She carefully placed her finds in a small box, intending to add this new treasure to her tiny collection of Egyptian artifacts that had made their way into her hands. Egypt seemed to be constantly reminding her that sooner or later she would board a ship heading for the Black Land. She felt stranded in the British Isles. There was so much yet to know, so much she couldn't truly understand until she had kissed the precious soil of Egypt and begun to unravel the mystery of herself.

The family tour did not interrupt her study of Egyptology; there were modest museums and libraries all along the way. The science of Egyptology was still in its infancy, but a prodigious quantity of publications about Egyptian history and archaeology were streaming onto the book market, written by world famous pioneers such as J. H. Breasted, Hermann Junker and Dr. Budge. As much as Dorothy appreciated their work – and Dr. Budge's especial kindness to her – there was one Egyptologist who warranted her highest esteem: W. Flinders Petrie (he would be knighted in 1923 for his work). On this giant of archaeology she bestowed her silent adoration for his meticulous attention to the protocols of excavation. In fact, he created many of the modern protocols, including systematic surveying methods and the use of seriation* to date sites and the artifacts found with them. Dorothy was interested in Flinders Petrie for another reason as well: He was the first archaeologist to dig in the early dynasty tombs in the ancient burial fields of Abydos.

I once asked Omm Sety what school of archaeology she belonged to, and she promptly replied, "First of all, I belong to the school of *life*, but if you are asking me specifically about excavating technique, my answer would be, I belong to the Flinders Petrie school."

---

*a dating technique based on establishing a chronological ordering of artifacts

33

More and more, Abydos haunted her thoughts and dreams, and not because Abydos was famous; it wasn't. Few people outside the Egyptological fraternity cared very much about Professor Petrie's excavations at Abydos. His discoveries in Thebes and Memphis, Dendera and Giza were far more glamorous to the average Briton in the 1920s. At that time there weren't even many Egyptians who had heard of Abydos. But thousands of years ago every Egyptian dreamed of making a pilgrimage to Abydos to witness the ancient passion play and see the blessed Lady Isis and Lord Osiris.

Isis in Plymouth

Reuben Eady's instincts told him he could make a go of it as a movie house impresario, and the port city of Plymouth seemed just the place. With his head fairly bursting with original ideas for such a venture he found the financing to set himself up in business.

His New Palladium Theatre was popular from the day it opened. He showed silent films and staged theatrical events that he wrote and directed. Often he featured his daughter, who would come out in costume and sing popular songs of the day in her high soprano voice. She was not always an enthusiastic participant in these musical interludes at the New Palladium; she was drawn to another kind of performance entirely.

Dorothy was part of a little theater group that once put on a play based on the story of Isis and Osiris. To anyone who knew of her obsession with Egypt it was no surprise that she took the role of Isis. When it came time for her to sing the words of the ancient *Lament* for the death of Osiris, she didn't use the music from the prepared score, but instead set the words to a melody she had sung over and over to herself when she was a child in London. The crooning melody had been in her head for as long as she could recall, and now she applied it to the rhyming lines that the writer Andrew Lang had adapted from a translation of the old hieroglyphic text. It begins with these words:

Sing we Osiris dead, lament the fallen head;
The light has left the world, the world is grey.
Athwart the starry skies the web of darkness lies;
Sing we Osiris, passed away.
Ye tears, ye stars, ye fires, ye rivers shed;
Weep, children of the Nile, weep – for your Lord is dead.

Throughout Dorothy's youth there were foreshadowings of Egypt, but it seemed unlikely that anything in Plymouth would take her in that direction. And the years were passing. As she approached her mid-20s there was no discernable plan for her life, at least not in the practical sense.

About those years in Plymouth, I have always believed that she was simply waiting. I think she had a fatalistic trust that the way would be shown to her. In the meantime she took classes at the local art school, which would serve her well later, and when she was about 26 she became involved in politics – in particular, the independence movements of Eamon de Valera in Ireland and Saad Zaghlul in Egypt. She was a natural-born partisan, always ready to jump into a fray if she thought there was a cause that needed defending. It was certainly that way with the growing Egyptian nationalist movement. In a roundabout way it was politics that brought her at last to Egypt.

Imam

In the early 1930s, Egypt had been in a state of prolonged unrest and turmoil under British occupation. The decades before had brought great wealth to some and reduced much of the populace to a grinding poverty. While on the surface the richly cosmopolitan society of Cairo seemed glamorous and optimistic, there was increasing desperation among Egyptians in general, and certainly among the young intellectuals, who resented the foreign economic manipulation and what they saw as the arrogant superiority of the occupiers. Egyptian nationalism was the inevitable result.

By 1920, the British had their backs to the wall trying to suppress the spreading movement for self-rule, and in 1922 they finally capitulated, giving Egypt its nominal independence.

But Britain did not go quietly back to her shores; she kept a large military presence in the Suez and elsewhere and she made sure that the new Egyptian government was attentive to British interests. Full independence was what the Egyptians yearned for, not this veiled colonialism. By the early '30s, acts of civil disobedience had led to suppression of dissent, which had led to riots and imprisonment of the leaders of the nationalists.

At that time there were a number of Egyptian students in the British universities. Two of them, George Wissa and Imam Abdel Meguid, had been best friends since they were boys, and had come to London to pursue advanced degrees. Imam was studying education and planned to be a teacher back home. But he was first of all a patriot; he spent long hours distributing handbills in the halls of Parliament and arguing eloquently for Egyptian self-rule.

By then, Dorothy had returned to London on her own, without her parents' blessing. They would have preferred to have her near them, but she was of age, and they knew very well that she would always do exactly what she had it in her head to do. A dear old friend of mine, Prof. Dr. Ali Fani, who was pursuing his doctorate at London University at the time, knew her then. He told me that she was really a very beautiful girl. This surprised me, because I had met her when she was already middle-aged and looking quite weathered. To prove his statement, he showed me a picture of her when he had known her. I saw an extremely beautiful young woman, and I was annoyed at myself that I didn't ask him to lend me the picture so that I could make a copy of it and show it to her. She didn't seem to have pictures of herself at a young age.

In London, Dorothy found work with an Egyptian journal devoted to educating the British public about Egypt and its right to self-rule. Here at last was a forum that gave her free rein to write her views on Egyptian independence. She could even put her artistic talents to work drawing pithy political cartoons. The work suited Dorothy's temperament perfectly. Now she was surrounded by people as passionate about Egypt as she was.

In such a charged political atmosphere every fighter for the cause becomes a comrade. And so it happened that Dorothy Eady found herself starting to fall in love, not with some pink-faced young English fellow, but, almost predictably, with an Egyptian – Imam Abdel Meguid.

The true man of her dreams, Sety, was impossibly separated from her by chasms of time, and she had all but lost hope that she would ever make contact with him again. Imam, however, was flesh and blood and he was right here, companionable, intelligent and attentive in a charmingly old-fashioned way. Imam's friends, especially George Wissa, weren't sure that this budding romance was a good thing, yet they could not bring themselves to tell him all that was on their minds. As good and amusing and forthright as Dorothy was, Imam's friends couldn't see how such a non-traditional woman, even by the rather laissez-faire British standards, would fit in with the refined Egyptian family of the Abdel Meguids. They tried to speak gently of these issues, but could not penetrate Imam's haze of love. He would leave it to Fate, *kesma*, to work it out.

The couple became engaged in the spring of 1933, just before Imam returned to Egypt. They could easily have had a civil marriage at the Egyptian Embassy in London, but they agreed that it would be more politic to have a traditional Islamic ceremony with his family in Cairo. They went together to the Egyptian Embassy in London to apply for Dorothy's entrance visa. It would be a matter of only a few weeks, they were told. And so Imam departed for home to prepare for his bride's arrival.

Speaking of those romantic days, Omm Sety later said, "The poor man did not realize he was marrying more of a Gypsy than a nice young Englishwoman. For my part, I honestly never suspected that King Sety would be part of my life. But I was quite wrong. We were – King Sety and I – on the verge of starting an odyssey of some sort. To be more precise, we were taking over from the point at which we ended 3300 years ago."

Summer dragged on, and into autumn, and Dorothy still didn't have her entrance visa. Just as troubling, she was having difficulty finding a vacancy on a ship going to Egypt. The routes to India and Australia took the ships through the Suez Canal with a stop at Egypt's Port Said. A British liner sailed once every two months to Sydney, Australia, and there was another that went to India, but the passenger lists on both of them were always full. Travel among the countries of the British Commonwealth was brisk at this time, because the turmoil of the world economic depression had caused waves of hopeful refugees to flee their homelands for opportunities they saw elsewhere in the Commonwealth. At last, after an almost unbearable delay, Dorothy finally had her visa in hand and she managed to secure a berth on a ship that was about to leave for Bombay. She sent a telegram to Imam saying she was on her way to Port Said. When she informed her parents of her plans they were not at all pleased to be the last to know. They had not even met the young man.

In her haste to prepare for departure, Dorothy neglected to pay a final visit to her dear Dr. Budge, who wondered for years afterward what had become of his remarkable young student – though he suspected that she had found her way to Egypt.

FIVE

The Journey Home

*"Oh, my Lady Isis…I am glad you brought me home again,
really I am!" OS*

O*ctober, 1933.* On a foggy October morning, a tearful mother and a perplexed father stood on the stone quay at Southampton looking up at a departing passenger ship, waving to their only child, who was leaving them for a doubtful and perhaps hazardous future in far-off Egypt.

The British ship blew its whistle furiously and moved slowly away from its moorings. On deck, Dorothy waved back at her parents, feeling sadness and joy, but mostly joy. She watched the quay as long as she could until the thick fog enveloped everything, and the quay and Southampton and then England itself disappeared from view.

Halfway across the English Channel the fog lifted, as though some giant hand had pulled aside a curtain, letting the sun shine gloriously through the fleecy clouds. At first the trip was uneventful as the ship steamed along the coast of French Normandy and southward into the Bay of Biscay, the large inlet of the Atlantic Ocean that carves a broad arc into the west coast of France and the northern coast of Spain.

The weather quickly turned again, as it does in the unpredictable autumn months; the ship heaved against the onslaught of ferocious, mountain-high waves and powerful winds, and the captain ordered all passengers to their cabins. By then, most everyone was seasick anyway and had already taken to their beds. But Dorothy loved the wildness and adventure of it all; she was the last one to leave the deck and seek the safety of her cabin, accompanied by one of the officers and a stern warning to obey captain's orders.

On the way back to her cabin, the officer told her a story about this part of the Bay of Biscay. Years ago, he said, a sarcophagus containing the mummy of an Old Kingdom pharaoh had washed overboard and sunk in a terrible gale. The seamen believe there was a spell on this spot because every ship that passes close to the site of the sarcophagus is badly shaken, no matter whether the climate is normal or stormy. That night, Dorothy couldn't sleep, fighting her own *mal de mer*, but also feeling terribly curious about the story of the sarcophagus and the fact of the awful turmoil outside. In the middle of the night she heard a strange groaning sound from somewhere inside the ship, then orders being shouted. If it was engine trouble, she thought, she would just have to swim to the Spanish shore.

By morning the sea had grown calm again, but the jarring mechanical sounds were louder. The now-disabled ship had managed to limp through the Straits of Gibraltar during the night. In the morning a small number of concerned passengers gathered in the dining room, and were assured by the captain that all was well. The ship was proceeding at slow speed to Marseilles, he explained, where it would dock for repairs for several days before continuing to Egypt. Most of the passengers took the news calmly, but there was one voice that would not be placated. "I must be in Port Said on Monday," Dorothy insisted. "People will be waiting to take me to Cairo and I haven't the slightest idea how to get there on my own."

The captain promised her that she could not possibly lose her way from Port Said to Cairo; nonetheless, he offered to try to find separate passage for her once they reached Marseilles.

He was as good as his word. At Marseilles, Dorothy boarded the French luxury liner *Esperia*, along with an elderly Lebanese couple from her ship who were returning home to Beirut. This most fortunate arrangement had been accomplished between the British captain, whose French was atrocious, and the French port master whose English was no better, but who successfully negotiated with the French captain to transfer the three passengers to his ship. The *Esperia*, "Bride of the Mediterranean," left port soon after.

Within a few hours the bright blue skies were again replaced by threatening weather. Not far from the *Esperia* an Italian troop ship was sailing eastward filled with recruits on their way to Abyssinia – part of Mussolini's grand imperial plan to control the Horn of Africa. The young men were singing in a formidable patriotic chorus that carried across the water with the wind. As Dorothy leaned against the deck railing of the Esperia enjoying it all, the sea began to roll with 20-foot waves and she was thrown to the deck. The sympathetic crewman who helped her to her feet made a little joke about Mt. Etna flexing its power again, a sly reference to the passing troop ship and the fact that the sudden storm was coming from the direction of the Italian boot.

The tempest finally blew itself out and the sea was momentarily at peace. Dorothy glimpsed a hazy line along the southern horizon: the coast of Africa. If she could have turned herself into a hawk in that instant she would have, and soared high above the ship until she spied Egypt far to the east along that beckoning horizon.

On this same day, Imam Abdel Meguid boarded a train from Cairo bound for Port Said. Having received no recent word from Dorothy, he thought it best to go a few days early, just in case, and await her arrival. In Port Said he went directly to the office of Lloyd's, only to be informed of the trouble with the British liner. The office had no information about Dorothy's current whereabouts. Imam was not the kind of man who tolerated uncertainty, especially in this sort of situation; he demanded that every effort be made to locate his fiancée. Late in the afternoon the Lloyd's office rang his hotel with news that Miss Eady would be arriving the next day on the *Esperia*.

As the French ship glided slowly towards the quay, a very impatient, very tall and handsome young man paced from one end to another, clutching a large bunch of flowers to his breast while the brisk wind whipped his overcoat about his legs. He scanned the ship's main deck and promenades, hoping to pick out one beloved face from all the others. Dorothy saw him first and waved frantically.

At last the boarding steps were in place and passengers could debark. She rushed to throw herself into Imam's arms, then pulled away and knelt to the ground, kissing it, murmuring her thanks to the gods. Imam stared and the passengers around her stared. In her excitement the flowers had slipped from her hands and Imam, completely at a loss, bent to collect them. When Dorothy stood again she saw the bewildered look on his face. "I am so sorry, Darling," she exclaimed, "it is just so wonderful!"

Her odd behavior did not escape the sharp eyes of the customs officials. They had never witnessed such a scene, and from a well-dressed and apparently rich Englishwoman at that. Very courteously, they insisted on thoroughly searching her suitcases before letting her pass. But the mere fact that she was considered a suspicious character only added to Imam's growing embarrassment. In all the to-do they had even forgotten to kiss. This was not the way Imam had imagined their first meeting after many months apart.

They exchanged but a few words as they sat together in the car that took them to the railway station. Imam knew she was overwhelmed by the new experience; he would give her time.

On the train Dorothy shut everything else out except for the wonders that were passing outside the windows on either side. The rail line paralleled the Suez Canal. Dorothy could see, on the far side of the canal in the direction of Sinai, a camel caravan moving in orderly procession over the golden sand. She had never seen a camel before, or Bedouins. Through the windows on the other side of the train car she was drawn into a panorama of an ancient time – ox-drawn plows, goats, a crystalline sky. *Oh, my Lady Isis,* she whispered to herself, *this is all so very beautiful! I am glad you brought me home again, really I am!*

The train made a stop in Ismailieh, a vast green park that was the administrative center of the Canal Authority, close by a row of elegantly arranged, tile-roofed villas where the canal pilots and other employees lived. An unexpected surprise awaited the couple on the station platform: George Wissa. George was too much of an old and sincere friend to refuse to accept, however reluctantly, Imam's decision to marry Dorothy. He met the couple with red roses and the best wishes he could muster for their future happiness together. The train stayed only three minutes and was off again.

With her hand firmly in Imam's, Dorothy sat hypnotized by the scenery around her – the donkeys loaded with grass, the waterwheels, the endless dark fields of the Black Land. Imam could only smile at her obvious joy. "Everything is taking my breath away!" she exclaimed, "I don't feel a stranger at all!"

The train pulled to its destination in the highly ornamented 19th century Cairo central station. Model T taxis crowded the streets outside. The Cairo Dorothy was coming to was not a part of her ancient dreams and memories. Cairo in 1933 was a cosmopolitan city of no less than twenty different nationalities, European enclaves and political refugees. It was noisy and bustling. Shop signs were in French, Arabic, English, Greek, Hebrew and more. And everywhere was the pervasive presence of the British occupation.

in the house of Haj Abdel Meguid

The taxi from the station drove through the narrow streets of Old Cairo and stopped in front of the house of the family Abdel Meguid. Dorothy took one look at the gate and was stunned by its enormity. Thirty feet high and ten feet wide, it looked more like the entrance to a caravanserai, a grand inn, than an arabesque-style house. Its lower third was solid sheet steel with a stylized wrought iron sunflower in the center. And above that, an amazing tableau in wrought iron, a piece of art formed of flower motifs, trees and different types of leaves. I can attest to its beauty, having seen it myself many years ago. The artist who made that masterpiece was really a genius, because the visitor only sees the beautiful flowers, trees, etc., rather than a massive, sheet of metal. The privacy of the house was thus protected while the entrance was inviting and anything but austere. The whole family was waiting anxiously behind that gate.

Dorothy was deeply touched by the warmth of their welcome. Imam's father, Haj Abdel Meguid (Haj is the honorary title given to any Muslim who has had the good fortune to make a pilgrimage to Mecca), was particularly openhearted in greeting his future daughter-in-law. Being especially fond of his son, Haj Abdel Meguid immediately approved of Imam's choice, as did the rest of the family. This loving, pious, upper-middle-class Egyptian family quickly enfolded Dorothy as one of their own.

The Abdel Meguid home was in Old Cairo close to the Mukattam cliffs, in an area of the Citadel, Cairo's highest elevation. The two-story building was arranged around a large inner courtyard with a brilliantly colored mosaic tile fountain at its center.

In families such as this, the Egyptian traditions and religion were respected, strictly followed and venerated. Imam and Dorothy had already agreed that they would be married according to Muslim religious rules. Naturally, it was left to Haj Abdel Meguid to make all the necessary arrangements. It is stipulated that the bride and groom should each have two witnesses to sign the marriage certificate and testify that it was done by common consent and in conformity with religious tenets.

Before the wedding, Imam and Dorothy slept separately in two richly furnished bedrooms. At mealtimes the whole family gathered in the vast dining room at a table that could accommodate twenty people. At the head was Haj Abdel Meguid and on his right, Imam's mother, a woman in her early 50s, extremely distinguished and beautiful, with evident Circassian blood from some remote ancestry in the Caucasus. Imam took after his father, Dorothy thought, elegant and handsome, with the wavy dark brown hair of a movie star. Dorothy's British beauty was appreciated in the household as well – her clear blue eyes that flashed with humor, her golden hair, and her sweet singing voice. Haj Abdel Meguid bestowed on her the affectionate nickname *Bulbul*, Nightingale.

In those first days in the Abdel Meguid house she woke early each morning to watch the sun rise between the slender minarets of the Mohammed Ali Pasha mosque. Often, while it was still dark, she would wake to the sonorous call of a nearby *muezzin* bidding the pious to perform the first prayers of the day. "The man's serene and beautiful voice sounded like a balm to the soul," Omm Sety said in recollection. "It endowed me with a curious interior peace that would stay with me through the day." She was enchanted and on her best behavior, still not quite believing that she was actually here. Each morning when Dorothy came down to breakfast with the family she found a sumptuous table laid with three kinds of cheese, boiled and fried eggs, fried mashed beans, fresh butter, marmalades and other delights. Dorothy was quickly exposed to traditional Egyptian cooking and delicacies.

On her third day, Dorothy (who was now called Bulbul) went on a tour of Cairo with Imam and his mother to search among the finest shops for the wedding trousseau. Her taste was politely consulted during the expedition, but when the moment came to select the wedding dress, she knew she had best defer to a more sophisticated taste. From London, Dorothy had written to Imam: "I have never been to any wedding in all my life, either British or any other nationality, so I will leave the choice to your mother. I have no doubt she will pick the most suitable dress." And so, in the chic showroom of the famous French-Lebanese *couturiere* known as Paulette, Bulbul was fitted for her custom-designed wedding dress.

In the meantime, Haj Abdel Meguid was making other arrangements. The traditional wedding must be conducted by a *Maazun*, a qualified sheikh authorized by the government to handle all matrimonial questions according to Muslim law. A *Maazun* must have completed his studies at Cairo's Al Azhar University, a revered, 1000-year-old institution dedicated to preserving the cultural heritage of Islam.

At that time there was usually a short period of engagement during which the bride and groom could get acquainted and discuss their plans for a lifetime together. There was always a chaperone. But for educated people above the age of 20 there was never a question of chaperones. Bulbul and Imam were nearly 30 and had already had sufficient time to get to know each other well, at least in the context of London and the consuming political drama that they were both engaged in there.

In the three weeks before the wedding Bulbul attempted to share her passion for the ancient world with Imam. Bowing to Bulbul's wishes, he agreed to visit the pyramids of Giza and Saqqara, and the Egyptian Museum. Unfortunately, he found it all a terrible bore. He was not particularly interested in the early history of Egypt, being entirely taken up with the present time and its problems; most pressing was the question of whether he would be able to find suitable housing for himself and his bride. He had no intention of staying indefinitely in his father's house, though the subject had not come up since Bulbul's arrival. Imam was becoming more aware of the incompatibilities between Bulbul's bohemian character and the orderly, disciplined life of his family, even though the family seemed to accept her with great affection. It was only a matter of time before the differences would become untenable.

an Egyptian wedding

The wedding celebration was a magnificent party in the Abdel Meguid house, with a guest list that counted many highly placed officials and notables, a reflection of the family's position in Cairo society. Many years later, sitting in her tiny village house in remote Abydos, she described the festivities: "The women, in particular, were very richly dressed in the most up-to-date fashion of the season, as imposed by *La Mode Parisienne*. I felt like Alice in Wonderland. There I was, accepting the compliments of all these people, like a princess. Can you imagine? Me, of all the persons present in the party – a princess..." And then she laughed at the absurdity of it.

The traditional weddings of the upper classes – before the 5-star hotel affairs with the Western rock bands – were romantic and lavish, a display of high fashion and wealth. The bride would be dressed in an expensive gown adorned with pearls or, in very rich families, sewn with diamond beads. Gold coins would be thrown over the happy couple's shoulders and women of both families would make that curious, piercing sound with their tongues known as *zaghrutto*, as the bride and groom walked slowly to their bed chamber.

Bulbul's wedding was no less elaborate. It began with a sedate ceremony in the courtyard of the house, during which the bride and groom signed the contract and pledged to accept each other according to Muslim law. Since the bride had no family with her (her parents had not yet reconciled themselves to the marriage) two of Imam's friends who had known her in London stood as her witnesses. For Imam it was his father and uncle. The ceremony was very simple, beginning with the sheikh's recitation of a verse from the Koran: "*In the name of God, the all-merciful, the most compassionate*, I open this proceeding."

One of Bulbul's witnesses, Ibrahim, served as an interpreter. He coached her ahead of time to nod her head as a sign of agreement or to shake her head and say plainly if she did not accept whatever the sheikh was saying. Imam and several others who knew Bulbul well held their breath that the brief contractual ceremony would go off without incident. There was the question about the dowry – in Egypt the bridegroom must pay a dowry and not the bride. The sum paid must be mentioned publicly and the bride must be satisfied. There was the question of divorce, how much money would be paid to the bride in case the husband wanted to leave the marriage. It is quite important to decide upon the sum ahead of time because it is meant to act as a deterrent to rash action. It is the bride's right to mention in the contract that the husband would not object to his wife's wishing to work, as long as the children were well cared for. Today, most of the marriages in Egypt put this condition in the contract.

After the ceremony, the great house rang with music and the sounds of jubilation, though several of the guests were not entirely joyful and were relieved when the ceremony was over and they could depart; those were some of Imam's friends, including George Wissa.

Achille Groppi, the owner of the pre-eminent restaurant in Cairo, catered the dinner for the 120 guests. During the feast, an orchestra entertained the guests with a repertoire that included *The Nile*, by one of Egypt's prominent composers. And then the real celebrations began, with lyre, flute, clarinet, tambourine and drum players parading into the courtyard, followed by belly dancers moving among the tables to loud singing and clapping. The reluctantly decorous bride wanted to join in, but she could only sit in the place of honor beside Imam and watch. She was proud of her restraint.

Hours later it was time for *el Zaffa*, when the principal belly dancer, accompanied by tambourines and drums, balanced a chandelier with seven candles atop her head and led the couple to the foot of the staircase leading to the nuptial bedroom. Because of the delay in Bulbul's arrival in Egypt, the family had had time to decorate the room in the latest Parisian style, according to Imam's mother's exquisite specifications. They had kept it a secret, even from Imam. The new couple was overwhelmed. "I had never dreamed of such a beautiful bedroom," Omm Sety told me.

After Bulbul and Imam retired, the party continued into the morning hours, and all of the people who lived in the area were invited to join the guests in an immense open banquet. The feast at the house of Haj Abdel Maguid was remembered for a very long time.

This was not the homecoming that Dorothy Eady had imagined for herself when she was a child in England dreaming of an ancient time, but Bulbul Adbel Meguid couldn't have been happier.

Bulbul

*"When she opened her eyes she saw a shimmering,
amorphous something next to the bed."*

The senior Abdel Meguids expected the bride and bridegroom to live with them for at least a year before setting up
housekeeping on their own. They also expected that by the end
of that year there would be a new baby in the family. Only their
second expectation came to pass.

When I knew Omm Sety well I asked her about when she
became pregnant. "After the third month of marriage I was sure
I was pregnant. So you see, Imam did not waste any time." I
said, "Well, *you* didn't lose any time either." We laughed.

I asked her how she behaved herself in the house of her in-
laws. "Oh, for the first ten days after the wedding it was the usual
procedure, and then after that, Imam was supposed to go and
resume his work. For entire days I was practically alone because
his father went to his work in the government office, his mother
didn't speak a word of English, and there was no other family
living with us in the big house. So one day I gave myself the
liberty to go out. I was really quite clumsy about it because as
a matter of courtesy to the old lady, my mother-in-law, I should
have asked her permission first."

Gypsies again

That was the day Bulbul set out on a sort of scouting tour

of the quarter, walking along el Muezz Street and stopping to admire the arabesque architecture, the street vendors, the people and their interesting attire. A boy of about 12, seeing a foreigner rambling aimlessly in the district, approached, saying, "Have you lost your way, Madame? May I help?" His English was excellent. "No, my dear boy," she answered, "I am discovering the area where I shall be living." That was a great surprise to the boy. "But," he said, "foreigners do not choose our quarter to live in. This is Old Cairo, Madame."

"This I know, young man, but I would like to live here, even if most foreigners don't. It looks good enough to me." She regarded the boy for a moment. "What are the most interesting things that I can see today? I mean anything nice and exciting…"

"There are lots of buildings in the old style; there are mosques, schools, and there is the Beit el Sehemy – it is very famous." Then he smacked his forehead as if remembering something quite exceptional. "There is a feast near Bab el Futooh, the Northern Gate. It is a long walk from here. Today is the feast of the Gypsies. They come from every part of the country and have a big festival with Gypsy dances and fire-eating and a lot of other strange things. If you wish, I can go with you to protect you. One should keep his eyes wide open because they are very sharp thieves."

At the word "Gypsy" Bulbul snapped to attention. She accepted the boy's invitation on the spot. His name was Tarek. And so began a strange adventure that would get the new Mrs. Abdel Meguid into trouble.

She and the boy walked the length of the famous road, starting from Bab Zwele, the Southern Gate of Old Fatimid Cairo, up to Bab el Futooh (also known as the Gate of Conquests), through which victorious armies had marched after campaigns in Syria and Mesopotamia – and beyond the gate into the largest and oldest Muslim cemetery in Cairo, where a large crowd of people was gathering. The cemetery had been in use since the Arab conquest of Egypt in AD 640, and the tombs were in every style imaginable, from step pyramids and pharaonic designs to domed buildings, in endless variations.

The sanctity of this atmospheric place was disturbed by the shouts of children, mostly foreign, running about. European sight-seers waited expectantly. The Gypsy festival was of no particular interest to the native Egyptians, although it was known that this pagan extravaganza always took place on a full moon in autumn. Perhaps the biggest reason Cairenes avoided it was that this was a gathering occasion for opium smokers and hashish addicts; the air was filled with the smooth, tingling smell of both drugs. Gypsies were extremely resourceful in running drugs past the watchful eyes of the coastal police, the young guide said, and punishments for smuggling were severe and swift. That was the story that Tarek related to her as they entered the cemetery grounds. He looked so absolutely innocent and well bred that she wondered if she should be protecting him, and not the other way around. "Last year," Tarek said, "there was a man who swallowed an entire sword right into his stomach. A German surgeon was able to feel. And there was a Gypsy girl who could roll herself into a perfect ball while her partner pushed her around in circles."

The hubbub of the growing crowd was punctuated by the loud voices of a group of Italians, while the Britishers, some in knickerbockers, talked among themselves in reserved tones as they waited for something to happen. And then a distant wailing sound became audible – sad, sad tones of painful tragedy, as if from some remote past. The Gypsies had arrived. An elderly woman wearing a head cap embroidered with seashells and swathed in bead necklaces and bangles began to call out to her troupe in short, croaking phrases, to which they replied with a rising hum of encouragement. Bulbul asked Tarek what the words meant, but he shrugged his shoulders. "Nobody but a Gypsy can tell you the meaning of the words, and even then you can't believe anything they say."

Bulbul and her guide wandered among the crowd. The real fair wouldn't start until evening. Tarek couldn't stay that long and he left the English lady to find her way back alone. She had brought a sandwich and a thermos of minted tea. Unaware of the passing of time, she moved deeper into the colorful crowd.

Meanwhile, Imam had returned home to find his dear bride absent. Worse, she had told nobody where she was going or when she would return. Not that Imam feared for her safety; Cairo was one of the safest cities in the world. Policemen were always in plain view with their heavy black boots hitting the asphalt hard with every step, announcing the presence and alertness of the law. I had my own experiences with them as a boy in Cairo. Occasionally they would declare their presence by an audible baritone cough, which we youngsters called the government cough. Sometimes when they felt uncertain about a pedestrian they would demand to know who was there, and one had to answer, giving his full name and address. If that satisfied the alert watchman he would say, *Maa el Salama* – Go in peace. Some of them we knew by their voice and cough and we would salute, saying, *Izzayak Ya Shawish* – How are you, Sergeant?"

No, what really bothered Imam that evening was that Bulbul had just walked out of the house without a word to anyone. This was un-Egyptian in the extreme and quite lacking in good taste – unacceptable from any member of the family. In the time they had spent together in London, Imam was well aware of her free, adventurous spirit and he had thought it charming. But now she was in Egypt. This would not do at all.

The eastern end of the cemetery is a large area of barren desert. There the Gypsies lit their fires at dusk and the fair began, with children excitedly watching first the jugglers, then the bareback horsemen with their wild, daring tricks. Bulbul found herself pushed into an area where a man was engaged in a comical performance with two monkeys. The female monkey did a double backward somersault and other acrobatics, but the male was rebellious. The Gypsy waved a stick at him and said some harsh words, then hit the monkey on his hindquarters. Losing patience, the man began striking him repeatedly about the face while the monkey cowered and whimpered. Bulbul couldn't bear to watch such cruelty. She rushed up and put herself between the man and the pitiful creature, wrenching the stick from the man's hand. A group of Gypsies pulled her away. "No good, Miss...no good!" one of them shouted to her. "Very bad luck for you...bad luck for family too!" Surrounded by the hostile mob she looked around frantically for a way out.

Miracles do sometimes happen. Tarek, perhaps feeling unchivalrous for leaving her earlier, was suddenly there again, and with the help of one of the gypsy men, waded into the mess and pulled her to safety. The man gave her a strange, intent stare as she left with Tarek.

When she was home again with her Egyptian family, explaining in utter truthfulness what had happened, she was not greeted with understanding but with extreme disapproval. There were no words to make her behavior acceptable. Imam was careful to keep his fury under control. It was unbecoming to make a row with his bride so soon after their wedding.

The next day his father went out before sunrise to perform his morning prayers in the nearby mosque, as was his life-long practice. On his return his face had the serene expression that Bulbul found to be a source of comfort and happiness each morning when he greeted her. At the morning's breakfast table he leaned towards her and said gently in a low whisper, "My dear daughter, do not ever do that foolishness you did last evening. We must know where you plan to go. You are new to this country and you have all the time to get to know Cairo well. But please do not choose such unwholesome places like the festival of those Gypsies. Besides, you must never forget that it is your husband's right to know where you are going." His voice became more firm. "In our class of people each married partner must know where the other is going and when he is supposed to be back home. This is indispensable to keeping the family structure in good order." Heavy silence fell upon the family at the table. There was nothing more to say.

the obedient wife

Now, when Bulbul wanted to leave the house to go to the museum or to the area of Giza to watch the excavations of the famous archaeologists working there, she abided by the rules. She would ask permission from her father-in-law or mother-in-law, but not before asking for the consent of her husband.

Things went smoothly until one day, a few months later, when Imam informed her that they would be moving into their new apartment on the Cairo island of Manya el Roda by the end of the month. Imam's declaration of independence came as a shock to his bride even though he had written his feelings about this in letters to her before they were married. His parents had dismissed his "too modern" idea of living apart from the family home so soon after the marriage and thought the matter settled. But apparently it wasn't.

Bulbul didn't want to leave the atmospheric beauty of Old Cairo. She wanted things to stay just the way they were. She always knew that sooner or later she would have to be mistress of her own house, but these pampered and spoiled honeymoon days in Imam's father's house were so pleasant! Here she never had to go into the kitchen; if she ever had, she would probably have been completely lost in it. So far, she had been saved the ordeal of having to actually cook for her husband, let alone manage a household. She could never be even a little like her beautiful mother-in-law whose every gesture spoke of nobility and the womanly virtues.

Imam's will prevailed, and they moved into the apartment he had selected in a very pleasant, tree-lined area of Manya el Roda. Bulbul tried to be a good sport, but she knew right away that being a good Egyptian wife would be an effort, especially the matter of cooking for Imam.

Earlier, during one of her ramblings in Cairo's business center she had visited the Anglo-Egyptian Bookstore where she found an English language book on French cooking. She thought she discovered a treasure, the solution to her culinary woes. Unfortunately, she was too optimistic about the powers of her "miracle book."

"From our first day living in Manya el Roda," she said, "I was destined to turn any kitchen into a disaster area." Even if Bulbul mixed the correct ingredients and put them on the kerosene stove to cook, she would often turn away and become completely absorbed in some book, not looking up again until the kitchen was filled with smoke. After the first incidents of burned or overcooked meals, Imam found it was no use making a scene about food that was, frankly, inedible.

As the couple settled into their new life, Bulbul Abdel Meguid found another reason to avoid the thought of food: She was having the first awful symptoms of morning sickness. Her pregnancy gave her an excuse to ask for some help in that most hateful part of the house, but a hired cook was beyond Imam's financial means and so his nightingale muddled along as best she could.

She had little in common with the wives of the neighborhood. Most of them were married to high officials, had French educations and preferred to speak French rather than English – English being a symbol of the hated occupation. Dorothy's education had been thoroughly English and she knew no other language, and Bulbul was having a terrible struggle learning Arabic. Even years later, after she could speak Arabic with relative fluency, it was still with a heavy English accent.

Imam had a warm disposition and he quickly made friends with the neighbors in the building, especially a fellow teacher and his wife who lived on the third floor. When Imam explained Bulbul's cooking problems the neighbor's wife reacted with compassion. Egyptians have a special weakness for children; a woman with a baby in her womb can always rely on neighbors, even total strangers, to offer their help. This neighbor promptly took Bulbul in hand and supervised the shopping and food preparation. Omm Sety never described how she and the woman managed to communicate, since they had very little language in common, but it had to be through the international language of hand gestures, facial expressions and laughter. However it happened, the thorny problem of the kitchen was momentarily solved.

the village of snakes and scorpions

One day, the friendly third-floor neighbor suggested an outing to the village of Kerdassa, several miles from Giza. Kerdassa is famous for its beautiful needlework and women's *galabeyas*, the traditional long cotton caftans. Bulbul bought herself two robes and a few things for the coming baby, which she knew with certainty was going to be a boy.

During lunch at a café in Kerdassa, they conversed with a woman at the next table who told them about a small hamlet nearby where the entire population had a very curious way of making a living. It has existed since the time of the pharaohs, the woman told them, and the children of the hamlet start from the age of three or four catching scorpions, cobras and horned vipers, which are then sold to laboratories and hospitals for making anti-venom vaccines. The people also catch wolves, hyenas, foxes and wild rabbits, she said, to sell to collectors and European zoological gardens.

Bulbul wanted to see this place for herself, and see what kind of people would be in such a trade. Her neighbor agreed to the jaunt, even though their driver showed only revulsion at the prospect. In the village at the edge of the desert they encountered a group of children who quickly surrounded the visitors in the usual way of curious children all over the world, and then one of the boys brought forth a horned viper, a highly venomous snake. Bulbul walked right up to the snake in a friendly way and offered her bare hand and arm to it. The small, dun-colored creature glided smoothly over her arm until it reached her neck, and then she extended her other arm and the viper slid the rest of the way down and returned to its owner. Her poor neighbor was speechless at the spectacle of Imam's English wife behaving like a snake charmer.

On the way home they stopped for a cup of tea at a rest house near the Giza Pyramids. Bulbul fell into conversation with a rather ample Englishwoman, a Mrs. Perkins, who had taken the table next to theirs. Mrs. Perkins happened to be the secretary of one of the leading archaeologists working in Egypt, George Andrew Reisner. She was gregarious by nature, and since she met very few English-speaking women in the area where her boss was doing his research, she was eager to find any subjects of mutual interest. Naturally, there was lots to talk about, even though it left Bulbul's neighbor staring into her teacup, no doubt now thoroughly disoriented by the unexpected changes in the day's itinerary. What must she have been thinking about Mrs. Abdel Meguid? Omm Sety never said what her relationship was with her neighbor after that.

When the conversation at the rest house came around to Bulbul's experience with the snake that day in the village, Mrs. Perkins mentioned certain spells in the ancient Pyramid Texts that can calm an agitated snake or make it lie low or turn back, or go away entirely. Bulbul was fascinated. She had not encountered those spells in her early studies of the texts.

The Pyramid Texts got their name because they were first discovered inside the 5th Dynasty pyramid of Unas. Even at that ancient time they were very old; no one knows just how old, except that they are among the oldest magical formulas ever written. When Dr. Budge had been her teacher at the British Museum he had spoken of the great power locked within the spells of the Pyramid Texts and warned Dorothy away from the practice of Egyptian magic – which was like telling a clever child not to try to open the locked cupboard with all the candy inside.

This chance meeting with Dr. Reisner's secretary rekindled her determination to perfect her knowledge of hieroglyphics so that she might go deeper into the meaning and the hidden power of the Pyramid Texts. She could not have known that day that within a few years she would be working with the most distinguished Egyptologists of the time, or that the chatty, heavy-set woman at the next table would become one of her good friends.

Unfortunately, this urge to explore and discover belonged to the part of herself that she couldn't share with Imam, and she knew it – one more barrier to her ever being the good Egyptian wife he deserved.   While she awaited the birth of the baby, Bulbul Abdel Meguid tried very hard to rein in her restlessness. In every other way life was actually rather pleasant in Manya el Roda.

someone in the night

And then, without warning, Sety appeared again – this time not as a mummy.   One night Bulbul was drawn up from sleep by a vague uneasiness, as if somebody had exhaled a long, deep breath very close to her cheek.   When she opened her eyes she saw a shimmering, amorphous *something* next to the bed, and a man's tall figure slowly taking form, but not quite fully materializing.   She knew instantly who it was – as she had 15 years before – but now he was dressed in regal attire with the double crown of Egypt* on his head.   She reached out to touch him but she was stopped by an invisible barrier.   He stood there in silence behind it, gazing at her.   Moments later he vanished, leaving behind an almost palpable energy.

Fifteen years of waiting, hoping and wondering.   She didn't know if this visit would be the last for another long span of time.

It wasn't.   He chose his own times and always at night – silent, watching, untouchable.   Bulbul never knew when to expect him, and she lived in fear that Imam would catch sight of this strange, imposing presence in their bedroom.   Yet he never woke, and she was careful not to stir or make a sound.   Barely sleeping for nights on end, she awaited every visit with rapt anticipation.   And she began asking herself the question that had no easy answer: Had her true purpose in coming to Egypt – in marrying Imam – been to meet the beloved vision again?   It was

---

*the crown representing Upper and Lower Egypt

an almost unbearable question. More than that, the timing of Sety's return couldn't have been more awkward.

In the sixth month of her pregnancy her mother and father had come to Egypt for a visit, hoping to reassure themselves that all was well with their daughter in this far-off land. They had made peace with the idea of the marriage. Imam had made diplomatic overtures in the past months, writing loving letters to Bulbul's parents that smoothed the way for a reconciliation. Any fears they had were laid to rest by what they found when they arrived – Imam's fine parents, Imam himself, who seemed to be such a kind and generous son-in-law, and the lovely apartment. All in all, Caroline Eady decided, Dorothy had got the better part of the bargain by far.

The visit was going well until it happened to coincide with one of Sety's appearances.

The Eadys were occupying Dorothy's and Imam's bedroom and Bulbul and Imam slept in a bed on the adjacent porch. One night, Mrs. Eady awoke before dawn, looked toward the French door and caught a quick glimpse a man's shadowy figure on the porch next to the bed. Thinking it was Imam, she just went back to sleep. But in the morning she thought about what she had seen, the man's peculiar attire, and the fact that Imam had stayed with friends that night and couldn't have been the tall man on the porch. Now very much concerned for her daughter, Mrs. Eady wanted to know who it was. Dorothy pretended ignorance, but she had always been a poor liar, and her mother was sure she was keeping some secret and she demanded to know what was going on.

Bulbul gathered up her courage. She told her mother matter-of-factly that what she had seen was the ghost of Sety the First, adding, "He has been a frequent visitor of late, but that is a long story." Caroline Eady didn't want to hear more. This latest "news" was just too much for her; it brought up all her old distress about Dorothy's strangeness. Carolyn Eady thought it best if she and her husband cut short their visit and returned to England. Mother and daughter agreed that Imam mustn't be told about Sety's appearance. What could Caroline possibly say about it anyway? When the Eadys left soon after, they parted lovingly with their daughter, with each knowing that they might never have a full reconciliation, because Dorothy's life would always be confounding to them.

During a conversation with Omm Sety in 1972, I questioned her about Sety's early visits. "He appeared to you in Manya el Roda, but how many times did he come to your room while you were living with Imam's family?"

"Oh, many times he would come – many times. Once my father-in-law saw him sitting on my bed when I was ill. And later Hassan Karam saw him." Hassan Karam was a close friend of Omm Sety's husband. He had a large shop in the Khan el Khalili bazaar where he sold jewelry and rare specimens of amber. "Karam saw only his arm, but my father-in-law saw him as a living king. But of course my father-in-law didn't stop to see if he was solid or not!" she laughed. "Bit of a shock for the poor old chap. He was a very religious man." And Bulbul was certainly not going to tell him what she knew about the ghostly visitor.

Three months after her parents departed, Bulbul Abdel Meguid gave birth.

SEVEN

Omm Sety

"I was unable to confess to him that
I had a secret life..." OS

It should not have surprised anyone that Bulbul Abdel Meguid would name her newborn son after an ancient king of Egypt. But it raised a terrible tempest.

In Egypt, as it is everywhere, choosing the right name for a child is of great importance. My own name was arrived at only after long discussions among my parents and all four of my grandparents. My father wanted to call me Hannibal, after the famous Carthaginian conqueror. He saw in that intrepid soldier the ideal man of courage, invincible will and resourceful planning. My grandparents were dismayed. Why this unusual name, they asked. And if it *must* be uncommon, why not choose a more classic Egyptian or early Arabic name?

My father had a sudden inspiration. He chose my actual name, Hanny, after an Arab Andalusian poet, which also happened to be the name of one of the most popular and talented football players in Egypt at that moment. Since my father was among the founding committee of the *Nadi el Ahly*, the National Club, which regularly fielded national championship teams, the elders of his family could see the reason for the name and gave their heartfelt approval. And my father had a son who would grow up with the name of not only a first-rate athlete, but an Andalusian poet and, more distantly, an ancient conqueror.

But back to the baby we are concerned with here. Bulbul spent the last days of her pregnancy in the Abdel Meguid family home. It was not yet the fashion to give birth in a hospital, and Cairo was world famous for its excellent midwives. Even in the earliest temples in Upper Egypt one can still see beautiful depictions of childbirth, blessed and helped by the presence of Isis and other goddesses concerned with this auspicious occasion.

Bulbul moved back into her in-laws' home willingly and happily, knowing that she would be pampered and saved from her loathsome kitchen chores. Imam was also spared the worry that he might come home from work to find that Bulbul had had another of her "adventures." In the benevolent custody of his mother she would be more likely to think before yielding to impulses that could put her in harm's way, especially in her condition. Bulbul behaved herself, often strolling with Haj Abdel Meguid in the evenings for a leisurely turn around the area of the great Mohammed Ali Mosque.

She never wavered in her belief that the baby inside her was a boy. There was no ultrasound then; she just knew. In ancient Egypt the sex of the baby was predicted in another way, by taking some urine from the pregnant woman, dividing it into two parts, and putting it into two flat plates. To one plate some grains of emmer wheat were added, to the other some grains of barley, and both were left to germinate. If the wheat came up first, the baby would be a male. But Bulbul did not know about this ancient ritual, despite her readings in Egyptian history. If she had, she would have been the first to prepare the two plates and watch to see which one sprouted.

"My delivery was a quick one," she told me. "It is really a credit to the midwife. She was so incredibly sure of herself, so calm. I was amazed. She just examined the lower half of my body quite deftly and when the pains started she smiled and did not make any attempt to help, saying, '*Ya Binti* (my daughter), you will have a nice, normal delivery. Help yourself with two or three deep, long breaths. Your baby is in a hurry to get out and see this crazy world.' She only assisted when the baby's

64

head was out and the rest of the body was gliding forth. I never pushed or cried out, and the midwife looked incredulously at this British phenomenon who made no remarks at all."

Everybody in the family was happy at the arrival of a boy. As in most parts of the world then, male progeny were preferred. The question of naming the child arose right away and the family discussions began in earnest. Bulbul knew what she wanted to call him, the name nearest to her heart – Sety – but she said nothing at first.

Though it was common to name one's boy after his father, Imam was not very enthusiastic about that and neither was Haj Abdel Meguid. They both favored an old romantic name from early Islam, like Khaled, Tarek, Hisham or Amr. Bulbul listened, growing more impatient while the names were debated. She wanted none of them. As if ridding herself of a heavy burden she stopped the argument by announcing: "I choose the name Sety."

Her tone had a finality that made all members of the family momentarily speechless. It was left to Haj Abdel Meguid to explain why the too-unusual name would never do. "My dear child," he said gently, "you must be aware by now that we are rather old fashioned and a bit conservative, too."

"I am quite aware of that, but I have chosen an ancient Egyptian name of a highly revered king," she replied. "Sety is a nice, simple name – and easy to remember."

"That is not the point," the older man said, intent on preventing a grave mistake. "Egyptians are not used to extremely ancient names, such as those of pharaohs. It will make of him a subject of ridicule. We can be merciless with our sense of humor, I must warn you."

His arguments failed to convince. Finally, all the family members retired in silent protest. But Bulbul knew she had won.

In those days it was (and still is) traditional to celebrate the naming of a baby on the seventh day after its birth. And so, on the seventh day after little Sety's birth, the large, extended family of the Abdel Meguids gathered for the ceremony of *el sebou*, the many children waiting in great anticipation of all the excitement that a *sebou* brings with it. The ceremony began with placing the baby on a large sieve that had been cleaned and purified and decorated with flowing ribbons.* As the sieve was gently rocked and shaken, seven children danced around the baby, singing songs sung only for this occasion, after which a large tart was brought in, ablaze with seven candles for the children to blow out. That was the signal for a woman to come forward holding a bronze mortar and pestle. She pounded the pestle three times into the mortar and the children sang to the baby, "You will obey Mama's advice." Then three more poundings and, "You will obey Papa's advice." The ceremony ended with a final series of loud poundings. The children of the Abdel Meguid family were then free to devour the tart and sweetmeats and drinks, and the cookies shaped like dogs, cats, teddy bears, lambs and donkeys, while the adults felt satisfied that the event was a success – in spite of the odd name the mother had bestowed on the baby.

In the festive Abdel Meguid house, Sety lay quietly in his elaborately swathed cradle, oblivious to the noisy goings-on around him. All the friends and family who came to look upon the new arrival could only exclaim, "*Masha Allah!* What a beautiful, smiling baby!" They were probably also thinking, *The poor thing will be teased with that name.* In addition to being the name of an ancient pharaoh, unusual by itself, it also sounded like the word for "grandmother" when pronounced a certain way; and if pronounced another way it meant "Mr. T."

Hor-Ra

One day, Bulbul was obliged to go to the commercial center of Cairo, the district around Midan el Attaba el Khadra – Green

---

*Elements of the ceremony harken back to ancient times. In Hatshepsut's temple at Deir el Bahri, visitors can still see the depiction of the female pharaoh's divine birth, with the god Anubis holding a sieve to determine the length of her life. As with so many folk customs, some of the original context has probably been lost, since the modern "sieving of the baby" doesn't relate to lifespan, but is now simply an auspicious ritual.

Park Square. Baby Sety was in need of some new underwear and warmer clothes for the coming winter. As inevitable as Fate itself, Bulbul found herself bumping into her Gypsy "friend" from the fair, the one who had helped Tarek get her out of the mess she caused with the poor, battered monkey. He was dressed entirely in black, with coal-black hair, eyes and moustache, and he looked to Bulbul like a figure out of some Greek tragedy.

He saluted her with a hard, expressionless face and began speaking almost incoherently about a grave wrong that had been done to him. For whatever reason, he wanted to tell her that he had been rudely displaced in the hierarchy of his clan. The odd encounter ended abruptly. When he shook Bulbul's hand goodbye she was relieved, but his sorrowful, dark wake left her feeling uneasy and apprehensive, as if the day itself were inauspicious. Even when she returned home she couldn't shake the haunted mood.

That night Bulbul woke up from the midst of sleep quite suddenly. Something, or someone, was whispering words in her ear in a language she could not quite comprehend. She knew it was not Sety, even though she had yet to hear him speak. She just knew that this voice could not possibly be his. Many years later, she described the visitation in detail: "He had a very strange, hypnotic voice. As he continued talking I believe I went into a sort of trance, although I remained half-conscious. A part of my brain was beginning to grasp the meaning of this whispering. It was somebody trying to tell me, in a patchy, disconnected way, the story of some previous life – which turned out to be my own.

"This came as a shock to me, although I had always been suspicious that I had some sort of a previous existence in this land. And now 'something' was trying to dictate to me the events of a remote life in an unknown past. At the start I was not able to understand a word. The voice was a monotone – not a normal droning voice, but rather that of an individual charged with a hateful mission, a commitment that filled him with suppressed revulsion. It was a moonlit night and I was feeling sort of hypnotized or mesmerized, entirely at a loss what to do."

She said nothing about it to Imam. Even if she had described it as a dream, which it certainly wasn't, she would have had to explain too much, and she hadn't yet satisfied herself about its meaning. Imam knew that odd things happened around her at times – her father-in-law had been quite vocal on that point – and up until now he seemed not especially concerned or disquieted. Shortly thereafter, on the next full moon, the visitor came a second time. It was just after midnight, Omm Sety recalled, "There was a desk near the window and when the voice woke me up I just slipped quietly from bed and walked towards the window to the desk. I said nothing and felt rather helpless. The owner of the voice altered his tone and became suddenly assertive. *'Sesh...sesh,'* he said to me several times. I had recently taken up my study of hieroglyphs again and I began to understand what he was telling me: *Write...write,* or *put down... put down.*

"But write what? The voice became softer and softer and I fell into an extended trance. I think I gradually lost all sense of time and surroundings. On the desk was an empty large black notebook with an inkpot beside it. I think I wrote for one hour, perhaps much more, I just could not tell. I know that afterwards I had put away what I had been writing.

"When I woke up the next morning I prepared a quick breakfast for Imam. He was in a hurry to be off to work and I was relieved that he said nothing to me about the night before. I was certain he must have noticed my absence from bed. When he had left the house I rushed to see what was written in my notebook. I was quite stunned to see that it was disjointed phrases in Demotic, the cursive form of hieroglyphs invented for public use and for teaching students in the *Per Ankh.**

---

*the House of Life, a school for scribes associated with the major temples

"I cried out, 'Damn you, Gypsy! Meeting you was a bad omen. Good Lord...as if I were not already deep in trouble with Imam.

"When I was in a trance I could understand what I was scribbling, but now in broad daylight I was as stupid as a cow watching a train go by. When a few years later I showed some of the pages to Professor Cerny, the scholar and authority on Demotic from London University, he was quite impressed and said, 'You write well indeed, for a beginner. If you continue to be so enthusiastic about Demotic papyri I may be able to find you a good job.' Luckily he never asked me the source of my writings. They certainly weren't any papyri he had ever seen!"

But trouble was growing in the household. The disembodied voice came to her again and again, demanding that Bulbul write what he was telling her, which meant that there were hours when she would sit spellbound at the moonlit window, listening to something only she could hear. "Imam never asked me what the hell I was writing night after night," she said, "What seemed to annoy him was that I was very careful to hide it from him."

For Bulbul Abdel Meguid, these, in her opinion, were the most difficult days of her life. "I was torn between two contradictory emotions," she said. "I was tormented by seeing the man I had always loved [Sety], and not being able to talk to him or even touch him. Just imagine sitting so close to him with no word exchanged between us. And then there was that other, I mean that hateful voice talking to me all the time and waking me in the middle of the night. An impossible situation – I should say really infernal: a man I cannot talk to, whom I loved so much, and a voice I cannot see, who was talking, dictating to me all the time, non-stop. His monotonous, tired, droning voice was both confusing and perplexing because I was writing something I could not fully understand. But worst of all, I had a person whom I *could* talk to, I *could* touch, I *could* make love with – and I was unable to confess to him that I had a secret life with a man from a remote past who appeared when Imam was not there, and a voice that could come any time late at night.

"Sometimes I hated myself. Imam was such a patient, tolerant and always caring husband to a worthless wife. Imam had a circle of friends, all of whom were of the same generation. Some I had met before in England in the company of Imam. They were not particularly interested in ancient Egyptian history, being far more involved with present-day Egypt, the shaky political situation, student unrest and the fight to end British occupation. There was little I could discuss with them of my own preoccupations. I was extremely anxious to pursue my study of hieroglyphs, and especially Demotic, to be able to decipher the dictation. It was a hell of a situation, being in that state of trance, unable to respond or ask questions that might help me understand to what kind of world I was being mercilessly driven."

Eventually, the messenger revealed his name: Hor-Ra. It took Hor-Ra more than a year to discharge his duty – and a tiresome one at that, as he made very clear to Bulbul by the disinterested tone of his voice. In the meantime, Mrs. Abdel Meguid did not pass her time idly. She bought some scholarly books on hieroglyphs and Demotic, and with fanatical persistence set herself to figuring out Hor-Ra's strange story.

Not surprisingly, Bulbul and Imam were quickly drifting apart. At this point his son was Imam's only source of joy. Baby Sety was a plump, healthy, smiling child who attracted attention wherever he was taken. Bulbul and Imam knew that it was only a matter of time before they would separate, though neither gave voice to the idea. It was as though they had silently agreed to adopt the old Sufi doctrine of "Leave it to God."

Finally, Allah intervened. Imam was offered a one-year contract to teach school in Iraq, at double his present Cairo salary. He promptly accepted, and a few days later he was on a plane for Baghdad, leaving his wife and baby behind with a monthly support stipend. It was October 1935, not quite two years into the marriage. Imam's quick decision had the support of his father who thought it was a good opportunity for his son to think things over alone and dispassionately.

Bulbul was happy to be alone as well. She had more time to study, to care for the baby and be spared the daily headache of preparing something edible for her husband. She had no talent at all for either housework or cooking. Her idea of cuisine was anything that came to hand. "I am like the Americans," she once said, "I'll eat anything." She was also resourceful. There was a small restaurant she knew about where artisans, taxi drivers and others, mostly bachelors, ate who could not afford to pay a cook. The food was excellent and Bulbul managed to make a deal with the owner to have a boy on a bicycle bring her the *plat du jour*. She was the only home-delivery client in the whole of the Manyal el Roda district.

Imam's departure left her free to do something else that she had been spoiling to do. One day, baby in tow, she went out to the Pyramid Plateau in Giza and asked permission from Professor Selim Hassan, the dean of Egyptologists at the time, to pitch a tent near his excavations and observe his work. She introduced herself as the English girl who had years earlier sent him her tiny collection of ancient Egyptian artifacts as a token of her esteem.

"So it was you who sent those coins and beads and statuettes?"

"Yes sir, that was me, Dorothy Eady," she replied. He said that she could stay, on condition that she watch the excavation from a reasonable distance.

On the next day she was given the name that she was to be called for the rest of her life: *Omm Sety*, mother of Sety. In the Egyptian countryside the polite and only acceptable way to address a married woman is as the mother of her firstborn; in this case it would be Omm Sety. Since the Giza area at the time was considered part of the countryside and not part of cosmopolitan Cairo, all the foremen and laborers called her Omm Sety.

Her keen interest in the work of Selim Hassan and the other archaeologists in the area did not escape notice. Her artistic abilities became known too, and very soon Professor Hassan took her on as a draftsman, even though it was without pay at first. She proved to be a talented designer, indispensable to the process of copying and recording the numerous artifacts that came out of Selim Hassan's dig.

As Bulbul's work at the Pyramids continued, her contribution became more and more important. Eventually, she undertook to edit parts of Selim Hassan's colossal ten-volume magnum opus, *Excavations at Giza*. When it was finally published several years later, he included "special mention with gratitude" to Dorothy Eady for her drawings, editing, proofreading and indexing.

If it seems like a lot for a woman with a baby to be involved with, along with her independent studies, it was. In the hindsight of her later life she admitted with regret that too often she was so absorbed in her work that she unpardonably neglected the care of her baby. There were times when she would drop little Sety off inside the handiest cleared tomb and ask one of the watchmen to look after him. The poor man would soon cry out, "Omm Sety, come very quickly, please! The boy wants to eat!"

In those months while Imam was away, other things were happening in Bulbul's life as well. The visits of King Sety were becoming more frequent, though without any fixed schedule. He never fully materialized to her, always appearing as a hazy shadow, a remote, silent, unapproachable vision – as if he were obliged to distance himself from her.

And there was Hor-Ra, whose droning voice spoke to her on moonlit nights, always at full moon, sometimes at impossible hours when she was badly in need of sleep. As the dictation proceeded, the material of the revelations became more and more disjointed. It was still quite bewildering to Bulbul that in a trance state she could write so correctly in a language that she was finding, in her waking hours, to be so very difficult. Demotic was rather "obdurate," she used to say. "It looked to me like nothing I could appreciate – as if a beautiful hieroglyphic text

had been run over by a lorry and distorted totally out of shape."
But she would not give up.

When Hor-Ra's dictation finally came to an end, Omm
Sety was left to discover the meaning of the words in her black
notebook. She knew this was the most important document she
had ever seen or ever would see. Bent over her Demotic gram-
mars long into the nights, she began to transliterate Hor-Ra's
dictation into English. Slowly, character by character, she pieced
the story together. The fact that she could do it at all, on her
own and without formal instruction, is a wonder in itself. Six
months after Hor-Ra's final visit, and just before Imam was to
return from Iraq, she finished translating the principal elements
of the story. As terrifying as parts of it were, she knew it was *her*
story and that from now on her life could never be the same.

The narrative started with a blunt, disturbing pronounce-
ment: *O, Bentreshyt, you have sinned, and your crime was punished by
death.* And then Hor-Ra told her why.

*Bentreshyt, ye sinner: It will take much time and many chapters
to tell of a tragedy that took place in the town of Abdu* during
the reign of the Majesty of King Sety...*

*You were born into a poor family not far from Abdu. Your
father was a soldier, your mother a simple vegetable seller whose
ancestors were from Syria. She had blue eyes and blond hair,
as did you. For this she was most visible among the women in
the countryside. But she was weak and fell ill quite often...*

*Your home was two hundred cubits from Shuna pa hib.** Your
father was on a mission in Men Nefer*** in the north, in the
company of the officer in charge of the Abdu garrison. Four
months later, when he returned he found your mother dead. He*

*Abydos
**Shunet el Zebib, an ancient fortress-like structure of unknown origin
***Memphis, the capital city of the early dynasties

loved her much and his grief was beyond words. He was worried about your future. You were still a child, Bentreshyt, and one day your father was ordered to join the garrison of Wasit*...

He was advised to hand you to the care of the high priest in the temple beside the Sacred Lake of Abdu. There he was sure you would be well fed, well clothed and looked after. It was the best your father could do for you, Bentreshyt....There, you were vowed as a priestess of our Lady Isis and you began your long training. You refuted all worldly pleasures. In time you grew out of your child's body...

O Bentreshyt: you were vowed to remain a virgin and you studied well for your role in the sacred drama of our Lord Wsir.** Your life was good...

The House-of-Men-Maat-Ra*** was under construction. The Majesty of King Sety came there to oversee the work when he was not abroad fighting the Asiatics or busy with state problems. He was a good ruler, a true, brave soldier. One day, after inspecting the work in the temple he went to rest in his palace, which was called Heartsease-in-Abdu, to the north of the First Court. In the afternoon he went for a walk in the garden south of the Hall of the Sacred Barques. There he saw a beautiful young girl. That was you, Bentreshyt. He immediately fell in love with you. That was unpardonable. Flesh is weak...

For him you were like a fresh lotus carried by the north wind and offering her perfume to His Majesty's nostrils. In a moment of weakness you both forgot to whom you were vowed as a priestess...

---

*ancient Thebes; modern Luxor
**Osiris
***the Sety Temple

Bentreshyt, ye sinner: In time the Majesty of King Sety departed from Abdu and your belly began to swell. It was noticed. The Chief Priest noticed. You had broken the holiest of the rules. It is true, he was the attorney, judge and executioner at the same time. That you were young and inexperienced did not diminish the horror of your crime. By the laws of Khem* no one could come forth to defend you. You were unlucky.

Bentreshyt: the first thing you should have done after eating the uncooked goose,** the very first thing, was to go and make ablution. Recite the words of remorse. Ask forgiveness from our Lord and our Lady Isis. Maybe you could have been spared. Had the Majesty of King Men-Maat-Ra been in Abdu he could have granted a royal pardon. But you lost the only chance that could have stayed your punishment and you chose to end your life by your own hand.

O Bentreshyt: this would not atone for His Majesty's crime and yours. In Amenti you would still have to be judged by the Council and be severely punished – both of you. And you were...

When the Majesty of King Men-Maat-Ra came again to Abdu he had to suffer the shock of hearing of your death. The Chief Priest asked for an audience and told the story in frankness. His Majesty's grief was beyond words. The palace dignitaries later saw him sitting alone in the garden where you first met. He sat with his head bent down into the two palms of his hands. Some swore that tears ran upon his cheeks. Until the day he died he never again returned to Abdu...

It is difficult to know whether these revelations from the Beyond were a blessing or some sort of pharaonic curse. Having

---

*Egypt, the Black Land
**illicit sex

known Omm Sety for 25 years and been witness to most of the events that came to pass in her life in Abydos, I can only say that Hor-Ra's recitation was both a blessing *and* a curse. One thing, however, is certain – they directed, guided and ruled her during her whole life in Egypt until she was finally buried in Abydos.

After she finished the translation there is little doubt she was a tormented woman. At times she felt like crying. "It was very strange," she admitted, thinking back on those days, "I can count on my fingers the number of times I have broken into tears in all my life." Too many things were happening to her. She could cope with one problem at a time, but the three or four that were before her were just too much.

At this crossroads she could not decide whether she could possibly create a happy marriage with Imam, increasingly convinced that she was simply making herself a burden, a nuisance to her husband. "Imam was a perfect gentleman...always. Even my mother was impressed by his sensitivity and kindness, and outraged at my utter incompetence as a proper housewife."

I don't know how much, if any, involvement the elder Abdel Meguids had in little Sety's life at this time. Omm Sety did not mention if there were visits, but one must assume that there were the usual family interactions while Imam was away, though I would imagine that Omm Sety "neglected" to tell them much about her work at the pyramids, especially the unusual baby-sitting arrangements there.

Imam seldom wrote from Baghdad. This year away from Bulbul must have given him the distance necessary to help him make up his mind about the future – with or without his wife – and to realize that theirs was an unrealistic bond.

Egyptians in general have never been enthusiastic about emigration, leaving *Misr Omm el Donya* – Egypt, Mother of the World, as they call it. The love of country is deep-rooted in the heart of every Egyptian. They would feel homesick as soon as they touched the soil of a foreign land. I was told by friends of Imam that he never felt at home in Baghdad. The pay was more than satisfactory and he had won the heart of all those he had to deal with – students, other teachers and bosses. At the end of the year he gently rejected attempts to convince him to renew his contract for one more year. He always said, "I cannot stay that long away from my son." It was a polite way of saying, "I have had enough. I am homesick."

In the spring of 1936 Imam was back home. The first meeting with his nightingale was cool and awkward, marked by an indifferent kiss on her forehead, but he couldn't conceal his eagerness to hold his son in his arms again. Bulbul understood the message. Later when they were alone she told him about the progress of her studies, and because she couldn't *not* mention it, she told him about her work with Selim Hassan out at the pyramids. Imam was appalled. It was bad enough that his wife was now an employee of some sort, but to subject the baby to the rough environment of a desert excavation was beyond his tolerance. Moreover, he had suspected that she had some peculiar second life that he could never be a part of.

Divorce was inevitable. It came without remorse, bitterness or emotional scenes. It was simply the only solution.

Amentí

"...and suddenly I was retracing my journey...
through the gray fog, then down into my bedroom
and my mortal body." OS

Very soon the ex-Mrs. Abdel Meguid found a small apartment quite close to the pyramids and the Sphinx, in the village of Nazlet el Simman. It had a nice roof terrace for sleeping during the warm summer nights. Her needs were simple; she had her child with her, she had quickly adopted three cats and she was living a stone's throw from her work with Selim Hassan. Only one thing was not yet resolved – the problem of her ghostly beloved. He continued to visit her in the middle of the night, sometimes almost fully materialized, but more often just a felt presence next to her. This went on for a long time, with not a word or a touch passing between them.

A year or so after she moved to the pyramids she woke from sleep one night to see someone else at her bedside. He was young and dressed in the manner of the lower echelons of the ancient priesthood. He spoke something to her in the old language and he beckoned to her, speaking other words of instruction that she could not completely understand. He identified himself as Ptah-Mes. His face was inscrutable but his voice was a welcome change from the monotones of Hor-Ra, who had always seemed to be speaking from the bottom of a tomb shaft. This young man's voice was clear and vibrant. She knew enough of the standard scholarly pronunciation of the ancient language to figure out that she was being summoned by "our Lord," and she knew that meant Sety.

Suddenly, Omm Sety found herself walking on air, literally, with Ptah-Mes beside her. Looking down, she saw that her body was still lying on the bed in her nightclothes, while the observing part of her was floating above, and quite naked.

Many years later, when she told me about the incident, I asked her how it felt to leave her body that way. "You feel light," she said, "and you have an overwhelming sense of freedom. In that first astral travel I followed Ptah-Mes. We flew high over the pyramids and I could see the whole area of the Giza Plateau. Then visibility gradually became obscured, as if we were passing through a thick, gray fog. I had no sense of time at all. I do not know how long I moved in that fog, but at some instant it suddenly lifted."

Emerging from the fog, she was surprised to find that they were in front of an imposing building. The astral highway had brought her to a place and a realm that she soon understood to be Amenti. She was led through a long passage into a great room, and seated in that room was His Majesty, King Sety – not as the phantom or the mummy, but as a man. Ptah-Mes made a sign of obeisance and retired to a corner of the room.

"My heart was racing," she said. "His Majesty addressed me and asked me to sit down. He set a cushion for me on the floor next to him. And then we talked, and to my great astonishment I quite understood every word he said. He was holding my hand all the time. It was as if a secret flow of strength, understanding and love was running from him to my whole body. As it was nearing dawn, Ptah-Mes came to fetch me and take me home again. I wanted to stay longer but His Majesty said very gently, 'It is time, my beautiful lotus, to go back.' He pulled me to him and we embraced and kissed, long and passionately.

"When at last we drew apart, I pleaded to be able to come again, by myself. His face became grave and he said, 'This form of travel is a dangerous practice – you cannot do it by yourself;

you must be accompanied by an envoy from my side. You do not know what evil spirits can do to you on your way to Amenti.'

"Ptah-Mes had begun shuffling impatiently. His Majesty smiled at him and gestured for us to go, and suddenly I was retracing my journey, back through the passage, into the air again, through the gray fog, then down into my bedroom and my mortal body. I remember that I sighed heavily and immediately fell into a deep sleep."

A few days later she was asked to report to the director of the Egyptian Museum, where she was offered an assistant's job. At this time she had been working for Selim Hassan, making herself useful to him in a number of ways, as an epigrapher copying tomb inscriptions and as his librarian making order of his office, all the while studying his methods of scientific excavation and learning scholarly lessons from this great Egyptologist. Her work had been without salary but she considered it the most valuable apprenticeship anyone could have found. Of course she was aware that Selim Hassan was behind this new job posting at the museum and she was delighted with this opportunity to have her first real job with the Antiquities Department. She was the first woman ever to be engaged as a member of the department.

There was a problem right away. She began arriving at the museum with her toddler in tow. She had always taken him with her at the pyramids, and no one had minded; everyone had loved the engaging little child. It didn't occur to her not to bring him with her to the museum. But the little boy was blessed with an intense curiosity and high energy, and his mother's new workplace was full of the most wonderful things – statuettes, coins, models of ships, houses, ancient toys – all residing temptingly behind the windows of the display cases, not to mention the larger statues and sarcophagi that stood within reach of his busy hands.

Omm Sety's immediate superior at the time was a German scholar named Englebach, a highly disciplined, methodical and orderly man who was extremely displeased to find a baby rampaging around his quiet domain. He could not tolerate the presence of a child still unable to walk properly, let alone handle artifacts, and he said so. Interventions by other staff members were to no avail and over time the situation only worsened, until Selim Hassan stepped in with a solution. He valued Omm Sety too much to allow the conflict to continue. When he offered her a contract to be his paid secretary and assist with his work excavating around the Sphinx, she jumped at the chance. He must have done some diplomatic work behind the scenes to arrange funding for the position.

Giza. After her divorce, Omm Sety lived in this two-story house in the village of Nazlet el Simman, close to the Pyramids where she was working. Her son, Sety, was a little over a year old. There were few houses there at that time and she had a full view of the Khafra pyramid and a grove of very old sycamores. (Hanny el Zeini)

In Nazlet el Simman, the village where she lived, she became the object of busy gossip because at certain times of the month she would go out late at night and lay offerings of bread and beer between the paws of the Sphinx, then kneel in prayer before walking slowly home. To give honor to the Sphinx as the embodiment of the great god Horus came as naturally to her as breathing. Was it something she remembered from the past, or had she learned it at the knee of Dr. Budge? Perhaps both.

And this was not all: Not far from her rooms there was (and is still) a very old sycamore tree. Every evening a beautiful hawk would come and hover over the tree, then settle on a branch and utter his cries. Omm Sety became his friend, leaving pieces of meat on the windowsill of her living room for the bird to snatch up. The villagers didn't know what to make of this friendship. He began to hover in front of her window each day when she returned from work, and call for her in a singing chant, then alight gently and devour the offering. She named him Horus, after the falcon-god, the son of Isis and Osiris. Among the poems that Omm Sety wrote during this period is one in which she extols the beauty of these birds and prays to Horus to protect them all.

Hawks forever circling, wheeling,
Utter their weird and mournful cry,
And hovering on motionless wings,
Hang like stars in the turquoise sky.

O Horus of Edfu, guard all hawks,
Strengthen their wings and protect their sight,
For they were held, in days long past,
Sacred birds in this land of light.

Sekhem

The astral visits to Amenti continued, not often, but enough to give Omm Sety's heart assurance of Sety's reality. She had no way of predicting when Ptah-Mes would summon her from sleep with the words, "Our Lord wants you," and guide her on the astral journey to Sety's world. Each time was as unexpected and startling as the first – and maddingly frustrating. Only there in Amenti were she and Sety able to actually speak to one another and touch.

In Amenti she met Ramesses, Sety's son, and other members of the king's household. Those were lovely evenings, she liked to say, which surely must have been an understatement. She met a priest named Mery, and his "silly" wife, she said, and the high priest Wen-nefer, and even some of Sety's officers.

During those astral visits Sety told her of his inconsolable grief at the death of Bentreshyt. "It was the news that your sweet body had been hacked to pieces, burned, and utterly destroyed, that plunged me into madness." After his own death several years later he searched for her, only to be told by the mysterious, all-powerful Council* that he would not find her because "she was sleeping in the blackness." But still he searched, anguished, unaware of the passage of the centuries, until he somehow became aware of the existence of a young girl who was living in the cold northern islands of Britain. He forced his way down through the levels of life to see her, and that was the night that his mummified figure appeared to 14-year-old Dorothy Eady, and Dorothy looked into his eyes – the eyes of somebody from hell who had finally seen the way out. But now, during her brief visits in Amenti he could tell her how happy he was once more. "I have found you again," he said, "exactly the same as when I first saw you in the temple garden."

For me, as Omm Sety's friend, I found the story of the king and the young priestess somewhat disturbing, since his violation of her had overtones of rape. But she insisted that that was not so, that it was entirely consensual in her memory of it. She reminded me that at 14 she would not have been considered a child, but a woman of marriageable age. I asked her to explain to me why their sexual relations should be considered a crime, and if the Council had passed some kind of sentence on him for it.

---

*According to Sety, the Council is responsible for keeping order in Amenti, and is answerable to Osiris. They exist in a great hall made entirely of black stone. Nobody has ever actually seen them; they are just voices, neither male nor female.

"Oh yes," she replied, "that was the whole trouble. It was only the fact that the girl was temple property. I mean, if she'd been one of the ordinary priestesses, she would be free to marry and nobody would say anything about it. If she'd been any ordinary girl and the king had picked her out, well, the whole family would have been overcome with the honor. But just because she happened to have been dedicated to the temple – because they wanted to bring her up to be one of these girls who play the part of Isis or Nephthys in the sacred drama – *that* was what all the trouble was about. Of course, in Sety's own eyes *and* Bentreshyt's eyes, it *was* a crime. And of course they were both judged by their own consciences."

One night in the autumn of 1952, the young priest Ptah Mes appeared to her in room and murmured the usual words before he escorted her on the now-familiar walk in the clouds that passed through the gray fog and ended in the palace in Amenti.

Sety could barely contain his emotions on seeing her. "My white lotus," said, gathering her into his arms, "I have wonderful news! I am permitted now to come and stay with you as a normal being." His voice grew soft. "You know what to expect." Ramesses was standing behind his father watching her like a lynx. She did not need to consider what His Majesty was telling her, and she answered quickly, "My Lord, I have waited for so long to hear this from you!"

"But my coming to you, my 'putting on flesh,' is conditional," he cautioned. "You must know that every time I materialize after my astral travel it will be necessary that I take some of your *sekhem** to be able to do so. The Council is very firm about this. And I must have your consent. Taking part of your sekhem could weaken you as time goes by.** So you must pray to our Lord Osiris to accept your consent and you must also present an offering to our Lady Isis to bless our love."

---

*vital force
**I believe that that did, indeed, occur.

85

Those were the terms and they could not be negotiated, since it was a matter of gravest importance. Omm Sety agreed at once. The days (or rather, nights) that followed were the happiest of her life. There was no doubt that he was a fully materialized man, as Omm Sety soon discovered. Not only was he the tender and skillful lover that she remembered, but he was utterly real in other ways.

> *November 28, 1973*
> *H.M. came early last night. He was cold, but got under the blanket and I put the hot-water bottle against his back. After a while I said that I knew that in this materialized body he could feel heat and cold, and asked if he could also feel pain. He replied, "This body that I use is exactly like that of a person living on the back of Geb.* With it I can feel comfort and pain, and as you know, I can laugh and weep, and you know what else I can do!"*
>
> *Then I asked, if he were cut or scratched would he bleed? He said, "Truly I would bleed. Scratch me and see." I wouldn't, as I could not bear to hurt him, so he scratched his own hand with his fingernail, and it bled. I wiped the blood away and kissed the scratch, and he laughed and said, "This body could be gravely hurt, it could be killed, but that would be of no importance; in a wink of an eye I can throw it away."*

I once asked Omm Sety to elaborate on the exact nature of their physical relationship: "Could you have a normal relation of husband and wife," I asked, "and could you produce children together?"

She laughed, saying that when he had first come in his fully materialized form he was able to exert his manly powers quite well. However, there was no possibility of having children with him, she said, because he had to depart before the sun came up

---

*Geb is the earth, consort of the sky goddess Nut.

and he could leave nothing of himself behind.* "Otherwise, by now there would be a counterrevolution, with a young man claiming the throne!" He told her he intended to marry her in Amenti. When she said that wasn't necessary, he insisted that it was. She laughed again, saying she would have to wait until she was dead before he made an honest woman of her.

One of the unbending rules of the arrangement was that he could only come at night and had to depart at dawn. Wherever she made her bed he would find her, he promised, which caused her to refuse invitations from friends to stay overnight in their homes for fear that others might see her visiting lover.

She had no reason to doubt that he would visit her regularly – and he did, for a while – but there was a time when he stayed away for weeks without a sign, and Omm Sety was frantic. Was that to be the end of it? There was no way she could send herself to Amenti on her own, to see for herself what was happening. She could only wait. When he appeared again at her bedside she gently chided him for his neglect, disguising her fear of losing him. He said, "But I was here yesterday – don't you remember?"

The simple explanation was that Sety had no sense of time between Amenti and Earth.

One night Omm Sety asked Sety to tell her more about Amenti.

August 28, 1973
*H.M. came early last night. I was still awake. He was in a good mood, so I thought I'd try a few questions. I wanted to know about life in Amenti, and if there was a "good place" and a "bad place." He said, "This is not easy to explain to you, Bentreshy.** In truth, there is only one place, which is good, but*

---

*from a conversation quoted in Cott, p. 65
**The proper spelling of her name is Bentreshyt, but by the 19th Dynasty the final 't' was no longer sounded. O.S. recorded it the way she heard Sety speak it to her.

*to evil-doers it seems to be bad. The place where I now dwell is bad, bad because it is full of memories of the terrible time I spent there after your death. My son Ramesses dwells near to me. As you know, he can visit me, but I cannot visit him."
I said, "Forgive my question, Lord, but what about your servants and the soldiers who stand on guard at your palace, what is their state?"*

He smiled and replied, "They are all good people who loved me in our life on earth. The soldiers are men of my army, whose happiness is to serve their old Commander, the servants are all my servants on earth. They were happy to serve me, and they ask for nothing better now…"*

I asked if it was true that every building and monument on earth had its counterpart in Amenti. He said, "This is true, but the dwellers in Amenti see only those buildings and monuments that existed when they were dwelling on earth, just as they see and contact those persons who were living during their own lifetimes."

From this, it would seem that all the people in Amenti are existing in special states of consciousness. I think the Hindus have a similar belief which they call "illusion." I asked, "Lord, do all the people who loved you on earth visit you now?"

He sat quiet for a while, looking very serious, and I was afraid that I had upset him. At last he sighed deeply, and answered, "No, Little One, not all. My mother, who loved me so dearly, has never visited me. On earth she was so good and kind that she was decreed eternal happiness. Our Lord, in his mercy, has made her unaware of the passing of the years. She knows nothing of my evil deeds, and perhaps thinks that I am still on earth

*This is in keeping with the ancient Egyptian worldview that in the heavenly realms the deceased is surrounded by all the people and things that were there in life, exactly as it had been.

ruling the Black Land. If she knew what I had done, and what I have suffered, she would, in the deepest misery, weep for me all day and night." After that, H.M. sat thinking, and looking very sad. I was sorry that I had asked that last question, and begged him to forgive me. He kissed me and said, "There is nothing to forgive, Little One. I alone am to blame for my unhappiness, and you are my greatest joy. What more do you want to know about Amenti?" I replied that I did not want to ask any more questions. "Then," he said, "we will sleep for a while, and be happy because we are together again."

I was intrigued by the idea of Amenti being a mirror of earthly existence. Sometime in the early 70s I asked Omm Sety whether in Amenti the House-of-Men-Maat-Ra,* was complete as it was in Sety's time – or did it appear in its deteriorated state, as it was when I posed the question. Her reply was that in Amenti "all those buildings from his period would be as they were when he built them. And that is why I think when the king says in the inscriptions, 'I have built this my temple of eternity,' they're not referring to the actual temple on earth, because they know that sooner or later it's going to go into ruin, but when they built this temple on earth they were building it for eternity in Amenti. I think that is the meaning of this. On many places in this temple is written 'This temple of eternity,' and in other temples too. And the idea was that they *were* building it for eternity."

If there was any shadow hanging over their blissful nights together it was Sety's knowledge that there would come a day when their physical intimacy would have to end. In order to gain an eternity together as husband and wife in Amenti, a great sacrifice was required of them by the gods: Omm Sety would have to return to Abydos – not now, but soon – to make restitution for the long-ago sins of the young priestess and the great king. Her return would be bittersweet, because her life from that moment must be chaste. She would live the life of a

---

*The Sety Temple

priestess of Isis, making offerings and observing the feast days and prayers. Sety knew this, but Omm Sety didn't, for the time being. Perhaps, as he contemplated their inevitable sacrifice, he preferred to bear the burden of that knowledge alone.

They would have four years of physical intimacy before her return to Abydos in 1956.

"And before that," I asked her, "you were leading a normal life with him?"

"A normal life – as husband and wife. Right up until the time I came here. Then he said, 'Now you belong to the temple, so you must always keep the Feast of Osiris.'* And so we have to keep this arrangement until I die. If not, apparently there will be trouble with the Council again. I'm supposed spiritually to belong to the temple. Temple property."

But that is getting ahead of the story.

---

*Sety's words quoted in Cott, p. 65

NINE

At the Pyramids

"If there is no temptation there is no test." Sety

O mm Sety's private life revolved around an extraordinary man and an unbelievable situation she could tell no one else about – while her outward life revolved around two other extraordinary men, Selim Hassan and Ahmed Fakhri.

From 1936 to 1939 Omm Sety was Selim Hassan's secretary, at first unpaid and then under contract with the Antiquities Department. Dr. Hassan was one of the bright stars in the archaeological firmament, world-famous for his methodical, systematic excavations on the Giza Plateau. Omm Sety felt fortunate and grateful to be under the tutelage of this no-nonsense but generous man.

Recognizing her multiple talents, he patiently guided her into the finer points of archaeological analysis. In turn, she became his all-purpose assistant, organizing tomb fragments, cataloguing what he brought out of his excavations, making epigraphic illustrations, and even acting as informal copy editor for several books of his renowned ten-volume work, *Excavations at Giza*. Working with Dr. Hassan, she observed the meticulous techniques she had so admired in Flinders Petrie when she was a girl immersing herself in the details of his excavations in Abydos.

Selim Hassan was the first Egyptian ever to be named deputy of the Egyptian Museum. Before then, the honor had been given only to non-Egyptians – most of the high positions in the Egyptian Antiquities Department being off-limits to Egyptian-born scholars. There was still a colonial mindset about the proper place of native Egyptians, no matter how intellectually accomplished they might be, and Selim Hassan's ascendancy ruffled some entrenched, non-Egyptian feathers. His early retirement in 1939 at the age of 46 was not voluntary. One of the immediate causes of it was a sharp dispute he had with then-King Farouk over a collection of monumental pieces in the Museum that the King claimed as his own. The Egyptologist ardently defended the position that the collection belonged to humanity and the Egyptian people and should not be in private hands – not even the King's. A short time later the decree came down, placing the outspoken scholar on early pension.

Ironically, this act freed Selim Hassan from the bonds of authority and propelled him into independent research into the whole span of Egyptian history, its ethics, arts and literature, resulting in many important books and scientific papers. In reference to his forced retirement, he dedicated one of the volumes of his encyclopedic work, *Excavations at Giza*, "to those who wanted to do me wrong, but did me right and set me and employment apart, but brought me closer to the service of science and my homeland."

It is easy to see why the tough, independent Selim Hassan and his British secretary would in many ways be compatible.

After Dr. Hassan's retirement Omm Sety moved to Nazlet el Simman for the second time and went to work for Ahmed Fakhri, another of the small cadre of outstanding Egyptian-born archaeologists. Omm Sety was living in near-poverty with her five-year-old son, sometimes even camping out in an abandoned tomb with him to be closer to her work. One of the things I could never understand about Omm Sety was why she insisted on living that way. With the generous alimony that had been stipulated in the marriage contract, and Imam's own desire to support Bulbul and their child, Omm Sety could have lived like a queen in Cairo with a suitable apartment in the heart of the city. But she refused. She wanted to be free and entirely on her own.

Giza. In trying to retrace Omm Sety's footsteps while she had lived in Giza, I came upon one of the abandoned tombs she sometimes inhabited (see opening at far right). For most of her life she preferred to sleep in the open and not be confined within a normal building, something that shocked her former husband and merely puzzled her friends. (Hanny el Zeini)

By 1939, Imam had lost patience with his ex-wife's haphazard living arrangements and took steps to assume custody of the child. Omm Sety could not argue the point. As much as she wanted to be a proper mother she knew she was not one and never would be; Imam was the sensible, reasonable, responsible one. After the divorce he had married a beautiful cousin who was happy to care for little Sety. Omm Sety was free to visit, which she did, but less and less often as time went on. Why, I never understood. Maybe she simply had little of the innate motherly instincts, or maybe she could see that the traditional

Egyptian upbringing was the best thing for her child in that society, while she was at heart still a Gypsy. She did confess to me once that when she visited Imam's home she felt clumsy and not comfortable.

Her comfort and ease was to be found on the Giza Plateau, in the presence of the pioneering giants of Egyptian archaeology. Several times she even met briefly with her childhood hero, Sir Flinders Petrie, and was duly impressed. As to Selim Hassan, with his imposing stature and authoritarian personality – when Omm Sety was in his presence she saw an important Old Kingdom vizier. She jokingly remarked to me that he must have been a descendant of the genius Him-Iun, the architect who planned the whole site of the Giza Plateau and oversaw the building of Khufu's Great Pyramid.

Omm Sety also knew Hermann Junker, one of the elders of 20th century archaeology. He had worked for many years at Giza and at Philae, and Selim Hassan had been his student. When Omm Sety knew him he was old and nearsighted and spoke slowly, but until his last years he conducted his excavations with youthful energy. Omm Sety was intrigued by the fact that, although he was a Catholic priest, he advocated for more honest study of the ancient Egyptian religion; he believed nobody had made a real effort to go deeply enough into it. Omm Sety's sincere belief in the old gods and rituals must have intrigued the old priest as well. Most of the early Egyptologists had approached the old religion with the moral condescension of Victorian-era Christianity, viewing it as "primitive" – a dubious starting point for balanced, scholarly interpretation. Omm Sety admired him for his open-mindedness.

One of her favorite Egyptologists was George Andrew Reisner, a professor of Egyptology at Harvard. He, too, was an old man when she knew him and partially paralyzed, but brilliant to the end. He died in Cairo in 1942. She thought he was one of the most fortunate of excavators because he had an unerring knack for pinpointing the exact spot for a successful dig. He was the one who found the tomb of Queen Hetepheres,

Khufu's mother, in a shaft next the Great Pyramid. Today, the Queen's elegant funerary furniture adorns the second floor of the Cairo Museum.

In her off-hours, Omm Sety explored the whole area of the Giza Plateau. The Sphinx was her neighbor and friend; Khufu's pyramid was there for the climbing, which she did many times, looking out at the scores of pyramids large and small that dotted the undulating sands all the way to the horizon. More than once she spent the night inside the King's Chamber. She lost no time paying a visit to the pyramid of Unas,* a few miles away at the vast necropolis of Saqqara. The smooth interior walls of the crumbling 5th Dynasty pyramid are incised floor-to-ceiling with columns of exquisite hieroglyphs – but not just any hieroglyphs; these were the ancient Pyramid Texts** she had studied with Dr. Budge. She was face-to-face with these magical texts at last. They had fascinated her as a child and they still did, because she had long suspected that the key to unlocking their power was yet to be discovered. She believed it had to do with achieving a more accurate translation than Budge or others had been able to do.

Around this time, Omm Sety began in earnest to make her own translation of the Pyramid Texts. By her arrival in Abydos she had finished it.

At Giza, Omm Sety developed a warm friendship with Mrs. Perkins, Professor Reisner's secretary, the jolly, talkative woman she first encountered several years earlier after her adventure in the village of snakes and scorpions. Omm Sety had friends and colleagues who cared about her and she had work that she loved, but in all the years since she arrived in Egypt she had never once gone to Abydos.

---

*2356-2323 BC; Unas was the last king of the 5th Dynasty

**These are the oldest complete representations of the religious philosophy of ancient Egypt, depicting the eternal journey of the soul. Far older than the 5th Dynasty, the texts are expressed in a kind of symbolic, spiritual shorthand whose original meaning is the source of great scholarly debate. Over the next thousand years, elements of these texts evolved into what we know as *The Book of the Dead*.

The question arises: Why? Why didn't she go there the first chance she got? She had had a few opportunities, but something always intervened to prevent it. She saw that as a sign that the time was not yet. And she also sensed – even though Sety hadn't yet told her – that once she returned to the ancient place there would be new rules for her life and for their intimate relationship.

Finally, in 1952, the way was opened and she was able take time off from work and go for a short visit. Immediately on her arrival in the village of Abydos, which was still called The Buried Hamlet, she found herself absorbed into the ancient atmosphere. Barefoot and alert, and in a state of vivid recall, she entered the haunted temple for the first time in more than 3000 years. There, she offered her prayers to Osiris, Isis, Nephthys, Ptah, Maat and the other gods and goddesses that inhabited its shrines and corridors – but most especially to Isis. Despite the general sad condition of the temple, the sculpted images around her were so lifelike, their flesh painted so delicately, they almost breathed from the walls. In the midst of the images was Sety, equally lifelike, making offerings and receiving blessings in the sacred company. By now, her dreams and fragments of remembrance had begun to take form as her true story.

In those brief days she walked the temple precincts with the assurance of someone who knew the place intimately. She ventured into the enigmatic half-submerged ruins of the Osirion, adjacent to the temple, looking down at the sodden, reed-choked chambers and remembering. In her recurring childhood dream she had been here in this place. This was where the priest had beaten her when she wouldn't reveal her secret. As a young girl in England dreaming this terrible scene over and over, she hadn't known what the secret was, but now of course she did. No amount of beating could force Bentreshyt to confess the name of the man who had defiled her body and offended the gods. She ventured in among the jutting, square pillars, remembering also that she had loved this place and held it in great awe.

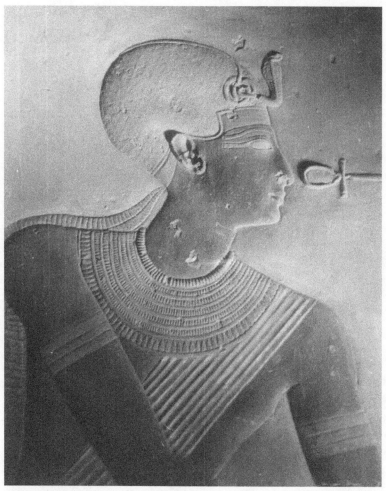

Sety being offered the Key of Life, the Ankh, to his nostrils by the god Thoth (not in picture; detail from the northern Chapel of Horus). "When you look at this picture intently," Omm Sety said, "you feel as though new life is being pumped into your being." She believed in the power of the images to do what they are shown to do. (Hanny el Zeini)

On impulse, she splashed her face with water from a well inside one of the small chambers of the structure. Before that moment Omm Sety had needed glasses to read and do close work, but for years afterwards, her eyes were those of a young woman. (Later, we will see what else the water from the

Well of Roarings could do and explore the other mysteries of the Osirion.)

Omm Sety knew that she was destined to live out her life here, but she couldn't stay; not yet. There would be no way to support herself without a contract from the Antiquities Department. At the moment, that looked almost impossible.

After Selim Hassan's pensioning-off, Ahmed Fakhri hired Omm Sety to be his own secretary.* As she had with Dr. Hassan, she took a secretary's modest salary but performed a research assistant's varied duties. She thoroughly enjoyed her years with Ahmed Fakhry. They worked hard and laughed often together. With Ahmed Fakhry she could not possibly have found happier company. Even better, his work always brought forth spectacular finds that stirred the admiration of his colleagues.

He is remembered most for his pioneering research in the Egyptian desert oases. In these remote places illicit digging has been going on for centuries. Nowhere else in the world does one hear such tales of treasure, particularly golden treasure. Not all of these stories were pure fabrication, as shown by the recent dramatic discoveries in the Valley of the Golden Mummies at the Oasis of Bahariya. Ahmed Fakhri, who died in 1973, had always believed that these distant outposts had been densely populated in times past and held a rich legacy, waiting to be found.

When Omm Sety worked for him he was in charge of excavations at Dahshur, located at the southern end of the necropolis of Saqqara, several miles from the Giza Pyramids. Dahshur is an extensive field of pyramids, mortuary temples and shrines in various states of ruin. Its principle monuments, the Red Pyramid and the Bent Pyramid, were both built by King Sneferu.** When Ahmed Fakhry's Pyramids Research Project began, very little careful exploration had yet been done.

---

*although O.S. continued working with Selim Hassan on his writing projects
**Sneferu (2575-2551) was the first king of the 4th Dynasty – father of
  Khufu and husband of Hetepheres

Omm Sety's work at Dahshur gave her the experience of assembling and then deciphering thousands of fragments from the pyramid field. It was invaluable training for her eventual work at Abydos. She told me that perhaps one of the reasons she could not go to live in Abydos earlier was that first she needed to know her way around a complicated archaeological site and understand the science of architectural reconstruction. She also needed to become more fluent in translating and interpreting hieroglyphs.

She was growing quite adept at working with hieroglyphic texts. We can glimpse her careful scholarship in the following excerpt from an analysis she wrote as assistant to Dr. Fakhri, entitled, "Remarks Concerning Some Texts on the Torch Shrine of the Chief Sculptor Ssnw* Found by A. Fakhri in Dahshur":

The ritual text on the top of the lamp-shrine is, for the time being, the oldest known copy and therefore especially important. There are parallel texts, partly with variants, in the Theban tomb of Neferhotep (N° 50, time of Haremhab); in the tomb of the royal scribe Tjai (N° 23, time of Merenptah); in the hypostyle hall of the temple of Karnak and in the Cairo Papyrus with the ritual of King Amenophis (Ramesside).

The following restorations in the Dahshur text are assured by the parallels. The concluding section (lines 12 ff.) is already known from Pyr. 1660f (dedication of the pyramid).

Translation:

To be spoken: hail to thee, thou lamp of this Osiris, the overseer of sculptors, Ssnw. Hail to thee (thou eye) of Horus that guides the gods in the darkness. ...Heaven is given to thee, earth is given to thee, the Field of Reeds is given to thee in this

---

*In Egyptian hieroglyphs, as in Hebrew, the internal vowels are not given. Most popular renditions of hieroglyphs offer "place-holder" vowels to aid the reader, but in a scholarly text only the original consonants would be given.

beautiful night of (the New Year, of the feast of 'establishing'), of the feast of the Months and of the giving of (young) water (to the gods). And likewise the gods have given you (young) water together with the stars in heaven....

the silver Osiris

During the 1940's Omm Sety found herself of necessity moving several times, always bringing her beloved cats along. By now, she was not surprised by anything in her life, but there were certain incidents that challenged even her idea of normal:

Nineteen forty-one was a strange, chaotic time in Cairo. The Axis armies were threatening British-dominated Egypt, Germans and Italians living in Egypt were rounded up and interned, and Cairo was bracing itself for bomb attacks. Spies and rumors were everywhere. Omm Sety was right in the middle of it, still working as an assistant to Selim Hassan, though no longer living in Nazlet el Simman; she now lived in three rooms on the roof of a high building Dr. Hassan owned in Dokki, a modern section of Cairo on the west bank of the Nile.

During a conversation with me on October 3, 1973, Omm Sety recorded her account of an inexplicable event. We were sitting outside in our favorite spot by the Osirion, where we liked to go when the evenings were cool, and she began:

In 1941, she said, "we were having air raids, although they didn't bother me. I wasn't afraid of them, but I *was* nervous about *where* they were going to drop their bombs. I thought they might drop them on the museum.

"One night I went to bed as usual. The terrace door was locked, there was no other entrance, and I had the only key; nobody could possibly come into my rooms. When I woke up in the morning one hand was closed and I felt something hard in it. I opened my hand and found a small silver statue of Osiris, about ten centimeters high. It was in perfect condition and not oxidized. One could imagine it was quite new.

"I didn't mention it to Selim Hassan because he didn't believe in anything supernatural. Anyway, I took it to a jeweler who said it was pure silver. It was really very nice. I bought a silver watch chain, which in those days was quite cheap, and I put the little statue on it. The ring for attaching it to the necklace was a heavy, thick one, not at all a flimsy thing. I had it cast solid with the statue itself; and then, to make quite sure it was secure, I had the clasp and the necklace soldered together, because it was big enough to put over my head – so there was no clasp to come undone.

"Well, I wore this statue of Osiris, and Selim Hassan said to me, 'Where did you get that?' I said a friend of mine gave it to me. It *must* have been a friend who gave it. I just don't know who it was!

"I wore it all through the war; I never took it off. Then a few days after the war ended I went to bed wearing my silver Osiris as usual, and when I woke in the morning it was gone. The chain was there still around my neck, the clasp was still soldered shut, but the statue was gone. I thought by some impossible means the statue had broken off the ring, in which case the ring would still be on the chain – but it wasn't. So I searched in the bed and all around, but I never found the statue, and there was never any explanation.

"How a solid object could have been transported to me, and how it was taken away, I don't know. There was no way anybody could have got onto that terrace. And another thing: If somebody else *had* a key – which they hadn't – they couldn't have put this in my hand or taken it off my neck to remove the statue without waking me, because I'm a light sleeper. One thing I *am* sure of is that it wasn't given and it wasn't taken by any human agency. I mean, it's quite impossible."

I interjected, "Did you ever ask Sety if he gave it to you as a protection during the war – or hadn't he begun making his appearances at that time?"

"He had made his appearances, but never in solidified form. Not as he does now – I mean, as a solid human being – not until the second time I went to live at the pyramids, when I was working for Dr. Fakhri. I never did mention it to him [to Sety]. Somehow, I don't think it was Sety. If he didn't come in a solidified form, how could he transport a solid object – and who took it away again?"

In one of the classics of 20th century spiritual literature there is the tale of another silver amulet that mysteriously appeared and then vanished. This one came to the revered yogi Paramahansa Yogananda (1893-1952) when he was a boy in India. In his widely read book, *Autobiography of a Yogi*, he relates the story of the amulet:

The small, round object materialized in his mother's hands one day, as she had been told it would by a strange holy man, a *sadhu* who had appeared the day before at her door. The talisman was intended for her son, the visitor instructed, and it was to be given to him at a certain time in the future. "When he has retained the amulet for some years," the sadhu continued, "and when it has served its purpose, it shall vanish. Even if kept in the most secret spot, it shall return whence it came."* When Yogananda was still a young boy it came into his possession. He kept it near him always, feeling that it gave him strength for his spiritual journey. He describes a certain moment when he was experiencing intense spiritual discomfort and he turned for solace to his "sole treasure," but when he opened the locked box where it was kept, it was gone. "It had vanished, in accordance with the sadhu's prediction," he wrote, "into the ether whence he had summoned it."** As he grew in age and wisdom, Yogananda came to understand the nature of the sadhu's gift and the possibilities that exist in the subtler realms of matter.

---

*Paramahansa Yogananda, Autobiography of a Yogi, Self-Realization
 Fellowship, 13th ed., 1998, p. 21
**ibid., p. 105

Such materializations are far more common in India than in Western culture and are often a part of the guru-devotee relationship, but esoteric traditions all over the world acknowledge the latent power of the mind to affect matter in ways that seem miraculous. In the West the sudden appearance of an object, an *apport*, is usually associated with mediums.

In Omm Sety's case, she had had enough experience with the other dimensions of reality to conclude that her silver Osiris was not brought by any ordinary means. But why – and how – did it disappear? A possible explanation can be found in a footnote to Yogananda's own story, where he wrote, "The amulet was an astrally produced object. Structurally evanescent, such objects must finally disappear from our earth."*

By the time Omm Sety sat with me on that October evening and told me the story of her amulet, I already knew that unexpected, and some might say miraculous, blessings came to her in times of great need. Perhaps by having no fear when the bombs began to fall, and by her utter faith in her Lord Osiris, she was rewarded with a tangible token of protection.

the phantom leopard

In her notebooks Omm Sety wrote about another mysterious encounter that involved appearance and disappearance. It happened in the summer of 1948.

At that time, she wrote, "The chronic housing problem in Cairo, plus a non-existent banking account, obliged me to take a flat in Abdine, one of the native quarters of Cairo. It was a flat of three large rooms in a house that, some sixty or seventy years ago, had seen better days. My neighbors above and below were Sudanese families, quiet and good-natured people. I lived quite alone, except for three cats, old and tried companions.

"I had been living thus quite uneventfully for some weeks; but one night I returned home about 8 P.M., and on opening

*ibid., p. 212

the front door, was puzzled, because the cats were not waiting to greet me, as was their usual custom. I entered the bedroom, which was well lit by a street lamp outside the window, and there, standing beside the bed, was a fine, full-grown leopard!

"There was a circus in Cairo at that time, and my first thought was that my visitor was an escaped performer. The beautiful creature padded softly over to me and commenced to rub his head and shoulders against my legs, just as a friendly cat might do. I could feel the force of the caress, the warmth of the body, and the ripple of the steely muscles under the soft fur; but by then the conviction was strong within me that in spite of appearances, the creature was not a real flesh and blood leopard, for no living creature larger than a mouse could have entered the flat, the door and windows of which had been locked all day. So, when I tried to stroke the creature's head, and it promptly disappeared, I was not particularly shocked.

"I lit the lamps, and while making a thorough search in the flat (just in case!) I found my three cats huddled in shivering terror under a divan in the living room. A few days later, I related this incident to some Egyptian neighbours, who were very much disturbed about it, and muttered verses from the Koran to ward off evil influences. But they either could not or would not explain the matter.

"A further two weeks passed without incident. Then I was awakened one night by the violent creaking of a small cupboard in the bedroom. The three cats, who habitually sleep on my bed, were wide awake and staring at the cupboard in alarm. Suddenly, there was a terrific thud in the middle of the room, as though some heavy creature had jumped off the top of the cupboard onto the floor. The cats, spitting and screeching, fled from the room and did not reappear until the morning. I lit the lamp, but could see nothing unusual in the room.

"The following afternoon, about five o'clock, I was in the living room drinking tea when I noticed a movement in the open doorway leading into the bedroom. Suddenly, in the doorway appeared the head and shoulders of the leopard! It was still broad daylight and I could see every detail quite clearly. The beautiful creature stared at me and I stared back, fascinated. Slowly it moved forward until it stood in clear view in the middle of the doorway, where it paused, still staring at me curiously.

"I extended my hand to it, calling, *Ta'la hena, ta'la hena,* come here, come here. The leopard cautiously advanced into the room, coming slowly towards me. The window was open, and some neighbors on the balcony of the house opposite began talking and laughing loudly. Their noise seemed to distract the leopard, for he glanced at the window and retreated a few steps backward; then he sat down and stared at me again. I called him, but he glanced up at the window and would not come to me. He yawned widely and I could see all his splendid white teeth and his rough, pink tongue. He licked his chops and then began to lick his left front paw and wash his face, exactly like a great cat. The toilet completed, he turned and entered the bedroom, I following. He crept under the bed, but when I looked for him there he had disappeared. I searched the flat, but could find no further trace of him.

"The behaviour of this strange beast was perfectly natural, except that he showed not the slightest sign of ferocity; in fact, he seemed to be somewhat timid. I have never been able to explain these incidents, and had I been entirely alone, I might have dismissed them as illusions, defective sight, or imagination. But why were the cats so terrified?

"About a week later, I had the chance to take a better flat, so I left the 'leopard house,' and my place was at once taken by another Sudanese family who, however, did not stay there very long! The flat has been constantly inhabited and vacated during the intervening two years, and now the landlord has taken upon himself the considerable expense of entirely remodeling and decorating it. And nobody wants to explain why."

the impossible

The archaeological season did not (and does not) extend through the entire year because the months of intense heat in most of Egypt made it impractical to conduct excavations then. This left several months of unemployment for a great many people involved in fieldwork, including Omm Sety. She filled in the gaps by writing articles under her maiden name for popular publications, and helping Selim Hassan with his books-in-progress. Being artistic and clever with her hands, she also made and sold items that she embroidered with ancient motifs. She was getting by on her wits and enterprise, but larger events were about to make her situation more difficult. It was now 1956, a year of political turmoil and uncertainty in Egypt.

Four years earlier, on July 23, 1952, King Farouk had fled from Egypt ahead of a revolutionary bloodless coup by General Naguib. Then, in 1954, the dynamic Colonel Gamal Abdel Nasser took power and re-energized the revolution with his vision and gift for oratory. But along with Nasser's socialist regime came new ills. I remember them well. By 1956 there was a feeling of malaise among the intelligentsia of Egypt because Nasser's government had its own set of priorities. Unfortunately, Egypt's ancient legacies were not among them. Only on one occasion did he demonstrate some interest in Egyptian archaeology, with support for the dramatic discovery and reconstruction of Khufu's Solar Boat next to the Great Pyramid. Beyond that, he showed no concern for our historical heritage, sharply curtailing funding for archaeological research and excavations. As a consequence of such a short-sighted policy, Omm Sety suddenly found herself, for the first time in more than 20 years, jobless.

Of course there were far graver troubles that year. Nobody who lived through it could ever forget it, for that was the year that Nasser seized and nationalized the Suez Canal, and Egypt was in turn invaded by Israel, Britain and France. We all passed the whole of 1956 in an anxious state of *prepare for the worst.*

As the new head of the Egyptian Sugar and Distillery Company, responsible for its mills and processing plant, I quickly found myself dealing with two almost intolerable situations: One was the American boycott and the Western European restrictions on delivery of spare machinery parts and vital equipment. The second and most personally painful was the obligatory departure of all French and British subjects, who were now considered "aliens." I said goodbye to many colleagues in the company, valued workers and good friends I had known since the beginning of my career.

Meanwhile, Omm Sety was enduring her own trials at Giza. The winter before, to his dismay, Professor Fakhry found himself with insufficient funding for her position. He tried very hard to create a job for her somewhere within the impoverished Egyptian Archaeological Department, but the problem was, no one else had extra funding either. However, as *kesma* would have it, a new inspector had just been named for the Abydos area. The Sety Temple at the time was in terrible condition, roofless and filled with fragments of stone from previous excavations. For a long time there had been warnings from senior members of the department that something had to be done to salvage the temples in the area.

Edouard Ghazouli, the new chief inspector for Middle Egypt, went to Cairo and begged for an assistant who could do some serious design work at Abydos and be charged with making precise copies of the inscriptions on each fragment. The Director-General, agreeing to the need, consented. It was left to Ghazouli to pick the right person. He soon met with Professor Fakhry in the department's main office in the heart of Cairo, where they discussed naming a draftsman for the Abydos temple project. Fakhry was delighted. It was as though the position had been carefully tailored for his assistant, who was now at the end of her one-month's notice of termination.

Omm Sety remembered that cool evening after a day of unusually hard work, when Dr. Fakrhi invited her to join him at the rest house for a cup of tea. "He asked me about my plans for the future and playfully teased me with some far-fetched scenarios," she said. "Finally he said, 'I have found a job for you. But it is in a remote part of the country and, mind you, the pay is not good – actually about ten percent of what you were paid here.'

"Well, I didn't much like the sound of that. 'Where on earth is it, and who is offering the job?' I said.

" 'Abydos. And your boss will be Edouard Ghazouli. He is waiting for me to give him your answer.'

"I almost fainted," she told me, laughing.

After the stunning news she walked back to her apartment in Nazlet el Simman, her mind racing with all the implications of her acceptance. The job started immediately. What would she do with her cats? How quickly could she be ready to go? And what about Sety...what about Sety?

In a later diary entry she wrote of that night: *"Sety stayed with me all night, and made love to me in a surpassing way. That was the last night that we ever made love together, and it was the sweetest."* Gently and with great seriousness, he explained to her that she now belonged to the temple, and that she was forbidden to any man until the end of her life in this body. She must observe all the feast days of Isis and Osiris and burn incense before their images in the temple and recite the *Lamentations*. Sety asked for her promise and she started to cry, asking him if she should refuse to go to Abydos at all. He said that this was to be their time of testing. If they resisted temptation they might be forgiven and be granted Eternity together. But, would she ever see him again? He assured her that he would come to her in Abydos. But in what form, if they were not to be lovers again? He would come to her as a living man, he said, because he could not forego the clasp of her arms.

The diary continues:

I said, "This will be a temptation." He replied, "If there is no temptation there is no test, but O Beloved, help me to be strong, and do not weep. I will never leave you or cease to love you." I said, "Why should I be forbidden to you? I am going to Abydos to help restore the Temple, not as a priestess, and you know well enough that I am not a virgin." He kissed me and said that I was a good girl. He thanked me for the years of happiness we had snatched while I was living at the Pyramids. He said a lovely thing: "Your love is an ointment poured on the wound in my heart." And I nearly started crying again...

A few days after this, I left for Abydos.

TEN

Abydos

*"He led me to a place on the edge of the desert
and said, 'Build for me a temple in this place.'" Sety*

B efore she left Cairo, Omm Sety sold most of her possessions,
managing to raise the modest sum of 130 Egyptian pounds.
She hadn't the slightest idea where in Abydos she would stay or
how she would find suitable lodging close to the temple, yet not
too far from the marketplace in the village. To any reasonable
person this looked like a foolish gamble, and indeed it was.

For the first few weeks she lived at the Antiquities Department's rest house, enjoying its privacy and comparative peace.
She needed the peace because she was beginning the enormous
job that had been put before her: making order out of the thousands of fragments of plaster and stone taken from the remains
of a small palace attached to the temple. A computer would
have been handy, but the use of computers in recreating fragments would come much later, most notably by Professor Donald
Redford, working with the fragments from Akhenaten's Temple
in Luxor. It is ironic that Omm Sety's first job at Abydos would
involve the reconstruction of what was believed to be Sety's
palace – *Heartsease*.

Since there was no electricity in the village, Omm Sety was
obliged to rise and sleep with the sun. She was happy at the
rest house until a new inspector arrived who wanted it for the

exclusive use of his family. Omm Sety quickly negotiated the purchase of a simple one-room peasant house of mud-brick for 80 pounds – a bargain, and well situated for her needs.

She had managed to bring two of her favorite cats with her and immediately began acquiring a new menagerie that eventually included a watchgoose named Sneferu, several snakes, a rabbit, a dog and a donkey named Alice. She called her ragtag companions her "mafia." Naturally, she was the focus of intense curiosity in the village. From the first day she arrived, she brought offerings to the temple morning and evening, reciting the ritual prayers before the images of Osiris and Isis and other divinities – and speaking her own personal prayers to the very real gods who oversaw her wellbeing. Except that she was living in the 20th century, she could have been mistaken for a 19th Dynasty woman, a Ramesside woman.

She walked the courts and halls of the Sety Temple with full knowledge of their ancient functions, familiar even with those parts of the temple that had suffered collapse or other extensive damage. This left quite an impression on Edouard Ghazouli and various Antiquities Department members. One day, shortly after her arrival, she pointed out where elements of the original temple gardens had been. When subsequent digging proved her correct, right down to the type and placement of the trees and the location of a well that still had fresh water in it, there was no doubt in anyone's mind that Omm Sety knew what she was talking about. *How* she knew, well, that was another question, and she wasn't saying.

My first meeting with Omm Sety took place a few months after her arrival in Abydos. It was mid-December, 1956. My personal journey to that day had taken almost as many surprising turns as Omm Sety's. I was 38. For several years I had been production chief of the multi-national European-owned General Company of Sugar and Distillery, one of the world's largest. A year earlier, I had been on an extended mission for the company to Western Europe, where I was assessing the industrial devastation left in the wake of the Second World War. In November

Abydos looking north, with the Sety Temple in the left distance. Beyond is the escarpment called "Lady of Life." (LL Company)

1955 I received a telegram at my hotel in The Hague, telling me to return to Nag-Hamadi at once. The wording was blunt and without explanation, and I had no idea what to expect when, 72 hours later and without much sleep, I arrived in Nag-Hamadi to hear the news: Colonel Nasser had confiscated and nationalized the Sugar Company. It was now the Egyptian Sugar and Distillery Company. There were rumors that major changes of high-level personnel were about to be implemented. My European colleagues feared for their jobs. Inside the Sugar Company's compound we had always been like a comfortable United Nations of co-workers, but the world's politics were about to change that.

In March 1956 the French Director-General was removed and shortly after, I was named to take his place. In July, Nasser took over the International Suez Canal Company* and all of its property – a bold, symbolic declaration of independence from more than 2000 years of Egypt's domination by foreign nations. In October, England, France and Israel invaded the Suez Canal

---

*jointly owned and controlled by England and France

Zone in a failed one-week "war," but their troops remained on
Egyptian soil until December, when they were finally ordered to
leave by the U.N. Security Council. I give this historical context
to help explain the state of mind of patriotic Egyptians at that
time. We were thrilled to have defeated the colonial powers and
taken back that important piece of our country for ourselves
– even though I and most of the educated people in Egypt did
not generally agree with Nasser's politics.

And so, on that day in December – with the excitement of
the war only a few weeks in the past – I decided to take a break
from the demands of my new job and go with a group of friends
to visit Abydos. After passing through the main entrance gate
of the Sety Temple, we heard an angry feminine voice insulting
and cursing all the foreign countries that took part in the inva-
sion of the Canal Zone. The curses were being hurled in a most
atrocious British-accented Arabic. Inside, we encountered four
inspectors of the Administration of Egyptian Antiquities. One
of them, Engineer Shandawily, was in the midst of an animated
exchange of views with a robust, middle-aged Englishwoman, the
hurler of the curses. At our approach, he introduced her to me
as Mrs. Omm Sety, the vituperations came to a sudden halt, and
she graciously offered to show our group around. I took note of
her blue eyes, engaging smile and very light blond hair.

As we proceeded together down a narrow flight of steps
I was startled to see that our lady leader – now speaking in a
clear, pleasant English – was walking barefooted. I could hardly
believe what I was seeing. She was the polar opposite of the
Englishwomen in Cairo, who carried themselves with the dignity and entitlement of the British Empire. That this barefooted
anomoly and I would one day be the closest of friends seemed
most unlikely.

Our next meeting was well into the following year. I
arrived at the temple, spent some time studying the famous kings'
list inscriptions in the Corridor of Kings, then dropped in on
Omm Sety, who I knew had her office in the adjacent Hall of
the Sacred Barques. She was sitting at a wooden bench, working

over her bits of limestone, basalt, sandstone and granite. She was again barefoot, and only too willing to stop what she was doing and talk about her hopes for the restoration of the Sety Temple. It was obvious to me that she had a keen analytical mind and more than a passing interest in the temple's wellbeing. I couldn't help thinking how much more money a person with her intelligence and knowledge of Egyptian history could have made as a tourist guide in Giza or Saqqara, and not be toiling here for pauper's wages.

I had been to Abydos before. The first time was in 1946, ten years earlier. Then, the temple was engulfed in sand. I remember feeling dismayed to see the toll that time had taken on this magnificent piece of pure pharaonic architecture. The thick mud-brick enclosure wall had been quarried through the ages by the villagers and was now just half its original width. The staircase was eroded and the first and second pylons were destroyed. The architrave* was intact and stood defiantly over-looking the two badly ruined courts that form the outer open-air parts of the temple, where in antiquity the general public was allowed to stand during the feasts and religious celebrations. What remained of the walls of both courts was covered with sand to a height of more than six feet, so that only the top of the walls remained visible. I recall praying that the sand would act as a protection for any surviving sculptures within.

Even with the blanket of sand and dust, the beauty of the sculpture in the two Hypostyle Halls was still breathtaking. Of course, I had been to Luxor before and visited the Karnak and Luxor temples, and had stood in wonder and admiration in the middle of those jungles of gigantic pillars – but I could remember nothing so beautiful as that sculpture in Sety's temple.

When I emerged from the temple I saw before me an enormous open pit and the colossal square pillars of the Osirion.

---

*a horizontal stone beam that rests on top of two columns (or across a doorway)

Sety offers the symbol of Truth, Maat, to Osiris (in the Second Hypostyle Hall.)
(Hanny el Zeini)

This was and still is one of the most intriguing mysteries of pharaonic Egypt. However, I was not prepared for something else I encountered: a woman standing bareheaded in the infernal heat, making some drawings of scenes on the outer western wall of the temple. I did not know, but I suspected, that she was English. She appeared to be not even slightly aware of my presence, even after I had said a polite, "Good Afternoon." Mad dogs and Englishmen, I thought. Later, the chief watchman of the temple informed me that her name was Miss Calverly. Elizabeth Calverly was a well-known scholar working for the Egypt Exploration Society of London. She was the second Englishwoman with a strong connection to Abydos; the

ABYDOS

first was Margaret Murray, who had worked here with Flinders
Petrie early in the 20th century. Professor Murray was the one
who discovered the entrance to the sand-shrouded Osirion and
named it in 1909, believing it to be the actual tomb of Osiris.
Now, with Omm Sety's arrival in 1956, there would be a third
Englishwoman devoted to the restoration of Abydos.

For those thousands of years when Abydos was the Mecca
and Jerusalem of ancient Egypt, pilgrims had come here to pay
homage to Osiris at his tomb. Contrary to Margaret Murray's
belief that the Osirion was the true tomb of Osiris, in Sety's
time the pilgrims made their devotions to Osiris at the mastaba
tomb of the 1st Dynasty king Djer, or at a modest temple to
Osiris that lay at the foot of the high escarpment, very close to
Pega, the gateway to the land of the dead. When Sety made
his plans to build a temple to Osiris, he did not place it in the
area of the royal tombs near the mastaba of Djer or the small
Osiris temple. Instead, he built it some distance away, alongside
the ancient Nif-wer canal, which during the four months of the
Inundation carried pilgrims' boats from the Nile.

Egyptologists have long wondered why Sety positioned his
temple, the House-of-Men-Maat-Ra, exactly where he did, since
it went against the existing traditions of kings building mortuary temples and shrines in the royal necropolis. In a diary
entry from January 1973, Omm Sety records this exchange with
Sety:

*I said, "Lord, when did you first begin to build the
House-of-Men-Maat-Ra?"*

*"Early in my second year," he said. "The high priest Entef
wrote to me saying that the temple of our Lord* needed repair.
I went, making my first pilgrimage to Abydos. I found the
ancient temple too crowded with later monuments. I passed the*

---

*the earlier small temple to Osiris that existed in Sety's time

117

night there, and in my sleep I dreamed that our Lord himself came and said, 'Follow me.' He led me to a place on the edge of the desert and said, 'Build for me a temple in this place.' I answered, 'My Lord Osiris, I obey your command,' and the god said, 'The House that you will build will cause my name and your name to remain forever in the mouths of men.'

"The next day I told the high priest of my dreams and he assented. I fetched the most skilled architects in the land and bade them to draw up the plan. In only one month the work was commenced, but I could not stay to see it, for I had to defend our frontiers."

There were some odd things about the way the temple was designed. Instead of the customary rectangular shape, it has a curious L-shape. This feature alone sets it apart from any other Egyptian temple. The interior layout suggests that the original plans were altered as it was being built. Had the architects encountered something beneath the foundations that they wanted to avoid? Ancient kings were not averse to building atop older temples; it happened all the time. What then might have caused the architects to reposition the entire western wall of rooms and annex them instead to the southern wall, creating the L? They would not have altered the traditional temple design unless there was some other building, a very important building, standing in the way. It was the Osirion, lying beneath the level of the sand and having existed (as we shall see) since at least the Pyramid Age.

Omm Sety writes in *Abydos: Holy City*, "It is obvious that it was the presence of this building which forced the architects to change the plan of Sety's temple. A certain amount of 'holiness' seemed to be attached to the building since part of Sety's temple is actually constructed over the ruins of an older temple, but the architect found it imperative to avoid building in any way over the Osirion itself. Had the temple been continued westward, as it should have been, it would have covered the roof of the older building. The Osirion was by no means just one of those old temples to be built upon!"*

Sety's temple is different in other key aspects as well. While a New Kingdom temple normally has a main sanctuary dedicated to its particular god – with two smaller sanctuaries for the consort and son of the god – the Sety Temple has seven chapels, dedicated in turn to Osiris, Isis, Horus, Amun of Thebes, Ra-Horakhty of Heliopolis and Ptah of Memphis, and the seventh chapel existing to perpetuate the eternal memory of a deified Sety.

"There are two possible reasons for these extra chapels," Omm Sety continues. "One is that Abydos, being a place of pilgrimage, received priests and pilgrims coming from those cities who would find their own local deities held in honor here. But it may also mean that the great gods themselves were coming as pilgrims to the Holy City of Osiris."**

Another unusual element is that the temple was built on rising ground. Normally, a temple's ceilings would become lower and lower as one penetrated deeper into the building to the most sacred inner sanctuaries. The fact that Sety's temple was on sloping ground allowed the architects to keep the roof levels even while the floor levels rose, giving the illusion of a descending roofline. Engineering the gradual incline meant that a great deal of extra work was required. Sety could have built on any number of level sites in Abydos, so why go to so much trouble with this difficult site that was far removed from the place the pilgrims believed was the tomb of Osiris? In light of Sety's oracular dream, he had no choice.

From the unwritten beginnings of its history Abydos has evoked a sense of majesty and the mysterious. Even long after Sety's time and the great pilgrimages, wealthy Greeks and

---

*O.S. & el Zeini, p. 11
**ibid, p. 45

Romans flocked here as tourists to marvel at the beauty of its monuments. They didn't have a *Michelin* guide, but they did have the writings of Strabo to tell them what was here. In 23 BC, Strabo remarked upon the invisible joinery of certain of the Osirion's limestone walls and said that the exterior roof was covered with a great mound surrounded by a grove of trees. Recent excavations have found several stone-lined pits on two sides of the Osirion, filled with earth and the roots of large trees. Little by little, the story of Abydos reveals itself. (For help in visualizing the layouts of the Sety Temple and the Osirion, refer to the drawings in the Appendix.)

Two thousand years later, Omm Sety came to this place of puzzles and mysteries uniquely qualified to add to the process of deciphering them. In me, she had the perfect accomplice. As a child and into adulthood I spent many solitary hours trekking into the Egyptian deserts, visiting archaeological sites and getting to know that special breed of dedicated adventurers who peel away the layers of civilization's secrets. By the time I met Omm Sety, many of those archaeologists were my personal friends of long standing. One of the great advantages of my working for the Sugar Company was that it had seven regional mills, each conveniently located near major archaeological digs-in-progress. I had worked for extended periods of time at several of the mill locations and there was never a question of where I would spend my off-hours.

When I was named chairman of the company and moved to its main compound at Nag-Hamadi, I found myself within easy driving distance of Abydos. But, as much as I wished to spend more time in Abydos with my new and fascinating English friend, the demands of my work meant that I could only manage the occasional short visit. Finally, in December of 1959 I arranged to pass a full day in Abydos. And so it was with real anticipation that I set out from the company compound at Nag-Hamadi with my driver Ali on a cool, refreshing winter's morning. My cook had prepared a special chocolate tart for me to bring to Omm Sety and I was looking forward to a leisurely tour of the temple precincts with her as my excellent guide.

My plans took another turn when I arrived and found two strangers sitting with her in the small cafeteria close to the temple. Ali stopped the car and immediately Omm Sety came to salute me, introducing her guests, two men in their mid-40s who were both curators at the British Museum. It was apparent that they held her in some awe, for reasons I soon learned.

Years before, at the start of their careers, they had worked under Dr. Budge, who had been the museum's Keeper of Assyrian and Egyptian Antiquities. Before his death in 1934 he had told his two young subordinates to search for Dorothy Eady when next they were in Cairo. He told them she had left England without saying goodbye and he was puzzled by her complete and sudden disappearance.

It was only now that they were able to find her – after 25 years and other trips to Cairo. By a stroke of luck they had met the chief watchman of the pyramids while touring the area. When they inquired if he knew someone named Dorothy Eady he said he was sorry, but he would ask someone about her. That someone turned out to be one of Selim Hassan's assistants. Dorothy Eady was now in Abydos, they were told.

The two Egyptologists had found her at last and were in the midst of reminiscences about Dr. Budge when I drove up. Fortunately, my arrival did not interrupt their lively conversation. It was a chance for me to learn more about my new friend. Budge had kept fond memories of his "miracle child," as he called her. I knew that she had had a childhood passion for all things Egyptian, but now I heard about her hieroglyphic training with the old scholar, and how precocious she was even at the age of ten.

One of the curators was saying that Budge had been astonished to see Dorothy again after she had spent the war years in the countryside. She had grown so, he hardly recognized her. "I recall that day quite vividly," Omm Sety said. "When he rose from his chair to give me a kiss and a hug I got the shock of my life. He had grown so short and fat! He jokingly asked me to 'come down' so he could kiss me." She resumed her studies with him where they left off before the war, and was grateful for his generosity, but Dr. Budge noticed that some of his other students were envious. "They couldn't understand why he was so interested in this giant of a girl," Omm Sety said, chuckling.

Budge was an ardent follower of the old religion. He cautioned Dorothy not to make the common mistake of thinking that ancient Egyptians were animal worshipers. To him, they were God-fearing, pious people, and he never tired of repeating that one must go deeper into the study of Egyptian religion. He had his own theory that in the remote past the Egyptian religion was a very abstract monotheism – but over time, with migrations from the adjacent countries, an increasingly materialistic priesthood turned it into a complicated multi-gods religion to suit the mentality of every local community.

I sensed that these three had much they wished to talk of privately and that this was the right moment for me to leave for a couple of hours. The Sety Temple would fill my time nicely. Passing through the temple gate I was pleased to see how much effort had been made to clean up the outer courts and the main halls inside since I was last here a few months earlier. The watchman, who knew me well by now, told me that the new khawagaya was very active and arguing fiercely with the inspector about the necessity of roofing the temple's exposed parts. It was obvious to me that this was the only way to save this wonderful piece of ancient architecture. Omm Sety was just the one to force the issue.

I returned to the cafeteria as the two men were preparing to leave. I offered to drive them back to Luxor if they would stay a while longer. Our conversation ranged among many subjects, but came back again to Budge and those early days. I knew that he had practiced magic and had written a great deal about Egyptian magic. Omm Sety recalled her last meeting with Dr. Budge. She had by then translated the Pyramid Texts under his guidance, and they had been speaking about magic. "With these texts in your hands," Budge said to her, "you will be the most powerful woman on earth, if you understand and decipher them properly and use them judiciously."

When the curators were taking their leave Omm Sety looked genuinely sad. They had brought back to her fond memories of her childhood, and of a man who had served as her teacher and mentor, and in many ways, a father. He may have been the only one who understood the strange and lonely child.

In my car on our way to Luxor the men never stopped remarking how on earth a woman like Omm Sety could have chosen to live in such miserable conditions. For them, she was like a priestess, with Budge as the god, and since the two gentlemen had loved and cherished the great scholar, they had equally warm feelings for her.

Before we set out I left the chocolate tart for Omm Sety. Early that morning I had felt urged to copy a verse from an old book of Afghani poetry and slip it into the wrappings around the tart.

> *Lo! After years in absence past;*
> *I hail my natal spot at last:*
> *And for one moment seem forgot*
> *The troubles which have vexed my lot.*
> *'Tis well that 'mid the changes round,*
> *The house in pristine state is found;*
> *The sight, no tawdry columns trick,*
> *No stucco hides the ancient brick.*
> *All wears the dull and solemn guise,*
> *As when the light first blessed mine eyes.* *

I don't know why I selected that particular piece of poetry; she and I were just beginning to get accustomed to each other. There was no exchange of confidences at that time. But maybe I felt that Omm Sety, who was very much at home in these

---

*Source information about original book and translation is not available.

impossible surroundings, somehow looked as if she truly did belong here. She rang me up two days afterwards to thank me for my gifts. Her voice was shaky when she said how much she appreciated my choice of poetry, how much it meant to her.

View from Omm Sety's first Abydos home towards the southern horn of the escarpment called "The Lord of Offerings." In the middle distance is an ox-drawn wheat thresher. When Omm Sety first came to Abydos she wanted a house that would allow her to have a wide-angle view of the whole landscape, something she had dreamed of since she was a child. (LL Company)

I did not know until many years later that on that December day in 1959 her contract with the Antiquities Department expired. She must have been terribly anxious for her future, but she had said nothing to me. Had I known, I would have called some of my close friends who would have willingly helped her renew her contract.

Omm Sety solved her problem in her own way: She took her case directly to the top, that is, directly to the god Osiris, who apparently set to work on her behalf. It seems there was a new inspector at Abydos, Dr. Abdel Hamid Zayed. I had never met him. He appreciated Omm Sety's zeal and her most unusual abilities, and felt impelled to write a long, praiseful letter to the director-general of the department, asking for an extension of her contract. That letter, or a copy of it, became one of her most valuable possessions. The extension was granted for five years. She was now 55.

Some months later, while we were sipping our cups of tea in the cafeteria after a tour of the temple, I was complimenting her on her vast knowledge of Abydos, particularly her unusual familiarity with the great, sprawling necropolis, the burial grounds surrounding Abydos. They were filled with the remains of monuments, tombs and an astonishing quantity of undiscovered archaeological burials. One of the more mysterious structures in the area is a massive walled ruin known as Shunet el Zebib, that dates back at least 4500 years. I had been intrigued by it and she had offered her opinion of its possible function in ancient times.

I asked her how she could possibly know so much about all of these things. She subtly evaded my question: "After all, I've been here for a while now," she said, "and in Dr. Budge's London collection there were many items that came from previous excavations around Abydos. Not that I was happy to see all those treasures outside the place where they belonged, but it opened my eyes to the enormous possibilities of future digs in this area."

It was evident that she was reluctant to tell me the whole truth, whatever that might be, and I felt it was not suitable to embarrass her with more questions. But those who worked with her told me that she seemed blessed with a very special "feel" for the terrain on which she trod. It was my understanding that Omm Sety's gift was at times invaluable to the work of the archaeologists, though it was never formally acknowledged by those who came to excavate, not even after they found, with her help, some remarkable pre-dynastic tombs that pushed the history of Abydos farther back than anyone had previously believed.

Omm Sety was relentless in her determination to have the roof of the Sety Temple restored. The priceless artwork on the walls had to be rescued from the elements. In an odd and indirect way I became the one responsible for her getting her roof.

So many stories involving Omm Sety are not what they seem at first. At my company's Nag-Hamadi compound there was a simple garden that extended for a short way along the Nile, a narrow greenbelt of sorts. Thinking that the garden could be made far more lovely and useful, I had it enlarged to four times its original length, with half of it reserved for the company's staff and families. I had recently invented a modification of the process of sugar production, and the Egyptian Cane Diffusion Process, as it was called, was then being introduced into the sugar industry. To implement it we had to demolish some old sections of the factory, removing considerable quantities of concrete blocks. Those blocks, in turn, were used to construct a new quay on the Nile for the company's fleet.

The old quay had been the only suitable landing place for floating tourist hotels in the whole of Upper Egypt. But now, with the enlarged quay and our beautiful and inviting Nile garden, more tour boats began to come, and Abydos became a destination for their tour groups. Soon, Omm Sety was a favorite guide through the Sety Temple, and her reputation began to spread. More tourism meant more money for reconstruction work on the temple, and now the new inspector had his funding for the enormous roofing project.

Once the work was completed I paid a visit to the temple to see the unintended fruits of my labors. I was walking with Omm Sety in the area of the restorations when I remarked how different the temple looked now, so clean and pleasant.

"Well," she said, "it now looks the nearest thing to what it was like when Sety and Ramesses built it."

"How do you know what it looked like then?" I asked, because I had the idea that it must have looked far different from what I was seeing at the moment.

She hesitated, then said, "Because I was there when it was being built, and before Ramesses made quite a few drastic modifications."

"So you were alive when this temple was being built," I said, going along with her joke. "Yes, I was," she stated quite soberly, "in another life – as a teenage girl. I came from a very poor family near a village a few hundred yards east of Shunet el Zebib."

I made no comment because I simply had none. I must admit I could not believe a word of what she had just said to me. As to whether there had once been a village east of Shunet el Zebib, at the time we spoke no such place had ever been found.

Now, so many years later, it has. I wish Omm Sety could have lived long enough to witness the recent (1997) unearthing by the University of Pennsylvania of an ancient village that had existed during the time that Omm Sety remembered. Where is it? *A few hundred yards east of Shunet el Zebib.* Just as she had told me that day when I was unable to believe.

ELEVEN

Magic

*"One day I asked Omm Sety if she herself
attributed any special powers to the Eye of Horus." HZ*

When Omm Sety invoked Osiris's help in her despair over losing her contract, or when she appealed to her beloved Isis for help with an illness, she was confident that her words would be heard. Some of her friends might have smiled at her seemingly naïve faith in the power of the gods, but more often than not Omm Sety got results, and no one could argue that point. She believed in magic, she had seen it work and had used it herself when the need arose. The magic she believed in was not trickery and games; it was not as small as that. It was the sacred power that flowed through everything, animate or inanimate.

Egypt's magic came first from the gods. In the story of Isis and Osiris, Isis invoked a great magic to bring her dead husband back to life. Magic was essential to creation and transformation. The energies of life were invisible, malleable, and responded to sound patterns, words of power and focused intention. Everything existed as potential, a living cauldron of creation waiting to be acted upon and brought into form. The gods possessed this activating power and to a lesser extent so did certain humans, but in humans there was always a risk of misuse. The foremost of the sacred practitioners was Isis, *Great-of-Magic*. In the Book of the Dead she declares: "I am Isis the goddess, and I am the lady of words of power, and I know how to work with words of power, and most mighty are [my] words!"* Isis worship eventually extended into the whole of the Greek and Roman worlds, and into the Christian era. She was the archetypal mother whose essence was compassion. Many scholars feel that the attributes associated with Mary, the mother of Jesus, have direct parallels to those of Isis. Even today, Isis has her "children," in the many groups around the world still devoted to the spiritual principles she embodies.

In his famous 1904 work, *The Gods of the Egyptians*, Budge describes her glowingly:

> [F]rom the earliest to the latest dynasties Isis was the greatest goddess of Egypt....Isis was the great and beneficent goddess and mother whose influence and love pervaded all heaven, and earth, and the abode of the dead, and she was the personification of the great feminine, creative power which conceived and brought forth every living creature and thing, from the gods in heaven to man on the earth, and to the insect on the ground; what she brought forth she protected and cared for and fed and nourished, and she employed her life in using her power graciously and successfully, not only in creating new beings but in restoring those that were dead.**

Omm Sety identified herself with Isis every day of her life. Isis was mother, sister, healer, companion, confessor. Budge had said of Isis, *what she brought forth she protected.* I began to understand what that meant after a certain incident in 1970.

---

*trans. by E. A. Wallace Budge, in *The Gods of the Egyptians*
**ibid.

Isis (detail from the Inner Chapel of Isis). Isis was Omm Sety's mother, sister, healer, companion, confessor. When she was troubled or sick she would receive help by kneeling in front of this image and making a small prayer. (Hanny el Zeini)

a warning in the desert

A young German archaeologist visiting Egypt had stopped by my office in Nag-Hamadi and asked me to help him get in touch with Omm Sety. I was not able to leave my work to escort him to Abydos, but I did provide him with a driver and a Russian-made Jeep. He had come here, he said, to visit the Archaic Cemetery at the foot of the western escarpment. He was looking forward to meeting Omm Sety for the first time. But I never saw him again because after that day in Abydos he told the driver to take him directly to the train for his return to Cairo.

What had happened during that very short visit to Abydos was, for all involved, unforgettable. First I should explain a dominant feature of the modern Egyptian landscape. High-tension cables carry the electrical current provided by the hydraulic power station at the Aswan High Dam to the whole of Egypt. They are supported by giant steel pillars or pylons, and one of the main lines runs north-south, paralleling the escarpment at Abydos.

At the time of this incident, Egypt was still at war with Israel, and the bases of all the pylons were surrounded with powerful mines in order to forestall enemy incursions and large-scale failure of the electrical grid. The local authorities were strongly advised not to allow anybody to come close to them, especially children.

Omm Sety was agreeable to accompanying her young visitor to the Archaic Cemetery in search of an unknown tomb. The trek would take most of the day. The archaeologist had brought food and plenty of water. However, the moment the Jeep started moving in the direction of the escarpment, Omm Sety began to feel an uncomfortable ringing sensation in one ear, which she thought was just a recurrence of an old infection and nothing to worry about. But as the vehicle proceeded out across the rough desert terrain, the noise that started in her left ear quickly spread to both ears and was growing louder. When the pain became too intense, she asked the driver to stop to allow her to take a painkiller. After a few minutes the pain and the noise subsided. Then, when the car began to move again, a shrill blast of sound exploded into Omm Sety's ears. The pain was so excruciating she screamed and covered her ears with her hands. The driver stopped the car again and the horrific noise stopped too, but now Omm Sety heard a low, admonishing voice calling to her in the old language: *"O Bentreshyt! Do you want to commit suicide again? Do you? Turn back...turn back, you fool! You are heading straight to your death. O you fool...O you fool!"*

Omm Sety immediately ordered the driver to turn around and go back. When he hesitated, Omm Sety flew into a fit, showering him with Arabic abominations until he gave in and turned the car around. On the way back, they encountered the chief ghaffir who had seen them set out and had been frantically waving to them to stop. Had nobody heard his cries of warning, he shouted. And why didn't Omm Sety tell him where she intended to go? "You stopped and I thought you had heard me, and then you drove off again!" he said in a voice furious with fear. When he saw her car heading straight towards one of the most heavily mined of the pylons, he knew she was driving to her doom. But no one was able to hear his voice over of the clatter of the Jeep's engine.

Omm Sety, still reeling from her experience, felt obliged to apologize to the men, saying, *"Maalish, maalish"* a mixture of *sorry*, and *no offence.* For the ghaffir and the driver, all was well again, although all was certainly not well with the German visitor, who was grateful to be alive but frustrated to see his day go so miserably awry. He had been told of Omm Sety's eccentricities, but this was extreme. Moreover, as soon as they got back to Abydos she left him to his own devices. She went straight to the temple and spent an hour praying in gratitude to Isis and presenting offerings inside her beautiful cult-chapel – apparently forgetting about the visitor who had traveled for five hours just to meet the old lady and spend a fruitful day searching for a hidden tomb.

Before making offerings to one of the gods, Omm Sety used to take hers, kneel before Isis and murmur a prayer below this Table of Offerings, which contains lotus flowers, figs, ducks and different forms of bread. Then she would leave her sanctified offerings on the ground beneath the deity in question. (Hanny el Zeini)

Omm Sety never said a word to the others about what had really happened to her in the car. It was enough for them to think that the real reason to turn back was simply the pain in her ears.

Months later she told one of her close friends from the UK that there had been nothing wrong with her ears, which felt fine until she got into the Jeep. What caused the pain was that unearthly sound. Omm Sety believed that it was a stern warning from Isis, who had been watching. In her merciful grace she had decided to send a messenger, apparently endowed with a highly efficient "siren," and a curt but effective message in the old tongue.

Magical intercessions and the practicalities of everyday life co-existed in Omm Sety's world; more than that, they were intertwined, as they still are in villages all over the Egyptian countryside. Much of the life of the fellaheen* might appear to be an ongoing ritual of actions taken for the purpose of assuring peace, happiness and protection. The origins of these ingrained rituals reach far back in time.

The world of ancient Egypt was infused with magic – magical spells, amulets, magician doctors and a priesthood of trained magicians. Magic was literally what made the world go around. Every day of the year had its magical aspects, complete with guidebooks of incantations, prayers and required behavior, if you wanted to stay on the right side of *Shay*.**

Bernard Bromage, a lecturer at London University in the middle of the 20th century, made a lifelong study of ancient spiritual practices that had carried over into the modern world, especially in Tibet and Egypt. He knew Arabic and taught himself hieroglyphs, and he spent much time among the temples and villages of Egypt. In his remarkable book, *The Occult Arts of*

---

*the country people
**Fate

---

*Ancient Egypt,** he writes about an experience he had one chilly night in the desert near Luxor.

He had wandered in the direction of some fellaheen dwellings and noticed that the huts were all dark, with no fires inside or other signs of light. The men were sitting silently in front of their doors and they were not smoking, which was itself unusual. The visitor offered one of the men a cigarette and was very politely refused. Writes Bromage: "I elicited the reason for the refusal and for the general air of taciturnity and reflection which was prevalent. Following on an ancient honoured tradition, they were observing an injunction which went back into the dim Egyptian past. It was one of those days on which fire of any sort must on no account be kindled. Not even the suspicion of a flame must be seen." And so the families had sat in darkness this night. One man explained that there was danger to everyone if a fire were lit. Bromage said that he could see no danger around and was told that he could not be expected to understand because he was not of their race. "If you must know," the man said, "our Faith tells us that such a flame, if lighted in defiance of the Law, would take its vengeance on us and all things near us." Reflecting upon this, Bromage wrote: "My mind played around the theme in the starlight, tranquil with the ancient Nile gleaming in the distance. Then I apologised for my curiosity and my intrusiveness and after wishing that Allah be with them, left them to their faith and their meditations."**

Omm Sety's Book of Days

Shortly after Omm Sety arrived in Abydos she created for herself a personal book of prayer and ritual. It was a version of an ancient Egyptian astrological calendar that contained instructions and prayers for every day of the year. This was a normal practice in the time of Sety and his son Ramesses. The famous

---

*Bernard Bromage, *The Occult Arts of Ancient Egypt*, Samuel Weiser, 1971
**ibid., pp. 167-168

Sallier Papyrus in the British Museum contains such a calendar, compiled in the Ramesside period (19th & 20th Dynasties) from the calculations of earlier astrologers. In it are the auspices for every day of the Egyptian year, from very favorable to very bad. Calendars like this, or fragments of them, are in museum collections all over the world. The most complete of them is the so-called Cairo Calendar, but whose title is in fact, *An Introduction to the Start of Everlastingness and the End of Eternity.*

No two are exactly alike, yet their basic themes are consistent: If something occurred in the mythological life of the gods on a particular day, then that day's human activities must be fashioned accordingly, in order to either invite good luck or avert disaster. Even though the Egyptians believed deeply in the immutable outcomes of Shay they were also not about to take any chances by offending the gods. The Egyptians were nothing if not practical, even to this day.

Omm Sety's book of days draws from these traditional admonitions because she had complete faith in them and followed them strictly, but she made her own additions as well, usually inserting additional passages from early wisdom texts that she respected. In hieroglyphs at the top of each page she gave the season, month and date – for example, the season of Inundation, the month of Thoth and the day – and then next to it she wrote the Coptic Egyptian date (which still uses the ancient month names) and the Gregorian Calendar date in modern script:

> *Saturday, January 19, 1957. Touba 11:*
> *Bad, bad, bad! Do not draw nigh to any flame on this day, for Ra entered the flames to strike all his enemies, and whosoever draws nigh to them on this day, it shall not be well with him during his whole life.*

> *"Show thou kindness to people of humble condition."*
> *(Amenemapt)* *

---

*a Ramesside period philosopher whose writings served as inspiration for the Bible's Book of Proverbs

Friday, January 11. Touba 3:
"Thou, O Amon, art Lord of the silent, who cometh at the cry
of the poor." (Stela from Western Thebes)

Thursday, January 3. Kiak 25: Mysteries of Osiris at Abydos:
Take wheat and paste figure of Osiris to the Temple of Soker;
leave it there until the end of the month. On this day must be
read the book of the Lamentations of Isis and Nephthys.

"It is a terrible thing for a man who knows his sin to be
charged with it." (King Khati)*

Omm Sety's religious practices were simple ones, but deeply felt. She identified herself as a worwhipper of Isis, but on certain occasions I found her in the temple offering flowers, beer and small loaves of bread to other gods or goddesses. I found out that when she had a problem with some of the ghaffirs she would make an offering to Horus, and when she needed some good guidance she offered flowers to Thoth, the god of wisdom and knowledge. Her favorite goddess, after Isis, was Thoth's wife Sheshat, who oversaw writing, mathematics and architecture. Before starting her day's work at the drafting table, Omm Sety would often recite a short prayer to Sheshat.

Those were her occasional practices for ordinary days, but always and without fail Omm Sety observed the long ritual prayers for the Feast of Osiris on the first days of each new year.

On the Feast of the New Year of 1965, on a day of freezing temperatures, I decided to pay a surprise visit to my friend. The factories at Nag-Hamadi had been running at full production for two weeks steadily, and I needed a respite.

As I passed through the main gate of Sety's temple I heard a strange, beautiful voice singing from somewhere within. I walked toward it until I could identify the voice and the words of

*10th Dynasty king (ca. 2150 BC)

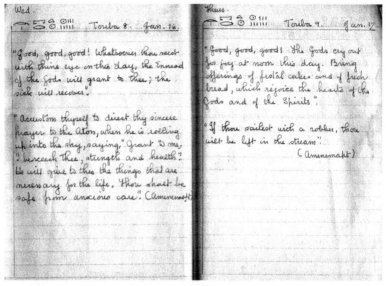

Omm Sety's Book of Days, her religious calendar of prayer and contemplation, similar to ancient calendars from the 19th Dynasty. These pages are from 1957, the year after she arrived in Abydos. The dates are shown in hieroglyphs, Coptic and Gregorian notations. January 16 starts with the auspices for the day, and reads: "Good, good, good! What-soever thou seest with thine eye on this day, the Ennead of the gods will grant to thee; the sick will recover." The meditation below, from the ancient Egyptian wisdom literature, reads: "Accustom thyself to direct thy sincere prayer to the Aton, when he is rolling up into the sky, saying, "Grant to me, I beseech thee, strength and health." He will give to thee the things that are necessary for the life. Thou shalt be safe from anxious care."

The next day reads: "Good, good, good! The Gods cry out for joy at noon this day. Bring offerings of festal cakes and of fresh bread, which rejoice the hearts of the Gods and of the Spirits." The meditation reads: "If thou sailest with a robber, thou wilt be left in the stream."

the song: The soulful voice was beseeching the dead god Osiris to come back to his loving people. I had never heard Omm Sety chant the *Lamentations of Isis and Nephthys* before, and now I was hearing such a deep expression of grief and unfathomable loss that I felt like a rude intruder to even be listening to it. I stopped my approach and stood some distance away in the Second Hypostyle Hall. The lament then gently descended to a soft, pitiful entreaty and ended in profound sadness. I passed through the doorway of the Osiris chapel and into the great

Osiris Complex.* I can't think of many moments in my life that have moved me more. There, near the wall on the left, I found Omm Sety weeping – kneeling next to the image of Nephthys who was herself kneeling beside the body of Osiris.

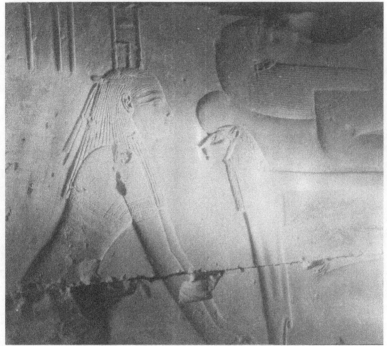

The goddess Nephthys mourning beside the dead body of her brother Osiris. The head of Osiris is seen upper right upon the lion-form bed. (Hanny el Zeini)

I stood quite still, watching the frail, rather shriveled figure of Omm Sety, entirely drowned in her grief, fully giving her soul for her dead god. In front of her, just below the head of Osiris, she had laid the bunch of roses that she had asked me to send to her the evening before. When she turned away from the scene and saw me, she took a few moments to collect herself. We walked from the temple together without the need for words.

---

*the large hall behind the seven cult chapels

In a diary entry for July 20, 1972, Omm Sety engaged His Majesty in a discussion about his own relationship to the gods:

Presently, I said, "My Beloved Lord, will you tell me some things about the Gods?" To which he replied, "I will if I am able to." I said, "Have you ever seen Set?"* He looked at me, and then looked away, with a very strange expression on his face, but did not reply. I was afraid I had made him angry and said, "If what I asked has angered you, Lord, be gracious and pardon me." He said, "I am not angry, I will tell you. I have seen him once; that was during my life on earth, when I was a young man. Bentreshy, do you know that I was once a priest of Set?" I replied that I did, and that a stela still existed, which Ramesses had made, recording the family history. Sety smiled and said, "The mouth of Ramesses was always as big as his nose!"

He said that for hundreds of years, all the men of his family had been military men, and that most of them were also priests of Set, whom they adored as a God of War and the patron god of their nome. He said, "This is not a good thing. One should not serve an evil being, even it if appears to have a good or useful attribute or function. Many of my companions in the Military School were also training for the priesthood of Set, but they did not take their studies to their heart. Most of them only passed their initiation ('entered the first gate') because the God had too few servants. I took everything to my heart.

"By day I studied and exercised in the Military School. At night I did not sit in the beer-houses or run after women like a dog after a bitch. I studied the cult of the Lord of Strength and I studied the magic powers that he offered. It is because of what I learned at this time that I am now able to come to you in the form of a living man. But those things I could have

---

*the god whom Sety was named after; the evil brother of Osiris *learned in the service of other Gods. After two years had passed, I asked to be allowed to try and enter the 'First Gate.' The Chief Priest agreed. For ten days I ate no meat and drank only water. On the eleventh day I fasted. One hour after sunset I was taken to the Chapel of the Great of Strength, which was lit by a lamp with three wicks. In a niche in the west wall was a statue of the God, a man with the head of a strange animal. I was told to kneel in front of the statue and repeat the God's name. I was not to rise from the floor; I was not to leave the Chapel. I was then left alone.*

"I did as I was ordered. After some time I felt the earth tremble, there was a terrible noise like thunder, and a bright light came from the niche. Instead of the painted wooden statue, there stood the God himself. Bentreshy, he was of a beauty that cannot be described! His hair was red as new copper, his eyes were as green as the great ocean, but he seemed to be the spirit and soul of all that is cruel and evil. His voice was evil music when he said, 'Come to me, my son and servant.' I jumped to my feet, I screamed, 'Never will I serve you!' I opened the door and fled from the chapel. As I did so, I heard the terrible mocking laughter of the God. The priests were waiting in the courtyard. They cried, 'Praised be the Lord of Strength! He has revealed his face to his servant!' They guessed what had happened, but they thought that my flight was caused by religious ecstasy. The next day, the Chief Priest wrote my name in the records as Wab-priest* of Set; but I swear to you, Beloved, that I refused to enter his chapel again, and I never served him, even for one hour."

"Did you ever see him again?" I asked. "No," he replied, "I have never seen him, but often I have heard his terrible laughter. I heard it on the day when my eldest son went to his death. I heard it on the night when I learned of your death. I heard it

---

*a class of priests who performed cult rituals for the deceased

*as I left the Court of Our Lord Osiris, after I had been con-
demned to wait in sorrow and loneliness for your return."*

*I burst out crying, and knelt at his feet and hid my face in his
lap. He comforted me; and after a while I asked, "Why did
you not change your name?" He smiled, "Silly child, the name
we are given at our birth cannot be changed before the Gods; it
is a part of us, like our ka and our glorified spirit. I always
hated my name until one night, in the garden of the House-of-
Men-Maat-Ra I told you to call me by it, and then it became
like music from my Harp-of-Joy."*

Omm Sety and I often talked about the persistence of the
old ways. Today, especially in Upper Egypt, one sees so many
amulets being carried and worn by people. Without doubt, my
own ancient ancestors attributed a lot of magical powers to amulets, in particular the Eye of Horus. One day I asked Omm Sety
if she herself attributed any special powers to the Eye of Horus
as an amulet.

"I certainly do! In fact, I might tell you I wouldn't go outside my house unless I were wearing one," she laughed. "The
idea of the Eye of Horus originated in the eye that Horus sac-
rificed in his fight with his uncle, Set, to avenge Osiris. And
then it came to mean anything that was good and beneficial. I
do certainly believe that there is a great, shall we say, 'magical
power' about the Eye of Horus."

I said to her, "I would like you to tell me something of what
you have seen with your own eyes of the remnants of the ancient
Egyptian magic, especially in the villages close to the desert's
edge, which have more or less preserved the ancient traditions."

"Well, I have a whole collection of similarities between
ancient and modern customs," she replied, "and they are very,
very similar. For example, around Abydos, when the women
give birth to a child they squat down on the ground and they
hold a large kitchen knife in their hand – all the while they're
giving birth. When I first saw this I said, 'Why are you holding

a knife?' The woman said, 'To keep away the evil spirits.' In the temple of Sety there is a scene of the goddess Mut in the form of a pregnant hippopotamus, squatting down to give birth and holding in her hand this enormous, great knife. Exactly the same as they do now. And no doubt for the same purpose.

"On the seventh day after its birth, they put the child in a sieve, and they put into the sieve some grain, some beans, some wheat – and then they shake the child. And after the ceremony they leave the child to sleep in the sieve. This is still done, not only in the villages. I have told you about the ceremony of the sieve after my son was born, and that was in a highly educated Cairo family!

"Now, in the temple of Hatshepsut at Deir el Bahri, in the birth scene you see Anubis bringing along the Great Sieve to shake the baby in. And in the Pyramid Texts you find the goddess Nut, as mother and protector of the god, being called the Great Sieve."

snakes

I knew that Omm Sety had an affinity with animals, even snakes, which is most unusual in Egypt where there is such fear of serpents, especially, and scorpions. And I knew that she had had a friendly encounter with a snake in the temple. I asked her, "Is it a special faculty you have, or is it just your natural love for animals in general?"

"I believe that there is a kind of telepathy between them and us. The snake you mentioned was a cobra, and they are unusually intelligent. So long as you don't attack them or even harbor ill will or fear of them, as far as I know they will never attack. An uncle of mine had been to India and had seen the snake charmers there and the fakirs, and didn't believe it for a minute. He thought it was all trickery, but I knew these things were possible."

There is a group of people in Egypt called Rifai who handle serpents – being bitten, or even eating them alive, without any harm coming to them. I said to Omm Sety, "There seems to be a magic formula of some sort that is transmitted through these Rifai people from father to son, and it must be very efficient because a serpent bite has no effect whatsoever on them."

"It is possible that some people have a natural immunity," she said. "For example, I have immunity to scorpion poison. I've now been stung eleven times and from the first time to the last I never had any real pain, only just the pain of the sting, and then a rather pleasant tingling feeling, like a mild electric shock."

The Rifai belong to something like a sect, begun over a hundred years ago by a chief called Ahmed er-Rifai. Some of them make their living going into gardens and collecting snakes. I told Omm Sety about a time 20 years earlier when I was in Kom Ombo, and the colony where we were living was absolutely full of snakes. In my garden there were seven or eight of them, and occasionally when I was coming back from the factory I saw several of them just talking together, it almost seemed, in a very easy way in my garden – just feeling very much at home. I was always scared of snakes myself, since childhood. I was never scared of anything else, not even wolves or foxes, but snakes were another thing.

One day, when everybody was complaining about the large number of serpents that were making free in all the gardens of the colony, we had to bring in one of those Rifai. And with my own eyes I saw the man come into the colony with just an empty sack (I checked it myself) and a small stick. He went right into every garden and he was reading something, just mumbling a few inarticulate words, and a serpent would come right out of a hole, and then another and another. At the end of the day he had in his sack 40 snakes of all types and all sizes. I thought it must be either magic or perhaps the man made inaudible sounds that could be heard only by the serpents, and on his call they would come out of their holes. I have no other explanation for this.

Omm Sety said, "I don't know about the genuine Rifai Dervishes. They seem to have some mysterious power, but of course there are a lot of fakers, people who come 'round the village and to a house where there are usually a lot of women, and they say they can smell a snake nearby. And so, of course, the women say, 'Oh, get it out, get it away from us!' And so he goes into a place and starts muttering and mumbling, and then presently he fumbles about and reaches up his arm and pulls out a snake. Well, I'm quite sure that that is his own snake.

"A man came 'round to some neighbors of mine a couple of years ago and he pulled out a horned viper – and you *don't* find horned vipers in houses, because they live in the desert. So I laughed at him and said, 'You're a *nasaab*, you're a cheat.' And he got angry. He had a basket full of snakes, including a cobra, a couple of horned vipers and a few kinds I don't know, and he tipped out the whole basketful in front of my bare feet. Well, if those had been genuine wild snakes, which he swore he had caught that day, they would either have bitten me or tried to run away. But they did neither; they all crawled back again into the basket!

"But the ancient Egyptians, they had magic spells for rendering serpents harmless. They never tried to kill the snakes. The secret word in the spell for ridding someone of serpents is to say *sebenn, sebenn, sebenn*. It means 'glide,' 'glide away.' I tried it that time when there was a cobra in the temple and some tourist was attempting to photograph it as it was swallowing a sparrow. A policeman who was supposed to be on guard, wanted to kill it. I said, 'Leave it alone; the gentleman wants to photograph it.' But this wretched man threw a stone at the snake. He didn't hit it, but it made the snake very angry and he quickly bolted down the sparrow and looked around for somebody to bite. So I said, *sebenn, sebenn, sebenn* and sweet-talked it, and it went back into its hole in the wall. And after that we became quite good friends."

I noticed that Omm Sety used a particular intonation when she said the words and I asked her opinion of the effectiveness of the ancient spells and how they were related to prayers.

"Certainly, all the Egyptian prayers were not directly speaking magic spells," she said, "but if you analyze it, *all* prayers, even modern ones – I mean, if they are set to a ritual – *are* a form of magic. It is an attempt on our part to get into contact with the heavenly deity. But it isn't what you'd call common, or garden-variety magic. There's another point: I believe that in the ancient days magic was a science that is now lost – because all the magicians of ancient Egypt were men of very high rank, princes of the royal family, wealthy men, not like these poor fellows that sit in the market place each day and write out love charms, how to get somebody's husband away from their wife, or something like that." She laughed again. "I mean, they were really educated, responsible men."

"You believe it was a science, then, a real science?" I said.

"Yes, I believe it was a real science, which we have lost. And now they are getting so many theories about the power of vibrations, and the ancient Egyptians were very insistent that when you are reading a magic spell you must read it in the correct voice and in the correct way. And so there may be something in the vibration of sounds that brings about this effect."

the Pyramid Texts

I knew that Omm Sety had deep knowledge of the spells inscribed on the walls of the 5th Dynasty Unas pyramid at Saqqara, and I asked her to give me her opinion of their efficacy.

"I think there is a lot of very real and effective magic contained in the Pyramid Texts," she said. "And there are certain spells in these texts that were used at least up into the 19th Dynasty, more than a thousand years later. For example, there is a spell that was intended apparently for the protection of the Unas pyramid and its complex. Well, that reappears again in the Sety Temple – exactly the same spell, but to protect the offering endowment of certain gods. It is in the Corridor of Kings, on the east wall, where there is a picture of the king presenting offerings to Amun- Ra. This text is inscribed, *"to protect the perpetual endowment of these offerings."* And then, in the chapel of Amun-Ra – in the cult chapel [in the temple] – where there is shown the presentation of ointment, there is the same formula that is used in the presentation of ointment to the dead in the Pyramid Texts. Word for word."

I said to her, "You once told me that in ancient Egypt they were very careful not to put the whole magic text entirely in one piece, that they used to divide it into several portions so that it would be difficult to put all the pieces together. Could you explain what you meant by that?"

"Yes. Quite by chance I noticed that certain spells in the Unas texts begin in one line and then continue in another line, far away from it. And then I tried this out with other magic texts and I found the same thing. It was very, very difficult to find. Some are fairly easy – you get the continuity – but some, I couldn't trace the ends of them, and I think this was done so that they shouldn't fall into the hands of just anybody. Because magic could be used for good ends and bad ends as well – as now."

Omm Sety was quite sure that she had stumbled upon a kind of "code" concealed within the hieroglyphic figures of the Pyramid Texts. And she believed that she was on the trail of discovering its key. Remember, she had made her own translation of the texts and had been fascinated by their mysteries since she was ten years old.

She was not the first to sense that there was a deeper secret in the spells than meets the eye. In the book *The Code-Breakers*, written by David Kahn, formerly a historian for the National Security Agency and generally acknowledged as the world's leading expert on the history of cryptography, the author pays special attention to the hieroglyphs of the early Egyptians. The first essential element of cryptography, he writes, is "a deliberate transformation of the writing....But many inscriptions are tinctured, for the first time, with the second essential for cryptology – secrecy. In a few cases, the secrecy was intended to increase the mystery and hence the arcane magical powers of certain texts. The Greeks were fascinated by the Egyptian hieroglyphs, he said, and "thought that a mysterious knowledge lurked behind this impenetrable veil. They came to regard Egypt as the fount of an ineffable wisdom of the East....The Greeks never really learned the complex writing system....They never grasped the relation between the sound and the image." The neoplatonist philosopher Plotinus, a Greek born in Egypt, felt that the Egyptians had "imbued these pictures – which transcended ordinary writing – with symbolic qualities that intuitively revealed to the initiated a vision of the very essence of things."* In other words, Plotinus was in agreement with the Egyptians themselves in regarding their writing as having magical powers.

The authors of the book, *Secret Messages: Concealment, Codes and Other Types of Ingenious Communication*, tell us that "some ancient writings have never been translated....These will probably always be mysteries. It just goes to show how easy it is to lose word and symbol 'keys' over time."**

I was curious about something else. I said, "With all those spells, this has not prevented the pyramids from being broken into and damaged, and also the tombs. Do you think that those spells, which were inscribed inside those tombs, ever caused harm to those who desecrated the old burial places?"

"I wouldn't be at all surprised. You know, the plundering of the tombs was done during the social revolution at the beginning of the First Intermediate Period.*** When the royal power fell, all these ka-priests who used to look after the tombs were left without salaries, and also the ghaffirs guarding the tombs. So, finding themselves starving, they began to plunder the tombs. That is quite plain because they would leave the doorway absolutely intact, and the descending passage, and they

---

*David Kahn, The Code-Breakers, Scribners, 1996, pp. 71-2 & 902
**W.S. Butler and L.D. Keeney, *Secret Messages*, Simon & Schuster, 2001, p. 142
***about 2000 BC, a time of turmoil and breakdown of central authority of government

would tunnel in from the outside, right straight down into the burial chamber. So it must have been done by people who were present at the time of the cutting of the tomb – maybe even the gravediggers themselves.

"I know one case from my own experience where retribution certainly did fall on a robber. A man was found in one of the tombs at Giza lying across a half-open sarcophagus with his hand inside. He was perfectly preserved by the sand that had fallen in on him; he was wearing a ragged loincloth and he was leaning over the sarcophagus with his hand grasping a beautiful wide collar on a lady who was inside the coffin. Apparently the thieves, instead of removing the filling from the shaft as they dug, had simply tunneled down, and the tunnel collapsed on the poor chap. He was in there for good until he was turned up in about 1933."

"I have another story to tell you," she said, "although I have no way of verifying its truth. In one of his visits to me His Majesty told me a very strange thing. We were talking about excavations and things still undiscovered, and he said that here in Abydos – as well as in Peak-of-the-West* – there are tombs cut deep into the ground in which are buried certain priests. These men were learned in things that even the most educated priests did not know about. They had achieved mastery of their minds and the laws of nature.

"His Majesty said to me, 'By their magic, their heka, they put their lives to sleep.' He said that at a future time, which they had decided upon before burial, they would awake, even after many thousands of years. I asked why they should do this and he replied, 'To teach men the knowledge they possessed.' But he said that while most of these priests were good and wise men, some of them were pure evil.

---

*the mountain that overlooks the Valley of the Kings at Luxor (ancient Thebes)

"I said, 'Can this be true? How could they exist so?' and he said, 'I do not know; it is something I was told by a very learned priest in Heliopolis.' I asked if he believed it, and he replied that it was difficult to believe, though he knew that some animals were able to sleep through the winter and wake again. 'If a simple little animal can do this,' he said, 'why cannot a very knowledgeable priest also do it?' "

Omm Sety had many conversations with His Majesty about things pertaining to magic and the power of the ancient spells. In one diary entry (August 17, 1972) she addressed him, saying,

> "O my King, will you please answer me one more question?" He nodded. "Why, in the pictures of the Solar Boat in the Book of Gates* are there always the figures of Heka and Sia, Magic and Wisdom?" He answered, "Remember that I told you that there is no Solar Boat, and that Ra, Iwf, and Ra-Hor-akhty** are only manifestations of the Lord of All? So too there are no beings called Heka and Sia. In our time there were some true magicians, and magic was a real thing. Magic is represented symbolically as Heka, and as you know, Sia means 'wisdom' or 'understanding.' They are shown together to remind all beholders that those who have and use Heka must also have Sia, or else they make a bad use of Heka. Do you understand now?" "Yes, I understand and will remember," I replied.

The idea of being able to manipulate the energies of life and death permeates the ancient Egyptian world. Inside one of the tomb shrines of Tutankhamen there is a spell designed to help the boy-king move in and out of the inner worlds. The action of simply writing the spell causes it to become animated. This one reads: *He will come out and come down out of the interior of heaven.****

---

*an 18th Dynasty funerary text that illustrates the nightly travels of the sun god Ra on his Solar Boat
**solar gods
***trans. by Alexandre Piankoff, in Bob Brier's *Ancient Egyptian Magic*, Morrow, 1980

the human body and its multiplicities

Ancient Egyptians believed that every person has several bodies, from the physical and corruptible to the most radiant and eternal. It is not possible for us to know in every respect how the ancients understood these various "bodies," and there have been many modern interpretations, but for the purposes of this book I will give some broad definitions.

- The *khat* is the physical, mortal body. At death it is subject to decay, unless it is mummified and becomes an eternal *sahu* (thus identifying with Osiris).

- The *ba* is sometimes called the soul, and is depicted as a bird with a human head. It is the universal animating spirit that gives life to the physical body. When the *ba* withdraws from the body, the body dies. It can come and go from the heavenly realms and visit the body in its tomb at will.

- The *ka* is referred to as the "double," but that term alone doesn't explain its many actions. The glyph for the *ka* is a pair of upraised arms. It represents the individual ego's life force, the spiritual, intellectual and creative energies. It can move freely after death between Amenti and the world of the living, it can eat and drink, it can inhabit a statue. Egyptologist John Anthony West adds a symbolist interpretation by saying that "*ka* is the power that fixes and makes individual the animating spirit that is *ba*." It is the I "that inhabits the body but is not the body." West says that there are many aspects of *ka*: "The animal *ka*, concerned with the desires of the body; the divine *ka* that heeds the call of the spirit; and the intermediate *ka*, which provides the impetus to those on the path for gradually gaining control of the animal ka and placing it in the service of the divine *ka*....If, during life on earth, the *ka* has degenerated to the point where it has been divested of all virtue, of everything truly human, then the *ka* disperses into the various lower animal and vegetable realms. This is the second death the Egyptian texts speak of with such fear and horror....The perfected man, to achieve immortality, united his *ka* to his *ba*: his individual essence to the divine spark within."*

– The *akh* is the shining, radiant form that inhabits a person's body, unites the *ka* and the *ba*, and as a spirit can come down from the heavenly levels to operate on earth – for good or ill. It is often shown as an ibis.

There are other aspects as well, among them the *khaibet*, which is the shadow, a ghostly, lower form with all the carnal desires and appetites of earthly life; the *ab*, the heart or conscience; the *sekhem*, the vital force; and the *ren*, the name of the person, which has its own magical powers and is essential to perpetuating the memory of the deceased.

In her diary Omm Sety recorded this conversation in which Sety speaks of his knowledge of the actions of the various "bodies" – and about magic:

Nov. 21, 1972
I asked H.M. if, in Amenti, he was able to meet the kings who had ruled before or after him. He said, "I meet only those people who lived during my lifetime, and not all of them, as some were sinless; others have gone back to earth, as I now believe my friend Hor-ra has done." I asked then how shall we meet in Amenti, since I was born only a short time ago. He replied, "Your body is of today, but your soul, your akh and your ka are of my day." I asked about the soul, the akh and the ka. He laughed. "Have you forgotten all that you learned in the House-of-Men-Maat-Ra, you bad girl?" I replied, "I

---

*John Anthony West, *A Traveler's Key to Ancient Egypt*, Quest Books, 1995, p. 64

*have not forgotten that I learned to love you." He was pleased
at this, and kissed me many times. At last I got him back to
the question of the ba, etc.*

*He said, "During life the ba, akh and ka dwell always in the
khat (physical body). As you well know, the akh may be freed
by one who knows magic, and it can travel to distant places or
even to Amenti. There are a few learned magicians who can
also set the ka free during life, but this is not a good thing to
do. If the ba leaves the khat, the khat will immediately die.
After death, the ba, akh and ka are reunited in Amenti, but the
ka may prefer to return and visit the earth. It is free to come
and go at will, and this makes no difference to the reunited ba
and akh, which have become as they were on earth. In Amenti
there is no sickness or physical pain. But how terrible can be
the pain of the heart."*

*He stopped speaking, and hid his face against my neck. I said,
"Forget that pain, it is all over now. We are treading a good
path together, so do not be sad anymore." He cheered up and
started calling me silly names. I asked if he knew and practiced
magic. He replied, "Of course I know it, do I not come to you
by magic? But all that I learned of magic I learned in the
service of the Great of Strength,* as I once told you. Therefore
I have never used it. Except for this power to use the sakhm**
of others, it is all evil, and even this power could be used for
evil ends. As I am at this moment, I could do anything that a
living man could do, perhaps more, for I am very strong (nakht)
and do not fear death. But if I misuse this power, I will lose
it, and I dread to think of what my punishment would be!"*

A few days earlier, Sety had come to her bed in a passionate mood. Omm Sety returned his kisses at first, then realizing

---

*the god Set
**an alternate spelling of *sekhem*

that they were entering dangerous ground, said, "Beloved! Do you want to lose me for another 3000 years?" He begged forgiveness. She sought to change the subject, and asked him to tell her, "By what road do you come to me?"

> He answered, "By the same road that your akh is brought to me in Amenti." I asked, "Do you pass through Pega-the-Gap when coming or going?" "No," he replied, "not always. Pega is the traditional gateway; through it the akhu* return every year to take part in the Great Feast of Our Lord Osiris. I was told that one year you waited for them; you joined the procession and went as far as the Great Wall within which is the most ancient temple."

> "I wanted to enter with them," I said, "but some power prevented me, I do not know how or why." He answered, "If you had entered, you would have died, and your lifeless body would have been found, and no one could have known how your life left you."

> "Why?" I asked. "Was I wrong to wish to enter?" "No," he said, "you were not wrong at all, but no mortal body could withstand that massed array of spiritual power all around you; it is a marvel that you did not die out there on the Sacred Road." I asked, "When you left this earth, did you go through Pega-the-Gap?" "No," he replied, "I was at Thebes when I left this world, and I passed by way of Peak-of-the-West."

> I said that I wanted to ask a question, but if it was something that I should not know, to please forgive me, and forget that I asked. He said, "Speak, Bentreshy."

> I said, "Do you remember your death, and what it was like?" He looked at me very seriously and replied," Do you not remem-

---

*the transfigured dead

ber your own experience, Child?" I shook my head. "So," he said, "I will tell you. The feeling is wonderful, just as you feel when your akh is released from your body. But one's thoughts and feelings remain the same. I was torn by longing, by doubt and fear. I longed, I even dared to hope, that I should find you waiting for me. But I also realized the full measure of my sin. For a brief while I was aware of my earthly surroundings. I saw my lifeless body lying on the same bed and in the same room, which you know. I saw my friend Hor-ra, weeping, and I saw my son Ramesses lying on the floor weeping bitterly and calling on me not to leave him. This was a terrible experience. Please, Bentreshy, tell the people that they should not torture their dead in this way, if they love them truly. Then the scene faded, and I found myself out under the starry sky."

"So," I said, "not every soul passes through Pega on its way to Amenti?" "No," he replied. "It is said that Our Lord Osiris passed through it, and also most of the people who died in Abydos. The priests taught many things that were not true, or were only partly true. They taught that the dead body must be preserved and transformed into a sahu (mummy). This is not true! A sahu may be useful to a ka wishing to become like an earthly person, but this is not necessary, and the ka of an evil person might use this power for bad ends. It is true that the body of Our Lord Osiris became a sahu.

"We all hate to think that the bodies of those whom we love turn to stinking corruption, and are destroyed. I used to grieve for my poor soldiers, slain in battle. Sometimes their bodies were torn by dogs or wild beasts and had become stinking, before we were able to bury them as best we could.

"It was very wrong of the priests to encourage people to spend their wealth on fine burials, wealth that could have been of use to the living." I answered, "And yet it is through those fine burials, those costly tombs, that the people of all the world today

know of the wonder and glory of our land. The tombs, as well as the temples, have kept the names of our gods ringing through the world. Perhaps the wise men knew that this would come to pass?"

Sety sat quietly, thinking about this. Then he said, "My little priestess is becoming a great thinker! Who put such thoughts into your heart?" "Lord," I replied, "in this earthly life I have seen with my eyes and heard with my ears. Men seek out tombs hidden in the flesh of Geb. They do this without a thought of gain for themselves, but only to know more and more about our wonderful achievements. Your name and that of your son, H. M. Ramesses, is known to people in far distant parts of the world, in places quite unknown in our day."

He seemed pleased at what I had said. "But what of the sahu, what use is a sahu today?" I replied, "It is a wonderful thing to look on the faces, to touch the hands of those who were once the masters of the world. Only in our land can one do that. Also, clever doctors can examine a sahu and see from what sickness or accidents the persons suffered and from what they died. In this way they can learn what are ancient sicknesses, and what have come lately to trouble mankind."

After that we sat very quietly, side by side, and holding hands. "You have brought peace to my heart, more than you can know," he said, and he kissed me very gently. And then he left me.

Aug 17. 1972.

H. M came last night at about 1 o'clock after midnight. I was still awake. I had put out the big light, but could not sleep, and was feeling rather fed up. Sety lay down beside me, and put his arms around me, and said: "Bentreshy, my Little Love, I had to come to you, I cannot bear to be far from you!" He began kissing me, and I returned them, but soon he became so passionate that I thought it wiser to change the subject. I said, "Beloved! do you want to lose me for another 3000 years? Stay quiet for a while. Please tell me by what road you come to me." He sighed deeply, and after a little silence, said "You are a wise little One, and I am a bad man to let my desire endanger our eternal happiness. But I love you so much; forgive me, Bentreshy". I said, "There is nothing to forgive, your love is very precious to me, but we must be wise and patient for just a little time longer". He got up, and led me to the chairs, and we sat down side by side. Again I said, "By what road do you come to me?" He answered, "By the

A page from Omm Sety's diary (August 17, 1972): H. M. came last night at about 1 o'clock after midnight. I was still awake. I had put out the big light, but could not sleep, and was feeling rather fed up. Sety lay down beside me, and put his arms around me, and said: "Bentreshy, my Little Love. I had to come to you, I cannot bear to be far from you!" He began kissing me, and I returned them, but soon he became so passionate that I thought it wiser to change the subject. I said, "Beloved! do you want to lose me for another 3000 years? Stay quiet for a while. Tell me by what road you come to me." He sighed deeply, and after a little silence, said "You are a wise Little One, and I am a bad man to let my desire endanger our eternal happiness. But I love you so much; forgive me, Bentreshy." I said, "There is nothing to forgive, your love is very precious to me, but we must be wise and patient for just a little time longer." He got up, and led me to the chairs, and we sat down side by side. Again I said, "By what road do you come to me?"

On a personal note, as I revisit my friend's private diary entries, I find myself somewhat uncomfortable with the apparent imbalance that existed in their relationship, the god-like king and the young girl of humble circumstances. But I have come to believe that the participants were existing in a kind of dream of themselves, a continuing moment in time at the height of their interrupted passion, for which they were, in all earnestness, trying to atone. My opinion was not important; their reality was theirs alone.

Ren: the power of name

The first time Omm Sety went to Luxor it was to track down an inscription that she had read about in Breasted's classic work, *A History of Egypt*. The inscription was to be found in the Hypostyle Hall of the Karnak Temple. This was an emotional journey for her because in Breasted's book she had discovered a reference to Sety's elder son, Pa-Remessu, and an ancient struggle for the title of Crown Prince – and by extension for the crown itself. Omm Sety already knew that Sety's eldest son Pa-Remessu had been buried alive in an anonymous stone sarcophagus, his name having been hammered out and the sarcophagus dropped into a deep pit. The inscription that Omm Sety found at Karnak confirmed for her in the most poignant way what happened to people – even a king's son – who committed grave crimes: Pa-Ramessu's name had been crudely hacked away, though a faint shadow of the hieroglyphs could still be seen. In its place, artists had inserted the figure of Ramesses, the younger brother.

Breasted wrote, "[T]he evidence of the bitter conflict of the two princes involving of course the harem and the officials of the court and a whole lost romance of court intrigue may still be traced by the trained eye on the north wall of the Karnak hypostyle."* Had Sety been the one who ordered this obliteration

---

*James Breasted, *A History of Egypt*, Scribner's, 1924 ed., p. 419

of his once-beloved first son's name after a failed palace coup? It broke her heart to know that he surely must have – here and in every other place it would have been inscribed. There could be no worse punishment. To lose one's name was to lose one's eternal life, to be cast into oblivion and erased from the memory of gods and men. This was one thing Omm Sety was never going to ask His Majesty about.

TWELVE

In the House-of-Men-Maat-Ra: the Temple

"I fear that one day men will find the Treasury." Sety

According to ancient tradition, all the kings of Egypt were given several royal names, each representing a special connection to the gods. The first of Sety's royal names was Men-Maat-Ra, which means Enduring-is-the-Truth-of-Ra.

Sety's temple at Abydos was known as the House-of-Men-Maat-Ra. In many ways and for many reasons this new temple to Osiris was unique in its design, but there were certain basic traditions that were always to be observed in creating a home for the gods. Egyptian temples served two distinct and separate functions, the sacred and the mundane. Specific areas belonged only to the gods and their attendant ritual priests, while other parts were open to the public and provided important services.

Among the pillared halls and chapels of the Sety Temple at Abydos (see temple plan in the Appendix) are several small rooms that once functioned as archives, where people could come to record their legal documents or check on the ownership of property. They would enter the Hall of Archives from outside, and not through the sacred areas of the temple. Today, the walls of these rooms reveal faded painting and incised relief work from the time of Sety and Ramesses and his son and successor

Merneptah. Images of the god Thoth the Recorder are featured prominently alongside his royal patrons. There are also images of several decorated chests, with descriptions of their contents, including "the King's annals, recorded in writing." Sety had confirmed to Omm Sety the existence of these annals, and that they were written in his own hand. I asked her if there were any possibility that the king's diary could still be found within the temple. Other royal annals that we know of are a compilation of events written by a royal scribe, and never by the hand of the king himself. If Sety's annals could be found, what a mine of information it would contain about a little understood and tumultuous period of Egypt's history.

"It would be a matter of great luck to find it," Omm Sety said, "because papyri are terribly fragile. While I was working here one of the chief inspectors made some investigations under the floor of the Archives, and we found a few pots, but from the Late Period. One of them contained papyrus, absolutely in powder. The largest fragment didn't measure more than 1/4 centimeter. Among the things in those pots – it must have belonged to a woman – was a double-sided hair comb and a spindle for spinning linen or wool, and a little workbasket, just like the ones they make today in the oases."

I asked if there were a possibility of tunnels or other structures beneath the temple that might be concealing a hidden cache of papyrus documents – and with luck, the annals of the king.

She replied in a knowing voice, "I believe that the Sety Temple protects a great number of important secrets, waiting for someone to discover them. Look at those inscriptions on one wall of the Archives that describe the 'Double Treasury' of King Sety. They say that it is filled with gold, silver, lapis lazuli and every precious stone. And in another room, an inscription over the lintel mentions *'the Great Treasury of the Temple of Millions of Years of the King of Upper and Lower Egypt, Men-Maat-Ra.'* On every side we find references to a temple treasury, and images of the god Thoth examining golden objects, offering tables and libation jars. These are the things that would be in a treasury, along with other sacred objects, like statues of gods and goddesses."

Did the inscriptions mean that the Hall of Archives was also the great Treasury of the temple? Omm Sety and I agreed that this could not be the case, for security reasons, if nothing else. The rooms were open to the public and there was easy access from outside and even from the rooftop that surrounded the open courtyard. No one would have put a treasury in such a vulnerable spot. But wherever it is, Omm Sety believed it was still intact, because if it had been discovered – and of course looted – it would likely have been left standing open. At the Temple of Dendera there was such a case when its crypts were discovered open and stripped of their treasure. The Treasury of the Sety Temple has never been found, but that doesn't mean that it isn't still there, somewhere, awaiting discovery.

"I will relate a strange experience that happened to me in 1958," Omm Sety wrote in our book, *Abydos: Holy City of Ancient Egypt*. She described a certain morning when she had been working in her office in the Hall of the Sacred Barques. She had been fighting off a case of Asian flu with aspirins, but to no avail, and decided she had best stop working and go home.

"At that time," she wrote, "work was in progress in roofing the temple." Heavy scaffolding had been erected around the temple to support the work. "Although I had the key to all the doors it was easier to get in and out of the building by going up the stairs to the roof, walking along the top of the southern wall of the unroofed Western Corridor and down the scaffolding at the west of the temple." This she started to do, but as she was walking across the wall of the Western Corridor she became quite dizzy and fell hard onto the stones, twisting her ankle. "I remember hearing a loud grating sound like that of a grindstone at work, and I rolled down a fairly steep slope; the grating sound was renewed, and I found myself in darkness.

"After a while, the dizziness passed off enough to allow me to stand up and grope for a wall. I touched some smooth limestone blocks and stood there wondering what to do next. Presently I sensed very faint threads of light filtering down from above as though through cracks in the roof, and as my eyes became accustomed to the gloom, I found that I was standing in a narrow passage less than three meters wide. A narrow path, perhaps about fifty centimeters wide, ran along the base of the wall, but the remainder of the width of the passage appeared to be completely filled with boxes, offering tables, vases, bales of linen, and everywhere was the gleam of gold."*

Limping and in pain, she felt her way down the long, crowded passage, past life-sized wooden statues of Isis and Osiris, and a statue of Horus, whose startling falcon face seemed to be gazing directly at her. Then she saw a golden vase, about ten inches tall. "It had an oval body, a long neck and a trumpet-shaped mouth and stood in a wooden ring stand. By the faint light I could see a cartouche engraved on its body, but it was too dark to read it. But by the length of the frame I knew that it was not the cartouche of Sety but one of the later kings perhaps from the XXV dynasty. I picked it up. It was very heavy, and at first I thought I would take it as evidence of what I had discovered by accident, but finally decided against it, and put it down in its place." She continued making her painful progress – "half conscious," she wrote.

"Suddenly, I found myself out in the open air almost blinded by the sunlight. I was standing beside the well in the Second Court of the temple, and approaching me was a young man, a stranger. He stared at me in frank astonishment and asked if I knew where the architect in charge of the restorations was. I told him, and still staring in surprise, he thanked me and left. I went to enter the temple by the main door only to find that the keys were not with me. I went around to the back of the temple in order to re-enter by the way I had left it, when I met two of the gaffers. They cried out, 'Where have you been? You are all

---

*O.S. & el Zeini, *Abydos: Holy City of Ancient Egypt*, p. 176

dirt and cobwebs!' And so I was; no wonder the young man had stared at me so hard!

"I replied that I had fallen down and hurt my ankle and had forgotten my keys. But I did not tell them any more. I managed to crawl back to the Hall of the Sacred Boats,* and there were the keys just as I had left them on the table.

"All that I am sure of is that I really fell, my ankle was swollen for a week, and I had a big bruise on my shoulder. Also I was really covered with dust and cobwebs, and having left the keys behind, there is no way in which I could have reached the front part of the temple except by going around from the outside, where the gaffers would have seen me and where, moreover, I would not have collected any dust or cobwebs all over my clothes. If this really did happen, then there is only one possible explanation. I must have hit a stone with my shoulder as I fell which turned on a pivot and opened into a sloping passage. This would account for the grating sound. But how did I get out again? All that I can suggest is that a deserted hyena's lair in the side of the well may have communicated with the 'Treasure Passage.' Later, the lair caved in, but its place remains still clearly visible. The Chief Inspector got interested and told me to try and find the supposed pivot-stone, which I did, in every possible place in the temple including the 'Blind Rooms.'** But no results, except some more bruises! I have spent many hours pushing and butting against the walls hoping to find a movable stone that turned on a pivot and that might open into a passage leading to who knows where or what. But all was in vain. This is real life; had we been in Hollywood, someone would have written a better script!"***

---

*Hall of the Sacred Barques
**two rooms, each 34 by 131 feet, built one atop the other and with no doors or windows. The uppermost has lost its ceiling stones over time, but the purpose of the two rooms is so far a complete mystery – one of many in the temple.
***O.S. & el Zeini, *Abydos: Holy City of Ancient Egypt*, pp. 177-179

She had been drawn to investigate the Blind Rooms, even though access to them is extremely difficult, because she was aware of a provocative inscription on one of the walls. The Blind Rooms do not seem to be part of the original plan of the temple and were most likely part of an older building, but what that was exactly is a matter of surmise. Omm Sety described yet another confounding clue pointing to the existence of a treasure (again, from *Abydos: Holy City*): "Like the lower room [Blind Room], the upper one is entirely undecorated, but on the western wall at a height of about thirty centimeters (one foot) from the floor level, is a most tantalizing grafitto. It is in well-formed hieroglyphs deeply scratched into the stone and reads: 'Travel to the north for three hundred and three paces and take to thyself the Eye of Horus.' Now the term, 'Eye of Horus' was often used for anything good and desirable; it could mean an offering, a gift or a treasure. But did the priestly writer mean true geographical north, or the local conventional north? Was he serious or was he pulling our leg? Above all, how in all the world did he get into this room to write the graffito? And in what period and for what real purpose?"*

If Omm Sety had allowed others to wonder if her experience in the dark corridor might have been the result of a fever-induced delerium, she herself never for a moment doubted what had occurred – because she had possession of the most intriguing proof of all. And she couldn't tell anyone about it.

the cloth

Omm Sety had written of the golden vase that she found in the corridor, and of her desire to take away some proof that her experience had actually happened. She said that she decided to leave the vase there. But that is not the entire story. Apparently, she did take something with her from that dark place – a

---

*ibid., p. 181

piece of linen cloth, the kind that was commonly used to drape the statues of gods. Early in 1971, Omm Sety showed it to me. The color of the cloth was yellowish brown, a clear sign of age. There were no fringes, and a big patch in the middle of the cloth was eaten up through age. Similar to the cloth in Tutankhamun's tomb that shrouded the majestic recumbent figure of Anubis, this cloth was about two by five feet in size. It had no great value as an artifact but I took it upon myself to have it properly tested. I cut off a small piece and gave it to the late Prof. Francois Daumas, who sent it a European lab to be carbon dated. I did not tell him the provenance of the sample. The resulting laboratory evaluation put it within the Ramesside period, within 100-200 years of Sety's time. As to where the cloth is today, unfortunately I do not know, since it was not among Omm Sety's personal effects at the time of her death, nor was the laboratory report.

I was not surprised that she had chosen to take the cloth and leave the gold vase, a far more important object. She respected the protocols of scientific archaeology. She had assisted some of the finest archaeologists of the time and scorned the careless mishandling of objects by some of the earlier men. I'm sure she was reluctant even to remove the tattered piece of linen. But it was her proof that she had actually been there, even though she could never speak of it openly.

Excerpts from Omm Sety's diaries reveal that His Majesty had his own thoughts about the subject, and about the existence of the Treasury:

Oct. 31, 1972
I began to tell H.M. about my adventure in the Treasury of the temple, but he said, "I have heard about this. I heard also that you were going to take away a golden libation vessel, but you left it and took instead one of the used garments of the gods. In this you did well; the garment should have been given away

long long ago.* But you must not take away the things of the gods; that is very bad."

I wanted to speak more about the matter but he refused, and wanted to sleep, but he promised to tell me more and said that he had something important to say in this matter, but that it could wait until his next visit.

Nov. 20, 1972
H.M. came last night at 11 o'clock. He was in quite a good mood. He laughed about Ahmed's dog, who was howling and barking... I asked again how I got into the Treasury of the House-of-Men-Maat-Ra. He replied, "The entrance is in the Pillared Hall of the Bearers of Beauties (the Hall of Barques, the sacred Boats). From it a long ramp (redwi) leads down to the Treasury."

I said that it seemed only a short slope, but he said that I had become partly unconscious ("had lost part of your heart"). I asked how I had got out and he said, "That I do not know. The stone closed behind you and you were trapped. Perhaps, by the mercy of our Lord Osiris, the animal which made its lair in the side of the well had dug right through into the Treasury, but of this I am not sure, but I will go and see it."

I asked if he would be angry if the Treasury was found, and the things taken to the Museum, where they would be much admired.** H. M. replied, "The things which are the property of the Gods must not be taken away from them. Surely you and

---

*Statues of the gods were daped in immaculate linen cloth, which was ritually discarded once it became worn or stained.

**I had asked her to ask this question of Sety. Many of Omm Sety's questions to H.M. were prompted by discussions that Omm Sety and I had had earlier. Sety was aware of my unbounded curiosity about his life and times.

I know that! I fear that one day men will find the Treasury, and in it there used to be a book, a book of magic, which should not again fall into the hands of ordinary men. If the Treasury is discovered, I will tell you to go in and search for this book and destroy it."

"But how shall I know it," I asked. He answered, "It used to be kept in a red leather case, sealed with my seal, and this was in an ebony box, decorated with gold, and on its lid was the golden cartouche of Iahmes the Hero.* I will go and see if it is still there."

I asked why he does not destroy it himself, but he said, "I can only enter now as an akh,** which has no power to destroy on this earth. I can only become as a man if I can take sakhm from you, or one like to you. But do not be anxious; it may be that the book is no longer there. I hope that it has been destroyed already."

I wanted to know more about this book, but he refused to tell me and said, "We have talked very much. If that dog will stop howling like the Son of Nut, we will sleep under your nice cover." Khalawi continued to howl and whine, but in spite of the row we fell asleep, and H.M. left without waking me up.

I have been thinking all day about what H.M. said about the entrance to the Treasury. If it is in the Hall of Barques, it must be the E. wall under the staircase. Certainly that wall is very thick. But if this is so, and the Treasury is under the aisle in front of Sety's chapel, then there must be a long, steep passage running from the Hall of Barques, right under the N. end of the Corridor of Kings.

---

*Iahmes is Ahmose, the unifier of Egypt after the Second Intermediate Period and almost mythical founder of the 18th Dynasty.
**the non-corporeal "body of light"

Nov. 21, 1972

H.M. came again last night, just after midnight. I was awakened by Mery,* spitting and swearing. I saw H.M. standing in front of my statues of Osiris and Isis, bowing politely, with his hands raised. Then he jumped into bed beside me and pulled the lahaf** over our heads. He was so cold that he was shivering, and would not talk sensibly until he got warm.

At last he said, "Little one, I have just come from the House-of-Men-Maat-Ra, and I went into the Treasury. I saw the libation vase that you left on the ground; it was made long after our day, by the Majesty of a King Owsarkan Mery-Imon.*** I searched for the book of which I told you. It still remains. But if the treasury is found in your time, you must destroy it entirely."

I said, "Tell me how to enter the Treasury and I will destroy it now."

He replied, very emphatically, "No, Bentreshy, you must not do that! It is said that the Majesty of King Iahmes will come again to the Black Land, and he will take the book and use it, but that time has not yet come, and I fear that the book may fall into the hands of evil or ignorant men, for you say that there are people who know our ancient language."

I said, "Perhaps it will be found after I have come to you in Amenti. What then?" He replied, "Then Shay must do as it will."

I said, "Did you find how I got out of the Treasury?" He replied, "Yes, as you thought; some animal made its hole in

---

*one of Omm Sety's cats
**a large head shawl that can be used as a blanket
***Osarkon I, 21st Dynasty pharaoh

*the side of the well in the Court, but it, or perhaps many of
its kind, dug and dug until they reached the eastern wall of the
Treasury. There, some of the blocks of stone had moved from
their places, I know not how or when, and one of them had
partly fallen into the animal's hole and left a small space, so
small I do not know how you could get through it! Now the
whole length of the animal's work has fallen in, but I think it
could be easily cleared out again. You may tell this to the Sad
Imy-ra Hani."**

When I first heard Omm Sety's story of the fall I was on
the borderline between doubt and belief. Some time later I was
able to spend a few hours investigating the path Omm Sety took
into and out of the dark chamber. First, I climbed over the roof
of the southwestern part of the temple. I stopped at the point
where she said the fall occurred and found nothing unusual. I
tried to venture into the passage by way of the well in the second
court, but an old, serious injury to my knee prevented me. Then
I questioned the only witnesses, the ghaffirs, interviewing each
one separately. Their testimonies were nearly identical. They
spoke especially of her appearance as she climbed out of the
sanded well – with her head, shoulders and most of her dress full
of dust and an incredible number of cobwebs. Knowing Omm
Sety's consistent honesty in all matters, I am quite satisfied with
her account, but not satisfied that we will ever know the whole
story of the Treasury.

One other thing that suggests the presence of an as-yet-
undiscovered room inside the temple is the difference of nearly
four meters between the floor height in the Archive rooms and
that of the Hall of Sacred Barques and Butchers' Hall immediately to the east of the Archives. Four meters of height would
be enough vertical space for a room or series of rooms to exist
beneath the known floor. We may never be able to know because
of serious structural problems in the temple itself, mostly caused

---

*Dr. Hani

by the rising of the subsoil water and the sinking of some of the pavement stones, which have compromised the integrity of the walls and made further investigations in that area extremely challenging.

When Omm Sety and I were writing our book about Abydos, I had to insist that she include the story about her fall, since I had come to believe it to be true. This turned out to be a good decision, because American businessman and independent archaeologist James Westerman* happened to read Omm Sety's account and right away contacted me. I arranged his visit to Abydos and introductions to the appropriate authorities within the Antiquities Organization. He was keenly interested in investigating Omm Sety's story of a lost Treasury in the Sety Temple.

Mr. Westerman financed the excavation, having engaged an Egyptian Egyptologist, Mr. el Sawy, and a prominent geologist, Dr. Bahay el Essawi. The work was supervised by the chief inspector and a civil engineer from the Antiquities Organization, under the aegis of Dr. David O'Connor. The project lasted only one season, 1999, during which I acted briefly as consultant. After doing radar soundings, we succeeded in clearing a pit leading to the underground part of the Sety Temple. But excavations had to be stopped because the passageway was blocked by a large stone, which looked to be part of an enormous pillar and was directly beneath the middle of the Second Hypostyle Hall. Unfortunately, no one in authority was willing to risk displacing the stone or doing the necessary engineering to make that possible, for fear of causing the entire Hall to collapse.

The excavation did, however, verify the existence of an underground structure of some kind, perhaps only one of many beneath the temple. And so the Treasury, if it is still intact, must wait for another day. My earnest hope is that it won't have to wait long, since the foundational structure of the temple is threat-

---

*James Westerman has done investigations at Machu Picchu in which he uncovered new clues to the astronomical significance of the ancient Peruvian city. He is the author of, *The Meaning of Machu Picchu.*

ened by the presence of a powerful acquifer, which was recently discovered by Dr. el Essawi. As to whether Sety's annals might be found intact, I very much doubt it. Ancient papyrus scrolls were usually stored in pottery jars and closed by wooden stoppers and tar – unlikely protection against long centuries of immersion in subsoil water. Water is the great, looming menace to the Sety Temple and its companion-in-mystery, the Osirion.

the mystery of the light

In Egypt, there have long been legends about mysterious ever-burning lamps left inside the tombs of the pharaohs. As I walked through the dimly lit halls of the Sety Temple I found myself wondering how in the world, in such poor light, the artists could have rendered such sublimely delicate sculptured portraits of the gods, and with such great subtlety of color. What was their source of light? As a photographer who has spent count-less hours inside temples and tombs, especially the Sety Temple, trying to "capture the light," it was only natural that Omm Sety and I would eventually have a conversation about this.

If you ask most archaeologists, they will say that the ancients used mirrors to bring the light to the interior walls, but I have never believed that was a good enough answer. I have tried using mirrors and found myself in a race with the sun, repositioning the mirrors every five minutes, and seeing how the expressions on the faces change with the changing light. It is a frustrating experience. This made me start to wonder, could those old legends about ever-burning lights be true – some type of technology beyond our current understanding? Or was the answer simply that the interior decorations had been done *before* the Sety Temple had its roof.

I was inclined to believe the "roofless" theory, because I cannot think that such perfection of sculptural art could be done without the help of a permanent and very strong source of light. In other words, in a place that was open to the sunlight. I asked Omm sety her opinion about this.

"No," she said, "I'm afraid I don't agree with you. I know that the whole of a temple building *must* be complete before they decorate it.* In your work with mirrors you used only a few. But if you had a large quantity so that you could get the light from different angles, and an army of men working them, it would be different. And this may account for the change that we see here in the expression of the figures. When you are working on them in one light, you work from a certain direction, and then when you work in another direction the expression appears to change. A little curl in the corner of the mouth, a little line beside the nose, a little line under the eyes. Some of the eyes of the figures seem actually to be smiling. I still think that it was done by mirrors, but rather an almost unlimited number of mirrors. As to the change in the expression of the figures, I doubt that the artists would have been annoyed by that. They might have thought that the expression actually *did* change. I'm sometimes inclined to think the same thing myself."

"But Omm Sety," I said, "with even the slightest inclination of a mirror the expression on the face changes. Those miserable people who had to hold those mirrors would have to have stood absolutely still, like statues – which is nearly impossible. So, I think that the wall sculptures would have been done while the chapels were without their roof, and the interior sides of the roof stones could have been decorated while still on the ground and later lifted into place. As to the use of multiple mirrors, I can't possibly see how they could have brought the light in through that forest of columns inside the Hypostyle Hall."

---

*The enclosed, consecrated areas of a temple were off-limits to anyone but the priests, and the innermost sanctuary could only be entered by the high priest. The images of the gods were not to be gazed upon by the common folk. On a god's feast day a small statue of the god would be brought out of the temple on one of the sacred boats to allow the public to see it, but the interior wall images were reserved for the eyes of the priests. The sacred art on those walls would not be commenced until the temple walls and roof were in place, secure from profane eyes.

Omm Sety later brought up the subject to His Majesty:

April 4, 1973
I asked how the very dark parts of temples and tombs were
illuminated. He said, "By silver mirrors or copper mirrors, and
in some cases by the tka.*" I said that I could not understand
how that could be, as the sun was always moving and the tka
gave only a bad and smoky light.

I said that I had heard of light being created by magic. He
replied, "This is possible, and was sometimes done by powerful
Kheri-heb priests.** But this was never done when the temples
were being decorated, as such things must not be performed in
front of the rekhyt.***" I asked if he knew how to do this, and
he said, "No, I do not know."

Heartsease

Sety often spoke of his small palace at Abydos, *Heartsease*.
That was where he stayed when he came to inspect the building
of his temple and when he came to celebrate the Great Feast
of Osiris. In modern times, there is scant indication of exactly
where the royal rest house would have been. An area of founda-
tion ruins adjacent to the temple has long been casually referred
to as "the palace," but Omm Sety, being intimately familiar with
the area in question, disagreed.

In the early '70s Omm Sety and I were standing in front of
the temple, next to remnants of the Nif-Wer Canal, the ancient
waterway that used to bring pilgrims from the Nile, several miles
distant. We were discussing the reconstruction of the broad stair-
way leading up to the first court and the remains of some ancient
houses just to our left, at the entrance to the temple. "From the

---

*a torch or oil lamp
**priests who are charged with reading the ritual words; lector priests
***common people

Late Period, probably Coptic," Omm Sety commented about the houses. "They are hollowed out of the thickness of the great mud-brick temenos wall."* I looked around at what little remained of the massive wall that once surrounded the temple precincts.

"You can still get a good idea of its original form at the southeast corner. It was an enormously thick wall and it had bastions. The bricks are huge, about 45 by 35 centimeters, and some of them are stamped with the name of the king. It extended far beyond the temple. There must have been other buildings inside this temenos, not only the temple. In fact, part of the magazines** can be seen on the south. On the north I believe was *Heartsease-in-Abydos*, the palace of the king."

I looked in the direction she was pointing. "You think that below that mound are the remnants of Sety's palace?"

"Yes, because there are the remains of a doorway in the eastern end of the northern wall, and the doorway must lead somewhere. We know that he had this palace. The other buildings inside the temenos to the south seem to be only magazines, and a sort of audience hall. Some of the Egyptologists wanted to say that that [the magazines and audience hall] was the palace, but it couldn't possibly be. The access to it would be too inconvenient. The palace would have been constructed of mudbricks, with the walls and the floor plastered and painted very beautifully. The doorways would be limestone, and the window grilles and the columns. There is a section of a column near the north wall of the temple, and it doesn't belong with the columns in the audience hall. The same style, the same type, but the measurements of the flutings are different. And I believe that this is part of one of the columns of this palace."

I noticed that the mound was quite a bit higher than the roof of the temple. Omm Sety explained that debris from a century of earlier excavations had been thrown on top. "But

---

*the wall around the outer perimeter of the ancient temples that defined the sacred space
**the storage rooms

among the fragments of pottery in this site," she said, "are small pieces of very fine pottery that do not appear to be either funerary vessels or temple vessels. It looks to be good domestic pottery. That's another reason I think the palace must have been there."

As we entered the first court of the temple we were surrounded by walls and porticos that Sety's son Ramesses had built. Sety had built the temple proper, but had not lived to complete the public areas outside the sacred inner halls. "In the original design," Omm Sety explained, "Sety intended that each of the seven cult chapels should have its own outer doorway in the façade, and this was allowed for. But when Ramesses came along he decided he needed a very big wall to say what a good boy he was to complete his father's work, and so he blocked up all the doorways on the southern side and gave us a long and very interesting inscription telling what he had done and why. And then on the northern half of the wall he blocked out the door to the chapel of Osiris and Isis."

One of the ongoing frustrations in archaeology is figuring out the correct sequence in the construction of a building, and the reasons why certain things were done or later altered. One night, after Omm Sety and His Majesty had been speaking of the technologies of modern times, she asked him a question about his temple:

August 23, 1972
I said, "Beloved, will you please tell me something about the House-of-Men-Maat-Ra that I do not understand?" He nodded. I said, "I can remember [from her other life] sitting in the first hall, and the walls and the shafts of the columns were not decorated, and yet the temple was in use. How was that?"

He replied that when the inner parts of the temple and the Second Hypostyle Hall were complete he decided to open the temple and consecrate it. Thus the doors between the First and

Second Hall became the outer doors of the temple. The First Hall became a kind of portico, and its wooden door leaves were never fitted. It was unconsecrated, and so the people could come there.

I asked why he had done this. He replied that he was not satisfied with the situation in W. Asia, and had determined to build a new capital near the old Avaris,* as Thebes was too far off if a sudden emergency arose. At the same time, his temple in Abydos was his dream, and he determined to have the pleasure of opening it, thinking that the unfinished parts could easily be completed when he had more leisure to attend to it. I did not ask why he never did complete it, as I knew from Hor-Ra's account that after the death of Bentreshy he never again set foot in Abydos.

the one in the many

I was interested in the way many of the deities had been portrayed on the portico columns of the Second Pylon, the thick wall between the first and second courts, because the gods depicted there have such overlapping characteristics and attributes. I had seen this before in 18th and 19th Dynasty representations, but not earlier. I asked Omm Sety why that should be.

"With the earlier figures of the gods," she said, "each one is separate, but later, and especially in the temples, they began to give each god attributes of another god. That is why I think that to the educated Egyptians the great gods like Amun, Ra-Horakhty,** Ptah*** and Min**** became only manifestations of one great god. A good example of this is here in the chapel of

---

*a city in the northeastern Delta, the old capital of the Hyksos rulers of Egypt
**Horus-on-the-Horizon, in combination with Ra, both solar deities
***the creator god of Memphis; creator of physical forms
****the god of generative energy, giving all creatures the power to reproduce

Amun, where you find Amun in his usual form of a blue-colored man, and then you find him in the form of the god Min. But instead of giving him the name Min, they give it as Amun-Ra. And the same in the chapel of Horakhty – even more so there – where you find a combination of different gods in one.

"I think that the ordinary uneducated people thought that all these great gods were different entities. They thought Ptah was one god and Amun was another and Ra-Horakhty was another. But I don't think the educated people did. It's rather like the Muslim idea that God has ninety-nine names, and each of these names is an attribute. Instead of just giving a name, they gave a form which expressed again the god's attributes or his functions."

the ones who watch

Oftentimes, Omm Sety experienced "presences" in the temple, in the sounds of a tinkling systrum* or a reed pipe, or as a light glowing softly from one of the small cult chapels at night; one time it was a benevolent voice. This did not surprise me, since she was so attuned to the energies of the temple, past and present. I myself have always felt some kind of non-physical presence when I was in Sety's temple. Alone for hours among its silent columns and shrines photographing its subtle beauty, I have been drawn many times into deep reflection and even awe. In those moments I knew I was anything but alone.

As Omm Sety once wrote: "One could imagine that these beliefs, held and practiced in this temple for more than a thousand years, have charged the very stones of the building with their potency. To be alone in the Temple of Sety is to feel watched over by benevolent, all-seeing eyes, and to know an overwhelming sense of peace and security."**

---

*a kind of rattle used in sacred music – often shaped like an ankh, the symbol of life
**O.S. & el Zeini, p. 71

By now, it should be clear that this chapter has not been a regulation tour of the Sety Temple. Any competent guidebook will offer the details of its architecture, but it may not give the visitor a sense of its compelling aura. In my travels around the world I have walked in many places considered sacred and felt the proof of it within myself. This is one of those places. And there is more here. There is the Osirion.

THIRTEEN

In the House of Mysteries:
the Osirion

"And the voice said, 'What is holy cannot be polluted.
Drink and do not fear.'" OS

If you walk through the Western Corridor of the Sety Temple you will pass by a famous scene of Ramesses and one of his sons lassoing a magnificent wild bull. The reliefs were added by Ramesses after his father's death and the meaning of the scene is obvious: the virile new king dominating the archetype of virility, the bull. But since this is Egypt, we must be aware of the deeper symbolism expressed in the depiction of everyday things. On the level of spiritual symbolism we see the king demonstrating the importance of controlling the primordial generative power. Another scene shows the king capturing a flight of birds in a net, symbolic of taming the undisciplined inner self. Both of these scenes end with a depiction of the king offering the animals (and what they represent) to the gods. These scenes in the Corridor of the Bull could suggest some sort of initiatory preparations, a subject of great interest to Omm Sety and me, especially in regard to the Osirion.

If we ascend a flight of stairs at the end of the Western Corridor we pass through the western entrance of the Sety Temple and out into broad daylight. And there, to our right, is the great subterranean structure itself, the Osirion. It is a place steeped in speculation: Was it the tomb of Osiris, or a cenotaph* of Sety as is usually thought – or was it built to be a hall of spiritual initiation?   Omm Sety and I had many discussions about whether the Osirion could have been an initiatory temple.   Only recently was I able to put the question to rest to my satisfaction.

At the Osirion, close to the spot where we would go when our recorded conversations were to be about religious, spiritual or esoteric questions – an appropriate setting. This picture was taken in January 1980, a couple of months before the fall that crippled her until her death in April 1981. (Hanny el Zeini)

I first set eyes on the Osirion over 50 years ago, during my first visit to the Sety Temple.   I had walked through the temple's Western Corridor and out the western entrance, and I found myself standing in the bright glare of Upper Egyptian sunlight looking at a mass of stone pillars and walls that jutted up from a great waterlogged depression in the sand.   I had never seen another temple or tomb like it.

---

*a ritual, symbolic tomb meant to receive offerings, but not to contain the body of the deceased; often erected at holy places like Abydos

I spent a long time just looking down into it, studying it. The focal point of the structure seemed to be the Great Hall. The perimeter was lined with retaining walls of dark red quartzite sandstone, faced on the inside with a number of small, square cells. In the center of this rectangular hall, occupying almost all of it, was a raised platform, an island made of larger blocks of red granite; and on top of the island stood ten monolithic* pillars, appearing to be at least 50 or 60 tons each – some even more. Strewn around the hall were the remains of the granite roof slabs and the heavy granite architraves that had once connected the pillars. Between the island and the outer wall ran a kind of channel about six feet wide. How deep it was I couldn't tell through the opaque standing water.

The cells were 17 in number, with six in each of the northern and southern walls, two in the western wall and three in the eastern wall. They opened onto a narrow ledge at the channel's edge. Two small flights of stairs descended from the island platform part way into the channel (see plan in Appendix).

On that first visit I felt an irresistible desire to walk down into the central hall and have a closer look, which I did by way of two long wooden planks. To the east and west of the central hall were two transverse halls. I waded through the eastern transverse hall. It was late afternoon and the slanting rays of the sun illuminated the remains of the saddle-shaped roof, revealing lovely scenes of the sky goddess Nut, stretched out over the world – the work of Sety's artists, I had read.

Yet, I just couldn't believe that this had been built by Sety, as most people believed, because the entire structure felt like something from the Pyramid Age. It shared the same stark simplicity and austere beauty as Khafra's Valley Temple next to his pyramid at Giza – the same massive, masterfully-worked granite stones that wrapped sculpturally around corners.

---

*cut from a single piece of stone, rather than constructed from blocks; a characteristic of Old Kingdom architecture

Osirion. In the Sarcophagus Room, the star-spangled body of the sky goddess Nut arches over the night sky, ready to swallow the sun and give birth to it again at dawn. Sety I is shown at lower left protected between her arms. (Hanny el Zeini)

Although most of the roof had been destroyed, what little remained showed a very curious aspect. At the northern and southern sides the roof sloped upwards, but the central part was flat. In fact, it resembled the undersides of a lid from an Old Kingdom sarcophagus. That alone made it impossible for me to accept the theory of most Egyptologists that the monument was a cenotaph of Sety. It differed from Sety's temple in another way too: It was constructed largely in granite, yet Sety's temple used no granite at all. It contained enormous monolithic pillars, but the Sety Temple's pillars and columns had been built up in sections. If Sety had built the Osirion, why were the architectural styles so completely different?

Remember that Sety's temple takes an abrupt L-turn just short of the Osirion, contrary to normal canons of 19th Dynasty architecture. Had the builders been surprised to find the presence of an older monument in their path? Because of the enormous dimensions of the roof slabs of the unexpected structure, did they think that it must belong to a very important ancestor, and did they then change the plan of the new temple?

This is not meant to suggest that Sety wasn't involved in some respect with the Osirion. The great archaeologist Henri Frankfort had excavated here in the 1920s and published his account in "The Cenotaph of Sety I at Abydos." He reached his conclusion that it had been built by Sety after he found two black granite dove-tailed tenons with the name Men-Maat-Ra on them, inserted between blocks of a red granite architrave. That, combined with the extensive 19th Dynasty artwork on the walls and ceilings, led to the assumption that Sety had built the monument for himself. "But," as Omm Sety later wrote, "when any king built a monument, he always put an inscription saying, 'He made it as his monument for his father, Osiris (or whatever was the name of the god to whom it was dedicated).' This formula, which is repeated over and over again in temples, is not found anywhere here."* Additionally, the tenons with Sety's name could indicate that his work was a restoration, rather than an original construction. A recent investigation by the Egyptian Antiquities Organization found no evidence that Sety I was the builder of the Osirion. And Sety never claimed that he was.

Strangely, in Sety's time there was apparently no way to gain entrance to the eastern transverse hall, which has come to be known as the Sarcophagus Room, for its sarcophagus shape. Yet he took great pains to decorate its walls and ceiling. We now know that the artists who did the decorations in this room, finding no other entrance, had forced their way into it through one of the small, square cells.

The Osirion's entrance, which Margaret Murray discovered in the early 20th century, was through a long passageway that starts outside the temenos enclosure walls and enters the Osirion on its western side. The passageway's walls are decorated with scenes and texts normally found in royal tombs; they were done during the reign of Sety's grandson Merenptah, the

*O.S. & el Zeini, p. 10

Omm Sety inside the Osirion's Sarcophagus Room. It took more than 60 sessions to be able to photograph the ceiling inscriptions on both sides, using four men and several mirrors. The sun's rays had to be reflected through the narrow entrance behind Abdel Ghani (my driver, right), who became an expert with mirrored light. Note the standing water.
(Hanny el Zeini)

son of Ramesses II. Now, no sacred structure within a temple complex would ever have its entrance *outside* the temenos walls. One explanation for the location of the entrance is that the Osirion had been built long before the temenos walls of the Sety Temple complex existed, and then at some later time had been forgotten, until Sety came along. The original passage is very ancient. It shows signs of later restoration, using the same huge mud-bricks that Sety used for the temenos walls around his temple complex.

Interestingly, Frankfort had also made several sondage* pits along the outside walls of the main hall and found Archaic Period and early Old Kingdom pottery at the bottom. Clearly, there was more to be known about the Osirion and its true age.

Omm Sety and I spent many hours together inside the Osirion. Visitors who enter through the corridor – which Merenptah decorated with vivid and often hellish scenes from

---

*a lateral excavation procedure for studying the vertical stratification of a site and establishing a timeline

*The Book of the Gates** – enter the Great Hall through a doorway that opens to the channel, and passing over this channel, they will come to the large island platform. The great stone pillars and architraves that once stood upon the island are in various states of ruin. Frankfort had made extraordinary efforts to clear up the dreadful mess of broken blocks of granite, a picture of destruction the scale of which is impossible to attribute to simple vandalism. The roofing slabs alone – especially the horizontal ones that covered the central part of the island – could weigh between 50 and 70 tons. Now, in many parts of Upper Egypt, some blocks from other destroyed temples were later shaped into round grinding stones to reduce wheat or barley to powder. But to actually dislodge and pull down a 50-ton stone for this purpose would be an absolutely futile effort.

Omm Sety and I agreed that after Strabo's visit to the Osirion an extremely strong earthquake must have shaken the whole area and caused considerable damage to this monument as well as many others. This is no flight of imagination if one considers an earthquake of the magnitude that struck Alexandria in the 14th century AD and sent the great Lighthouse plunging into the harbor.

Frankfort made a determined effort to clear the Osirion of its standing water, which had prevented thorough examination of the monument. After a month of strenuous preparation – including the installation of a gravity railway with which to dredge up the sand that continued its centuries-old drifting – the pumping began. After Frankfort had pumped about six feet of water the engine broke down. Within half an hour the water was back to its original level. Since that time the water level has risen and fallen, but not in any way that would indicate its true source. It appeared that seepage from the Nile, the obvious source, might not be the source after all.

The channel around the island is always full of water and until recently the water covered the island. The level varies occa-

---

*depicting the journey of the soul in the Underworld

sionally, but never in a regular monthly or even seasonal pattern. It was once thought that the variations were connected with the Nile flood and the subsequent rise of subsoil water, but hydrologists proved that to be wrong. Strabo gives the opinion that the water was originally introduced through a long underground roofed passage that connected to the ancient Nif-Wer canal, but no trace of this passage was ever found.

Omm Sety loved a mystery and a challenge. She was determined to find the source of the Osirion's water, and she was also curious to discover if the island might have contained something within it that would be accessible from its usually-submerged side walls – an ancient burial chamber, for instance. In the early 1960s Omm Sety and I tried to measure the depth of the channel by dropping a steel chisel tied to nylon fishing line. We found in one spot that some fallen blocks obstructed the chisel at about 12 feet below the ledge. In another spot the chisel dropped as far as 24 feet below the ledge before hitting a hard layer of soil. In January, 1964, Omm Sety celebrated her 60th birthday by diving into the channel fully clothed. She wanted to feel by hand those blocks that our chisel had hit against, to determine if they had curved lines indicative of broken fragments of a statue. I was away in Western Europe on a business trip, but a month later she told me about her adventure.

The water in the channel was cold but she dived well below the lowest part of the eastern staircase, carefully examining with her hands some pieces of broken roof slabs. On her second and third dives she examined other pieces of granite, but none had any curvature. She couldn't see farther than three or four feet, but she did ascertain that the entire eastern side of the island was one complete, unbroken wall. The assumption could be made that the entire island block was made of tightly fitted stone and contained no openings or chambers. Omm Sety was left with more questions than answers. She had suspected, as had I, that this place was connected with the initiatory rites of the Osirian worship, and that it could actually be the tomb of Osiris as well.

One of the many stories about Osiris is that after he was murdered by his brother Set, his body was cut up into pieces and the parts buried all over Egypt. In the story, the head of Osiris was buried at Abydos. Was the head of Osiris buried within this ancient monument? If that were the case, then it would follow that his tomb would become a place of spiritual initiations as well. In many ways the architecture resembles a large tomb. Evocations of death are a common theme in initiatory processes all over the world: The initiate enters a deathlike state, goes through psychological trials and tests, and emerges triumphant as a higher spiritual being.

Sometime in the late 1950s the island inside the Great Hall was dry. Omm Sety and I studied the floor carefully and found four rectangular holes, two to the east and two others to the west. The four holes were identical and looked as if they had been carved to fix four pedestals that would have supported a large reclining statue, most likely of Osiris. This could explain the presence of the two staircases of 13 steps each on both the east and west sides of the island.

Going on the assumption that this was an Osirian initiatory hall, what might that process have involved? How did the initiates live and what were the procedures? Was solitary confinement in the small cells around the island a part of it? We can see remnants of this, perhaps, in the mystical ascetic practices of Coptic monasticism that are still alive today in the desert monasteries of Egypt. I discussed with Omm Sety my earnest desire to learn something about the Osirian ceremonies of initiation. She never pretended to know anything about it but felt that some record must exist in the Cairo Museum or elsewhere.

an ancient initiation

By an unexpected piece of luck, in 1989 I met Antoine Seronde, an anthropologist and amateur Egyptologist who was researching religious music in Egyptian temples. He was among a group of American tourists to whom I gave a lecture at Abydos, and we became friends immediately. He was making acoustical studies of temples and was convinced, as I had become, that the Osirion was a temple of initiation and the burial place of Osiris. I was thrilled when he told me that in addition to pursuing his research into Egyptian temple music, he would search for documents concerned with the process of initiation. He paid another visit to Egypt at the end of 1992, and a few weeks later he wrote to tell me that he had made an exciting discovery in the library of the American University in Cairo (AUC). He wrote:

> I chanced upon a volume by Max Guilmot entitled, *Les Inities et les Rites Initiatiques en Egypt Ancienne* (Initiates and Initiatic Ceremonies in Ancient Egypt), published by Robert Laffont, Paris, 1977. I found this book especially compatible with my own anthropological point of view since it placed initiation doctrine in the context of the doctrines or "rites of passage" observed in many cultures.

> Broadly speaking, initiatory rites of passage include the following elements or themes: the separation from this world, the entry into the other world, the meeting of challenges along the way, the help received from a guide, the entry into the inner sanctum, the illumination, the assimilation of this mystical experience, and finally, the return to this world. Guilmot then recognizes this same general pattern in the description of a visit to Abydos during the 8th century BC by an Egyptian priest named Horsie'sis. In addition, Guilmot describes some representations of the tomb of Osiris buried under a mound on which trees have been planted. Taking this information together with the description of an initiatory process previously mentioned, he proposed that the Osirion was in fact an underground initiatory temple with trees planted over it. The description of the initiation of Horsei'sis, as

it appears on a Leyden papyrus translated into French
by Guilmot, goes as follows...

The translation that my friend sent me is a long and poetic
one. It begins with the initiate being welcomed with a garland of
flowers, a divine favor from Osiris, meaning that he has in effect
been accepted as an initiate. The ceremony continues with the
entry into the domain of Abydos, guided by the god Anubis who
leads him across the frightening world of the dead. Horsei'sis
descends into the earth *("Geb is opening to receive you!")* and moves
through the underground corridor leading to the sanctuary of
Osiris *("You come to the subterranean hall underneath the sacred trees.*
Near the God Osiris, the God who sleeps in his sepulchre").

Horsei'sis then goes through the judgment of the gods and
is declared "True-of-Voice" and "Justified" – after which he takes
a ritual bath in the waters surrounding the central platform, and
he is reborn. Now he crosses to the holy island on which lies
the sepulchre of Osiris, and here receives enlightenment *("For*
you will open the doors of the horizon of the Netherworld, the doors of
Eternity"). That night he sleeps next to the holy waters *("You sleep*
in the spot reserved for mysteries"). The final stage of the initiation
is the Return to the World, which is left unsaid, except for the
single word *"Then..."**

My friend Antoine Seronde ended his letter with an equally
hopeful statement: "Here is the first really plausible explanation
of ancient Egyptian initiation I had seen...and at the Osirion, no
less. Little did I suspect that this book would become the instru-
ment of my own paradoxical initiation – into the labyrinthine
halls of Egyptology and the deep mysteries of reincarnation."

Bless your heart, Antoine, was all I could say on finishing
his letter.

---

*parenthetic quotations from Max Guilmot and Robert Laffont, *Les Inities*
et les Rites Initiatiques en Egypt Ancienne, Paris, 1977. Excerpts translated into
English by HZ.

the Well of Roarings

On that first visit to the Osirion long ago, as I was passing by the northern pillars of the island I was surprised by a strange and rather eerie sound that was difficult to locate. It sounded something like the gurgling noise that comes out of a *narjila*, a device for smoking tobacco widely known in the countries of the Middle East. It is often called a hubbly-bubbly. Trying to locate the source of that peculiar bubbling noise, I thought it came from inside one of the cells on the northern wall.

This was the famous Well of Roarings, described by the historian Strabo who had given a full description of the Osirion's appearance in his time and said that the water fed into the Osirion by way of a channel from the Nif-Wer canal. As I suggested earlier, that proved not to be the case. Additionally, we may now know the water's source: the newly discovered aquifer beneath the entire area of the Sety Temple, found when geologist Dr. Essawi used ground-penetrating radar during his work with James Westerman in 1999. It is possible that this same pure aquifer is the true source of the water inside the Well of Roarings. It is also possible that, before now, the only people who knew about the existence of the aquifer were the ancient Egyptians.

Omm Sety told me many stories about the water of the Osirion and its curative effects. One of them had to do with an appendicitis attack.

"It was early in 1958," she said. "I had a very bad attack of appendicitis and I went to the doctor, and of course he wanted to send me to the hospital and have the operation. And I couldn't go because I had a very particular cat at that time who was old, and she thought the end of the world would come if I wasn't unto her beck and call. I thought, if I go to work I shall forget about it. So I went to work, but it got very bad and I couldn't do anything but just lie down in the cult chapel of Isis. And I went to sleep.

"I dreamed a very beautiful woman's voice said to me, 'What is the matter?' And I said, 'I have this pain in my side.' And the voice told me to go and drink the water in the well. I said, 'I can't, because the workmen now are using this well to wash in when they finish their work – they wash in the well before they go home, and so it has become dirty.' And the voice said, 'What is holy cannot be polluted. Drink and do not fear.'

"And then I woke up. What woke me was some talk and rattling at the gate, and it appeared that a high official from Baliana had come with some officers and they wanted to see the Orision. I didn't want them to see me lying on the floor, so I got up. They said, 'Omm Sety, take us to this *Hammam*' – the Osirion. And I said, 'Well, I will if I can.'

"I managed, struggling, to get down there, and I went over to the well and drank the water, and it was very cold. I could feel it go down my throat, right down until it reached the spot of the pain. And then I felt the pain sliding down from this place in the lower side, right down to the thighs and from the thighs to the knee and from the knee to the lower leg, from the leg to the floor, until it disappeared – as though it disappeared into the stone. And I was completely cured. I felt nothing at all and I didn't have this pain again."

Osirion. Through this doorway is the Well of Roarings in whose curative power Omm Sety had deep faith. Note the cornerstone hewn from a single piece of granite. This was a typical feature of Old Kingdom architecture, not of the New Kingdom style of Sety's time. It is one of the many reasons Omm Sety and I could never accept that the Osirion was built by Sety to be his cenotaph (symbolic tomb).
(Hanny el Zeini)

I have not been able to check the authenticity of all of Omm Sety's stories, but I can testify to the truth of an experience that both my wife and I both witnessed. We were passing one holiday with Omm Sety in Abydos. She was very ill, having caught a bad flu; she was feverish, coughing and sneezing incessantly. I thought it would become necessary to take her back home with us to rest, but for the time being I promised to send her some medicines as soon as we arrived back at our compound in Nag-Hamadi. That day in Abydos we were staying in the rest house of the inspectors. On our way to our car, as we were departing, Omm Sety suddenly left us and walked toward the Osirion. We wondered what she was up to. To our consternation, she went down the stairs leading to the Great Hall and plunged into the water with all her clothes on. We watched, really quite furious at her reckless behavior. My wife declared her crazy. "She will not live to see another day."

I had to act. I went down the stairs, pulled her out and expressed my anger in very clear terms. We drove her quickly to her house, where Gowhara helped her to change out of her wet clothes and almost forcibly put her to bed. The next day, having returned to Nag-Hamadi, I rang up the telephone office in the village, close to her house. "How is Omm Sety?" I asked. The operator said she was well and he would go to fetch her. After a short while I heard her voice loud and clear: "I'm perfectly OK. The Osirion water did it. You needn't bother about medicines!"

Another incident, which I personally confirmed, was the case of the epileptic child in the village of Nazlet el Simman, beside the Giza Pyramids. Omm Sety had once told me that she had cured the little boy, sick with epilepsy since he was six years old, by washing his head with some water that she had brought back from her first brief visit to Abydos. I saw the same boy 12 years later. He was a handsome, healthy young man who had never suffered another seizure since the day Omm Sety anointed him with water from the well at the Osirion.

I am sorry to say that the Well of Roarings could only help Omm Sety so much. Her hard life in the sun-baked village and her disregard for her diet – and probably the years of depletion of her vital energy from her psychic interactions with Sety – had taken an awful toll on her physical body. I knew that at some point Omm Sety, despite her enormous willpower and enthusiasm for life, would have to deal with her own mortality – and I always prayed that she would have an easy time of it.

FOURTEEN

The English Fellaha*

"I replied that I hated to sleep under a roof, and I liked to see the stars."
                                    OS

I always thought that her self-deprecating humor was one reason for Omm Sety's resilience in the face of hardship. She wrote on the cover of one of her diaries – which were ordinary school notebooks – *Name:* Omm Sety. *Class:* Low. *School:* Life.

On the eve of September 28, 1970, the television news was carrying live coverage of the Cairo summit of Arab nation leaders. My wife and I watched as the last departing dignitary waved his hand to President Nasser, who returned the wave, but without his usual vigor. We could see that he was pale and perspiring, clearly exhausted from yet another ugly inter-Arab squabble session. We saw the President's legs start to give out under him and several presidential guards rush forward to help him – and then the television screen cut to black for a few seconds before resuming with repeat footage from the day before. It happened so fast we could hardly believe what we had just seen.

The truth of the situation was soon revealed to an uneasy public when a recitation of verses from the Koran replaced all of Egypt's television and radio programs. Gamal Abdel Nasser,

---

*Egyptian peasant woman

the President of the Republic, was dead at age 52, after ruling Egypt for 18 eventful years. He had been an absolute monarch, beloved by Egypt's poorer classes, the peasants and laborers. But in his zeal to reframe the nation's economic and social structures through redistribution of land and other extreme measures, he had deliberately ignored the cultural pillars of Egyptian society – the academicians, thinkers, writers and creative artists. Between Nasser and the intelligentsia the gap couldn't have been wider, but for the average Egyptian citizen the President represented hope and a renewed national pride. The night of the announcement, in towns and villages up and down the Nile, people took to the streets in an outpouring of grief.

A few days later I was notified by the worried chief ghaffir at Abydos that Omm Sety had dressed herself in black and locked herself inside her house. She heard the news and had simply fallen apart, unable to stop crying. She refused to speak with anybody or hear a word of consolation. She had adored Nasser; he was her hero, the new Pharaoh of Egypt.

It was the sorrow of her fellow villagers that brought Omm Sety out of her isolation. I was told that the whole village of Abydos had turned to her as if she were the only refuge in their deep sense of loss. There weren't enough words with which she could alleviate their sorrow, so she did the only thing she knew she could believe in: She chose a day of prayer and offerings for each of the gods represented in the temple, fervently praying to Ra, the principal lord of the Universe, then to Osiris, Isis, Horus, and the rest of the Egyptian pantheon. Her sadness was so genuine and so protracted that in my subsequent visits I avoided discussing with her the damage Nasser had done with his political blunders, which in my opinion tarnished all the positive achievements he made during the first half of his rule.

Omm Sety was 66 now and technically retired. Six years earlier, her previous contract had expired, and once again she had faced the loss of her job. As before, she had invoked the aid of her "higher authorities" – and with the gods on her side, and with high praise and recommendations from all the inspectors

Omm Sety in mourning for Nasser. When President Nasser died in September 1970, Omm Sety's grief was very deep. She believed him to have been the reincarnation of an ancient pharaoh. She wore black and stayed in mourning for seventy days, probably an ancient Egyptian custom. I was told she went to the temple every day and then to the Osirion, carrying her book of hymns. Here at the Osirion I caught her unaware of my presence one evening in mid-November 1970. (Hanny el Zeini)

with whom she had worked, she was granted one final five-year extension. At 65 she had reached the compulsory retirement age for government employees.

But she was anything but retired. She was still a vital woman, blessed with a dynamic energy that few of us have at any age. She worked every day at her table in the Hall of the Sacred Barques. This was her true home, this temple, and there was still work to be done, whether or not she was paid for it.

But now that she was unsalaried she had to find ways to supplement her meager pension. From the start of our friendship I was worried, as was my wife, about how she managed to make ends meet. She flatly refused to take any money from me for all those times she had generously offered to be my guide in the temple. I did find a way to help, however. When VIPs from Western Europe would come to Nag-Hamadi on business with the Sugar Company and wished to explore a bit, I would send them to Abydos. If they hadn't known much about Egyptian antiquities before, they returned from Omm Sety's guided tours as newly-minted enthusiasts. I insisted on paying her a fee for her services to my company's clients, and finally she accepted. Her artistic gifts provided her with a little extra income as well. She had always done very beautiful needlework and paintings depicting the ancient gods and pharaohs, and she continued to do so, selling her pieces or giving them away to friends who had admired them.

People came from all over the world to see her and take one of her famous tours of the temple. But mostly, people came to be in the presence of a person who was clearly from another time and who could bring the past to vivid life for them. She enjoyed most of her visitors, though she had met one too many Hatshepsuts and Nefertitis over the years. I recall her complaints to me that she was plagued by "those absurd reincarnations." She never put herself in the same category since her own memories were of a girl of the most humble origins, and not from the top of the pecking order.

Floating hotels like the Hilton's *Isis* and *Osiris* stopped regularly now at the port and quay of Abydos. As a result of this newly flourishing tourism, The Buried Hamlet was beginning to come awake from its long slumber. Before that, tourists would look around at the impoverished village in dismay and pity, but I believe they were not truly seeing. Every house had a small kitchen garden, fractions of a hectare in which all their needs for vegetables and seasonal fruits were met. The people had bread called *shamsi* that was fermented by the heat of the sun, and there was always protein, sweet-meats and fat available from chickens and geese. This was the fare of the fellaheen as it had been for thousands of years. The remains of these kinds of foods have been found in archaic tombs, nourishment for the *kas* of the deceased. It is not likely that the pioneering archaeologists who worked in the Egyptian countryside, like Petrie, Selim Hassan and Junker, felt undernourished on this traditional diet. Which is not to say that Omm Sety availed herself of the bounty around her.

My wife, Gowhara, often invited her to pass the day with us, as much for Omm Sety's delightful company as to make sure she occasionally had nutritious meals. Omm Sety was extremely negligent about her health. We regularly sent her, either by way of my driver or mutual friends who were on their way to visit Abydos, a mixture of fresh vegetables for her to cook, and this arrangement pleased her. The stories of her absent-mindedness around food were legend in the village – like the time she had put some potatoes on to boil early in the morning, shortly before she was called for by a group of British tourists. She forgot to turn off the butane cooker under the pan and when she returned late in the afternoon she found that the potatoes had been rendered into a dark, glutinous mass. Her solution was to add some carrots, tomato and a pinch of pepper and put the whole mixture on the boil again. The concoction stayed in the pan, uneaten, for two weeks, and then I received a phone call from the post office in the village reporting that Omm Sety was convulsing and had a high fever. I immediately sent our company's physician. He treated her for severe food poisoning and told me that she could have died. She had come home that afternoon famished, and had reheated the first thing at hand, which was the weeks-old toxic potato stew. At least she hadn't given it to her animals.

Omm Sety's ground and marine mafia

Most of Omm Sety's tourist clients were curious to see where and how she was living, and Omm Sety was happy to oblige. The little garden through which they had to pass to reach her mud-brick house was always full of all sorts of pets – mostly cats, usually between ten and fifteen of them. The other members of her fauna, which she called her "mafia," were rabbits, guinea pigs and geese, and also some occasional visitors such as cobras, dogs and a few foxes – and for some time, the donkey named Alice. The master of ceremonies was her giant blue-eyed gander Sneferu, who had an aristocratic air about him.

The only real nuisances were the geese, but Sneferu knew how to keep order in the improbable circus.

To anyone observing her morning ritual of the feeding of the animals, it was more like watching a fractious kindergarten class. The first lesson of the day was always how to respect law and order. Instead of letting this uncouth gang of undisciplined, noisy beasts start their morning chaos, Omm Sety gave them their daily lesson in how to keep their mouths and bills shut and wait patiently until she was done with her cooking. The dogs sat on their haunches and listened to every word she was saying in English, but the cats she would address in Arabic, for whatever reason.

One of Omm Sety's closest friends, watching all this, asked her if she had ever read the Bible. "Not much," she replied, "I went to church where the chanting was beautiful and joined in singing some hymns, but that was all. Why do you ask?"

"Because, my dear Omm Sety, I was anxious to know if you had read the Book of Job."

"I was more keen on reading the Book of the Dead," she answered. And then her friend quoted from memory:

Ask the very beasts, and they will teach you;
ask the wild birds — they will tell you;
crawling creatures will instruct you;
fish in the sea will inform you;
for which of them all knows not that this is the Eternal way;
in whose control lies every living soul;
and the whole life of Man.

"Things must have run this way since the beginning of creation," Omm Sety said, "man and animal living closely together; no barriers to separate them. The barriers were erected later, much later."

Omm Sety always cooked for her animals before eating her own breakfast, but sometimes, as we know, she would get too involved in other things and forget that the stove and the animals' meals needed tending. If it turned out that she had ruined yet another pot of food for them, they made other plans for themselves, usually at one of the two village butcher shops where they might have better luck. Omm Sety had told me more than once that she was a "goddamn dangerous cook." If her mafia rejected a burnt meal she would carry the whole awful thing out to the ducks and geese that had gathered at the main irrigation canal not far from her home. At the sound of Omm Sety's voice, every living thing swimming in the canal would join in an infernal anthem of welcome. And when the last bit of that "thing" she had managed to make a mess of was gone, she would salute her "marines" and say, "Bless your stainless steel tummies."

Omm Sety's cooking produced sometimes unrecognizable results, even for her cats and the rest of her rag-tag menagerie. Instead of throwing away the rejected meals, she would offer the questionable delights to this flock of ducks and geese near her house. "They can eat anything," she said jauntily. "Real strong guys, my marines."
(Hanny el Zeini)

Omm Sety's relationship with her animals went very deep and had a very poignant reciprocal nature. I was witness to some of this and was told of it by others. At times when she was ill all the cats would jump onto her bed and stay there. Even a few strays jumped on, licked her face and then left. Others with better manners would warm her feet and her joints whenever she had rheumatic pain. Most of them would ignore their need for food and spend days refusing to leave Omm Sety's side, except to answer the call of nature. No less obliging were the dogs, who stayed close, but more astonishing was the similar behavior of the rabbits and guinea pigs – they all seemed capable of tender affection. Her neighbors didn't know what to think about such devotion.

Even Sety commented about it – and in so doing he revealed something of himself:

August 7, 1973
H.M. came last night at about midnight. I was not yet asleep, and the "club"* was still alight. He was in a good and cheerful mood, and we sat under the shelter in the garden. Just then, Ahmed's dog Khalaur started howling, and I shouted to him to shut up. Sety said, "Leave him to sing as he pleases. He feels that I am here and he is afraid." I asked if he liked dogs. He replied, "Yes, they are good animals, and useful, not like your spoiled cats." And did he have dogs himself, I asked, to which he said, "I have five lion dogs,** but they stay outside in the stables. When you come to me, you can feed them with honey cakes and make them lazy and stupid, and I am sure you will also spoil all my good horses too!"

"But perhaps," I said, "I shall be too busy spoiling their master to trouble myself about them." That pleased him and he hugged me very tightly. "We will spoil each other!"

Just then, my new little white rabbit ran by, and seeing H.M. sat up, as if frozen by fear, and the light made her pink eyes

---
*pressure lamp; pronounced "kloob" in Arabic
**hunting dogs

shine red like two rubies. H.M. cried, "Ah, the beautiful little rabbit (wen). She has reminded me of the time when I was hunting lions in the land of Ta-sti (Nubia). My dogs went shouting into some long grass and bushes in the valley, and a lion came forth. I raised my bow to shoot, but could not. He was so beautiful. He was white like moonlight, and the hair on his head was the colour of electrum; his two eyes shone red as fire, like those of your rabbit. I lowered my bow and called off my dogs, and the lion and I gazed at each other for a while, as though we were two men of equal rank. Then we each went our ways."

One night when Sety came to her he found her upset and crying because two of her favorite cats had disappeared. His Majesty comforted her in his bruskly affectionate way:

October 4, 1972
"What a stupid girl you are! You know you will have all your cats again; they will be waiting for you and I swear to you that you shall keep them all in our dwelling. Now stop weeping. Your tears are like arrows piercing my heart."

I asked why he had not come to me for more than a month and he replied, "I dared not come. You were too weak.* I dared not take from you the sakhm that I need. If I did, it would kill you. You must take better care of yourself, Bentreshy!"

Omm Sety had always had a rather a precarious coexistence with her neighbors. She was as unlikely a villager as had ever lived among them. Being well versed in ancient Egyptian practical magic, she had quickly rid the children's play area of snakes and scorpions, and with her knowledge of native medicinal plants (sometimes using water from the Osirion's Well of

---

*Omm Sety had been sick for several weeks, suffering from the excessive heat.

Roarings) she was able to effect a number of dramatic healings
– all of which earned her the love of the women and a certain
wary admiration, if not outright fear, among the men. If the
crazy khawagaya wished to keep a shrine to the old gods in her
house and make offerings in the temple ruins, that was her own
business. It was best not to challenge someone who talked to
cobras. And so, by the strange virtues she brought with her she
unwittingly ensured her own safety.

About Omm Sety and magic, there were only two times
that I suspected that she might have used it rashly. One involved
her beloved watchgoose Sneferu who one day just disappeared.
Omm Sety knew that a certain man had taken her pet and she
knew that he had most likely served Sneferu for dinner. She was
outraged and devastated. Shortly afterwards, the man contracted
rabies and died. Another man made the mistake of forbidding
Omm Sety to enter the temple, and he too died suddenly soon
after. Had she used the power of ancient spells on the two men?
She certainly knew the words to say. She never mentioned the
deaths to me – I had to hear it from others – and I simply hated
to ask her about them. I rather think that she believed she had
been the agent of their demise. I also think that the unfortunate
men's kesma was their own, and had little or nothing to do with
the anger of the village khawagaya.

Abydos may have seemed remote to the average tourist,
but for the community of Egyptologists it was an important
destination because of the intriguing work that was ongoing in
the Archaic Cemetery and at the Sety Temple and the nearby,
smaller, Ramesses Temple. Omm Sety often entertained visiting friends for tea, many of them Egyptologists she had become
close to over the years – Dr. Labib Habashi, dean of Egyptian
archaeology; Dr. Kent Weeks, director of the Theban Mapping
Project, and his wife Susan; Dr. David Silverman; Dr. Lanny Bell;
Dr. William Murnane, (before his recent death, director with Dr.
Bell of the University of Chicago's Epigraphic Survey at Chicago House in Luxor); Dr. Ray Johnson, now Field Director at

Chicago House, and others. Omm Sety and I took several trips to Dendera, Aswan and Luxor, enjoying some happy occasions in Luxor with our Chicago House friends. Often, the occasion was Omm Sety's birthday, during which she held forth with her entertaining wit and wonderful intellect. In that setting she was among equals and well appreciated.

Omm Sety and Dr. David Silverman, prominent American Egyptologist.
(Hanny el Zeini)

But most of all, I think, she enjoyed her times with my family at Nag-Hamadi. Gowhara always cooked special treats for her and our daughter Kotkot had a special and very loving relationship with her. Some of our most pleasant conversations took place on the verandah of our home, where we would all sit after the evening meal and watch the sunset colors on the distant cliffs, listening to the music of Mozart or Liszt or Beethoven. Omm Sety's favorite was Beethoven's Pastoral Symphony with its evocations of nature in all its varied moods. Very much like Omm Sety herself.

changes

In the spring of 1972 I got another phone call from the post office agent in Abydos, one of Omm Sety's few male friends in the village. In a trembling voice he told me that she was in very bad shape, suffering from terrible chest pain and having difficulty breathing. He begged me to come and see her. I was at that moment dealing with some urgent problems in the factories and couldn't drop everything, but I sent our company's chief of medical services, the physician who had seen to her before. He brought along a nurse and an assortment of medicines, and quickly determined that she had had a mild heart attack and needed to be hospitalized. Over her strenuous objections and her refusal to leave her animals, the doctor and the nurse carried her to their car and drove her to the government hospital.

When the doctor returned to the company compound, this normally even-tempered man was quite upset. "Just imagine, sir," he exclaimed. "Just imagine, this impossible woman is now living in a *zeriba*! She is going to kill herself!"

That was the first I knew of her new living arrangement. Under different conditions I would have smiled, but this was really too much. Without telling anyone, she had, out of the blue, sold her house of 16 years and built for herself an open shed in a field. Zeribas are made of dry maize stalks covered with mud and bundled together to form a roofless room – a place for domestic animals to take shelter in at night. I immediately called our mutual friend Labib Habashi to report the latest developments. It was summer now, but the nights would soon be getting cold. What could she have been thinking? It takes the poorest of the poor, the most deplorably deprived, to choose to live in a zeriba. I could not understand what was going on inside her unfathomable brain.

Her hospital stay was brief and her recovery satisfactory, though she needed to begin taking better care of herself. She was perfectly happy to be back in her zeriba with her animals, she insisted. About the delicate question of a toilet and where to take a decent bath, some kind neighbors were sensitive enough to search for her each morning and ask her to come use their bathrooms. In the Egyptian countryside such human relations become so strong, so natural and so binding that a woman in Omm Sety's situation becomes a personal concern to her nearest neighbors. In spite of that, the rest of us – Omm Sety's non-village friends – were appalled.

It happened that one of her neighbors had a small piece of land close to his house. Labib immediately made an agreement with Ahmed Mahmoud to build her a comfortable wattle-and-daub bed-sitting room and kitchenette. It would measure 3½ by 5 meters, with a staircase leading to an open terrace on the roof, where she could sleep during the warm nights of summer. It would return to his possession upon Omm Sety's death. She would name it *Heartsease-in-Abydos*.

unfinished business

In her life Omm Sety was always forthright and honest. She would expect no less from me in writing this book. All of us who knew and loved her were aware of her shortcomings – she could be stunningly impulsive and childlike, side-by-side with a great maturity of mind and intuition. Sometimes I even wondered if certain parts of her emotional development still belonged to the young Egyptian girl, Bentreshyt.

One of the things I had never been able to understand, and that concerned me, was her failed relationship with her son Sety Abdel Meguid. She had given him away to his father as a small child and had seen him only intermittently for a number of years after that, but she never spoke of him the way a mother speaks of a child she loves. I knew he lived in Kuwait, but beyond that I knew almost nothing about him, and I had long wondered why he made so little effort to maintain a connection with his mother. In fact, I had written him off as a poor excuse for a son.

I had considered not telling the story that follows, because I didn't want the world to think the less of a brave and unique soul. But I know she would say, "Tell it, warts and all."

Before the new house could be built, as fate would have it, Omm Sety received a surprise visit from her son Sety, accompanied by his wife – the first time mother and son had seen each other in 20 years. I can only imagine the poor man's shock to see his mother coming out of a zeriba to greet him.

Later that day, the telephone rang at my home in Nag-Hamadi and I heard an unfamiliar voice saying, "Good evening, Dr. Zeini. I am Sety talking to you from Abydos. I want very much to see you privately. Can I come to meet you tomorrow?"

I told him he could come now and I would send a car to bring him to my place. He thanked me, but he wished to stay with his mother for at least one night. "One of her neighbors has already sworn on the Holy Koran that my wife and I will pass the night in his house," he said. He would come in the morning, and he would come alone.

When Sety appeared at my door the next day I encountered a handsome, tall young man with a well-trimmed moustache. It was hard to believe this man was Omm Sety's son. Except for his mouth and chin, he had inherited nothing from his mother, and was probably a younger version of his father. His manner was respectful and refined, but almost at once he said to me, "I have seen my mother and I cannot allow her to stay in such a place." I told him how much his mother was admired, and that she had many friends who were looking out for her – even at that very moment raising money to build a comfortable home for her. I wanted our meeting to be convivial, as did he, I'm sure. "Tell me something about your life," I offered. "We can speak of your mother afterwards."

He described scenes from his early childhood. He remembered vividly the tombs of the Old Kingdom nobility in which he and his mother used to sleep. And he even remembered his ramblings in the Egyptian Museum, and the problems that had caused with the man in charge. It seemed astonishing that a baby who was barely walking would remember in such detail. Sety confirmed that an amiable relationship had existed between his father and mother after the divorce. He said that until he was 18 he had made a point of seeing his mother at least every few months, and then he left Egypt for Kuwait because he thought he would have a better future there. To his deep dismay Omm Sety had accused him of going to Kuwait to avoid recruitment in the army. "That was not true, sir," he said with great intensity. "I was exempted from military service at the time." He was quiet for a while, then made a casual remark that I felt was quite meaningful: "Only deep wounds have strong memories. Happy moments seem to have a very short life." Sety shook his head in despair. "I did not come all the way to this goddamned hole for this. I am counting on your help, sir. For the past ten years I have been writing her. I have begged her to come and live with me and enjoy being among her grandchildren. But everything I wrote has been ignored."

I began to feel pity for the young man. I had made quite another picture of him in my mind. I had thought him a negligent, indifferent and unaffectionate son. Omm Sety had never mentioned the letters, except for once a few years back, when I had visited her unannounced and found her reading one of them. I said, "Good news, Omm Sety, I hope?" And she replied, "Oh, that...well, it is a letter from Sety, my son. He wants me to play the baby sitter for his five kids. I can't do that. I was a complete failure as a mother with only one boy, what do you think I would be with five grandchildren? You just tell me."

I didn't mention this to my guest. I was thinking about what he had said about military service and why Omm Sety would accuse her son like that. But I knew the answer. After Nasser died in 1970, she had mourned for months and only stopped wearing black when I told her we were preparing for another round of war with Israel over the Sinai. A righteous war, if you asked any Egyptian, including Omm Sety. She told me that she had always wanted her son to become an officer in the army, and that she was devastated when he left Egypt for Kuwait, by unhappy coincidence at the age of recruitment. In the back of her mind she had this deep-rooted belief that he should become a military man like her own Pharaoh Sety. Instead, according to her thinking, he had chosen the dishonorable way out. I knew I had found the deep wound that had never healed and was never forgiven or forgotten – by either of them.

Sety looked at me with real anguish. "How can I possibly leave her to live like this? She is my mother. She must come with me to Kuwait." His voice was shaking.

"Consider me as your older brother," I replied, "and take my advice. Don't pressure her. Right or wrong, this village has been her whole life. Even the Egyptian Antiquities Organization's highest authorities say it frankly, that the Sety Temple is her private property. It was roofed on her insistence and she was indeed the guardian angel of this monument. She was the prime mover behind all the repairs, restorations and upkeep of the temple. Abydos is a tourist attraction, thanks to her. So, my friend, we have to approach your proposition with a lot of tact and, if possible, good humor."

We agreed that we would arrange a family meeting the next day. Meanwhile, Sety intended to have a serious talk with his mother in Abydos and help her to see reason. Hearing that, I knew he had lost the battle even before it started.

The three visitors came to my home early next morning. Our conversation was strained from the start. My elder daughter Zeinab, whom we call Kotkot, was home on holiday from university in Cairo. She and Omm Sety had always been especially close, so I held out hope that this would be a gentle and reasonable encounter. Kotkot began by warmly declaring her love for Omm Sety and urging her to think of her health and security and to at least consider her son's proposition. Then Gowhara took her turn, then Sety, and then me. To no avail.

"I don't know why we are all here," Omm Sety said rather petulantly, after we had each spoken our piece. "I am quite content just as I am and I have no plans to be otherwise." After that, the affectionate words quickly devolved into a stalemate of mutual misunderstanding. I couldn't recall many times in my life that were more distressing.

The phone rang, and it was Labib Habashi calling from Chicago House at Luxor, where he had been collecting donations for Omm Sety's new house. I told him the dilemma we were in at the moment and he said, "Why are you wasting your time, my friend? You know damn well she won't budge. She is like a fish in a pond – she will never be able to live outside Abydos. Just say that to the son. Let them separate with no hard feelings." I prayed to God things could be that easy. As we talked, I could hear Sety starting all over again with the same arguments and frustrated concern, and Kotkot joining in with more of her furious enthusiasm.

I returned to the fray and added my (I hoped) calmer voice: "My dear Omm Sety, you know that sooner or later I will be going away. I don't know of anybody who will take care of you. You take better care of your cats and dogs than you do of yourself." I thought I saw a slight smile move across that stubborn face. "I honestly believe you should accept your son's wise and generous suggestion," I said. And then Kotkot jumped in with, "We are five against one and we cannot all be wrong and you the only one who is right. What do you say now?" Omm Sety drew into herself and refused to reply. Hoping to break the tension, my wife suggested that we have lunch in the garden. There, Sety pleaded, almost prayed on his knees, for his mother to relent. After an hour of this misery, Sety asked to walk with me in the garden. He put a hand on my shoulder. "As my elder brother I ask you, what do I do now? Neither my wife nor I were prepared for what we found yesterday. I feel responsible for the abject misery in which my mother lives."

"It is not you," I said. "You must understand how she is. Sometimes when I have come to see her in Abydos and I would be told that she was inside the temple performing some kind of ceremony, even I at times have felt unwilling to intrude or trespass into the territory she has claimed so convincingly. I truly believe that we have no choice, you and I. We must accept her decision in good grace and with no hard feelings."

"But how can I leave my mother in a roofless shed?"

I said again that we were all concerned with her safety and health, and that within three months Omm Sety would have a comfortable, small house. The governor of Sohag Province had even given instructions that the work be given priority. "She is in good hands," I promised.

"But where is my part in all this? Where do I come in?" Sety said, near tears.

"She loves beautiful things around her, as strange as that may seem to you. You can send her money for new furniture. That will make her happy."

When we returned to the table I put my question to my stubborn old friend: "Well, Omm Sety, what have you decided? We will abide by your choice."

"Dr. Hany – and you, Sety – you know well that I have always wanted to come to Egypt, live in Abydos, work in Abydos, die and be buried in Abydos. At no point in my life have I ever regretted my decision. And that is how it shall be, *Inshallah*." She smiled, looking at each of us in turn, and I saw the glint of victory in her eyes.

So, that was that. I took a few photographs to memorialize this sad, disheartening day. A family that could never be a family – I felt for them all. The Abdel Meguids would be leaving for Kuwait the next day. In the morning Sety rang me up from Abydos to bid me farewell and thank my family for their support. He said that he had left his mother a sizeable sum of money in a savings account in the post office. I wished him well.

Later, I heard through Labib Habashi, who had seen Omm Sety shortly after Sety's departure, that the final words between mother and son had been bitter ones. They had had a last showdown in which Sety accused her of having neglected him as a child and having "thrown him to the dogs," and Omm Sety defended herself saying she could not have done better under the circumstances. In the end, they shook hands and exchanged a cool embrace.

As Shakespeare said in *Hamlet*, "and the rest is silence."

Omm Sety and her son Sety in 1972, together for the first time in 20 years. This picture was taken during the "family meeting" that we arranged to try to convince Omm Sety to go to Kuwait to live with her son's family, where she would get the care she badly needed. But Omm Sety refused to leave her beloved Sety Temple. (Sety's wife in black; my wife, Gowhara, seated at left; our daughter, Kotkot, at right) The meeting took place inside the garden of our residence at the Sugar Company in Nag-Hamadi. (Hanny el Zeini)

They never met again. I believe that he continued to send her letters and that she never answered them.

A few months later she had her new house and all of her friends were relieved. But Omm Sety had not changed in certain fundamental ways. She was still a *fellaha*, still rooted in the earth and not ever to be "the lady of the house." I saw this clearly when I came across a diary entry from shortly after she had moved into her new home:

November 13, 1972
I am very lucky these days! H.M. came again last night, and in a very good mood. It was cold, so he came in under the lahaf and pulled it up over our heads. "Truly, Bentreshy," he said, "you should sleep in the house now." I replied that I hated to sleep under a roof, and I liked to see the stars. He said, "Sometimes I think that you are a wild animal and not a human girl at all!"

politics and the road to Abydos

In many ways Omm Sety would always be an outsider in her adopted village. The villagers were fortunate that she brought some of her very British sense of right and wrong with her. To her mind it was decidedly *wrong* that the village had no electricity, no school and no clean drinking water. Shortly after her retirement she took it upon herself to attend all the meetings of the local council to see what she could do to improve things. The council was a branch of the Arab Socialists Union, the only political structure that existed at that time. Though she was not officially a member of the Union, she had the right to attend whenever she wanted, but each time there was a terrible row and she ended up insulting everybody. The members laughed at her bad Arabic and apparently did not take her very seriously. Omm Sety knew that the key to any progress lay in getting a paved road into Abydos from the main Cairo-to-Aswan road.

After a number of squabbles and no improvement in the political will among her fellows, she decided to go directly to the governor of the state of Sohag. The new governor was an energetic army general who decided to take Omm Sety's complaint seriously. Very few people in the village knew about her flurry of visits to the head administration office of Sohag. They only knew – when a road crew suddenly showed up to begin asphalting ten kilometers of dirt road – that something miraculous had happened.

Shortly after the road was completed I paid a visit to General Wassel, the governor, on other business. Right away he smiled and said, "Your friend Omm Sety is an incredible woman. I wish I could find someone like her in every village who fights to improve the situation in this appalling poverty."

Over time, the new road made life better for everyone in Abydos. It facilitated travel to and from the village, and it brought more tourists from Luxor, which meant money to build a school and bring electricity and water to every house.

I would like to report that Omm Sety lived happily ever after with the village council, but then you would be reading a fairytale. Omm Sety continued to find ways to help her fellows when they were in need, and she continued to insult people in power when she thought them fools and idiots. I could never convince her of the wisdom of restraint.

Omm Sety on her 70th birthday, January 1974. She was full of energy, having recovered from a mild heart attack two years earlier. His Majesty was a frequent visitor at this time, which meant that her health was good, because Sety would never visit her when she was ill or weak, since the process of his materialization drew upon her vital energy, her sekhem. She often joked that Sety still saw her as the young girl he had loved in the past and not as the aging, weathered woman she was now.
(Hanny el Zeini)

FIFTEEN

Ancient Evenings

"O Bentreshy, how you would have loved it then!" Sety

Before her retirement, Omm Sety had always kept detailed work diaries relating to her job with the Antiquities Department, but she had not kept a personal diary. Now that her life did not "belong" to the Department she felt free to begin keeping a private diary. I was glad of this because I had always hoped she might leave a written record of her relationship with Sety and their discussions of the ancient world.

Since Omm Sety and I were by now the closest of friends and had been through so much together, she sometimes invited me to read her diary entries and make notes about things that I did not understand from her conversations with His Majesty. She would lend them to me for two or three days at a time. She was quite happy to include my questions in their further discussions. Apparently Sety was agreeable to having a third party in their exchanges as well. It made for some interesting historical forums. In her career with the Department, Omm Sety had always been a stickler for accuracy and intellectual honesty; so too with her diaries, as she attempted to apply a rudimentary "scientific method" to an otherwise very unscientific situation. In an odd way, all three of us at different times became fact-checkers for each other concerning details of Egyptian history. Sety would often revisit a topic to correct a previous statement after he had consulted an authoritative "source" in Amenti, or investigated a certain place for himself (as he did with his visit to the Treasury in the temple).

After her heart attack in 1972 her health never returned to its earlier vigor. Whether this was from the many years of offering her sekhem to Sety and depleting her vital energy, I am not in a position to say. She had had illnesses before, but this was the first time in her life that she had felt physically vulnerable. She was concerned about what would become of her possessions, mostly her books and papers, if something should happen to her, and she started sending her completed diaries to me at the end of each year for safe-keeping. Now that she is gone and I have been reviewing the record of those years, I see how often I made notes in the margins, asking her to inquire further of His Majesty.

Next to the entry for August 29, 1972, in which Sety spoke about the Great Pyramid, I found this notation in my writing: "What about the Sphinx? Is it truly the work of Khafra?" My own opinion, contrary to accepted thought, is that the head of the Sphinx does not represent the 4th Dynasty pharaoh and must be far older. Two weeks later, Omm Sety brought the question to Sety:

> *"Please tell me about the image of Hor-em-akhet* that lies near Akhet-Khufu."** He replied, "In our time it was said that the great image was carved in the likeness of Our Lord Horus, to commemorate his victory over Set." I told him about Prof. Selim Hassan's theory that it was made by and in the image of Khafra, and explained the reason for this theory. He thought that over for a while and said, "That also may be true. It could have been made by Kha-fi-Ra*** as a memorial to Our Lord Horus. It had always been connected with Horus in the minds of both the priests and the people."*

---

*Horus-on-the-Horizon: the ancient name for the Sphinx
**the Great Pyramid
***Sety's phonetic pronunciation of Khafra

"What did it look like then?" I asked. *"Oh,"* he replied, *"it was very beautiful. On its head was a god's crown of disk and plumes. This was made of copper and flashed like fire in the sun. The nemes* was painted and gilded, and so was the collar and the great falcon's wings that covered its back. Of course, the face, body and legs were red. When I was a child I loved to visit it with my mother. We used to go by boat when Hapi** flooded the land, sailing from Memphis. My mother always took great bunches of flowers and papyrus reeds as offerings. O Bentreshy, how you would have loved it then!"*

With or without my suggestions, Omm Sety was a tireless interrogator. There was so much she wanted to know. Her direct memory of the ancient past was fragmentary, since it was the memory of a young, unlearned woman, Bentreshyt, who had little access to the greater world in which she lived. As to Sety's knowledge, it seemed to spring from several sources: his own personal connections with the characters living in his time; his understanding of history as it had been handed down by the scribes; his access to certain wise individuals in Amenti; and his exposure to the prevailing attitudes, rumors and royal gossip around him.

Here are a few of the topics that were under consideration in the small house of Omm Sety while her neighbors slept, unaware that a king was among them – except for Ahmed's dog.

the first Egyptians

November 20, 1972
H.M. came last night, in quite a good mood. He laughed about Ahmed's dog, who was howling and barking. After a while I asked him if he knew from whence the first Pharaonic Egyptians

---

*the crown that covered the head
**the Nile god

came. *He laughed at me and said, "What a strange thing you ask! They did not come from any other place. The Blacklanders have always been in the Black Land where the Great God put them. What makes you ask this, my Little One?"*

I said, *"Some learned men say that the pat* from the time of Mena** came from the east because their ways of life are the same."* H.M. *thought about that for a while and then said, "The learned men of which you speak are as stupid as little boys! Of course the ways of life and learning were the same. Did not our Lord Osiris teach the easterners, after he had taught the Blacklanders? I have heard it said that the people of Pa-woont*** claim to have the same ancestors as we have, but this also I do not think is true. They do not look like us, they live in a way worse than the marsh-dwellers; their gods are not our gods. But they are a good people, friendly and honest. I wish for them good fortune."*

the Nile's dams

November 20, 1972 (continued)
I spoke about the High Dam. He said that he had not seen it, but had seen the Aswan Dam. I explained about it as well as I could and asked his opinion. He answered very seriously: *"Bentreshy, this thing could be very good, or very bad. If it waters more land, more food will grow, and the rekhyt will become fat and shining like the cattle of the gods. But there is great danger! What if it breaks, for how shall the work of men defy the might of Hapi forever?"*

---

*the aristocracy
**or Menes; about 3000 BC, first king of the 1st Dynasty, thought to be the first unifier of Egypt. Sety calls him "Meny."
***Punt, a land visited by Queen Hatshepsut's expedition in the 15th century BC; thought to be in eastern Africa near Eritrea

I replied that it is very strong, much bigger and stronger than the dam which Mena built, and which is still strong and intact. He said, "Yes, I have seen the dam (djanet)* of Meny when I was a boy. Who built the new djanet ga?** I said it was Egyptians, helped by some barbarians called Russians. He frowned at this: "Since when have the Blacklanders needed the help of barbarians in building; this is a very shameful thing!"

the Great Pyramid

The question of who built the Great Pyramid and why and when is a matter of heated debate. The accepted theory, in spite of very little specific evidence, is that it was built by Khufu to be his tomb. The debate exists because there is no record of anyone else having built it, yet its technical perfection is unique in all the world, and its mathematical measurements suggest a grander symbolic purpose than merely a king's tomb; so we have theories of extra-terrestrial visitors, Biblical prophesies, ancient mystery schools and more. One other theory about Khufu and the Great Pyramid is that it was already ancient in his time and had suffered damaged, probably by earthquakes – and that the king did extensive restoration work on it, intending to use it as his own tomb. It was only natural that Omm Sety would bring up the subject with Sety. But we might remember that he lived 1200 years after Khufu's time, and that history has a way of losing its clarity in the absence of written records.

August 26, 1972
I remembered one of the questions that Dr. Hani asked, and I asked H.M. if he remembered what the Pyramids of Giza looked like in his day. He replied, "They looked far different to what they do now. It saddened my heart to see them when

---

*a massive 50-foot wall that protected the ancient capital of Memphis from the floodwaters of the Nile
**High Dam

I used to come to you in the shadow of Akhet-Khufu.* I first saw them when I was a small boy and my mother brought me to see them. In those days the doorways were hidden under a smooth casing of the stone of Ayan,** and the eastern temple was still standing."

I said that an ancient Greek traveler has visited the Pyramids, and that he said that there were inscriptions on Akhet-Khufu telling how much lentils, etc., the workmen ate. He said, "He was a big liar! There were no inscriptions on Akhet-Khufu, but there were scenes and inscriptions in the eastern temple, and in the small offering-chamber that stood near the middle of the northern side, and which is now gone."

I said that the Greek could not read, but the priests told him what was written. He said, "Perhaps the priests read to him the names of the offerings, and being a stupid barbarian, he did not understand." (Poor Herodotus, called "stupid barbarian!") I asked if any of the pyramids had been damaged or robbed. He replied, "The middle small pyramid had been robbed, and some of its stones removed, some say by the Hyksos, and most of the Houses of Eternity had been robbed, but I know not by whom.

I asked however did Khufu build the Great Pyramid in the space of 23 years of reign. He replied. "No, Bentreshy, the Majesty of King Khufu ruled this land for 44 years!" He said that 5 gangs of 200 men worked all the year round. These men were sent in by the different nomes, and were fed and clothed at the state expense. Their families were provided for by the Nomarchs of their respective nomes, and if there were any justified complaints about this, Khufu dealt very seriously with the Nomarchs! The men were supposed to work in shifts of 3 months, but many volunteered to keep on working.

---

*Sety's pronunciation of Khufu was Khu-**fiu**.
**white limestone

The bulk of the core-masonry was quarried locally, and only the granite (from Aswan) and the limestone casing (from Tura) was brought by raft during the time of the Inundation. The Chief Architect was Sneferu's son, Him-Iun (Khufu's brother), and Ka-Aper worked under him. (This is the same man whose wooden statue in Cairo Museum is called "Sheik el Belad). Him-Iun died before the pyramid was completed, and Ka-aper finished it.

I asked how the stones were raised, and H.M. said that they were rolled up a "redur." That can mean staircase or ramp. He said that in his day the N. and E. ramp were still in good condition and used as roadways around the plateau. At his time also, the casings of all the pyramids were intact and their entrances hidden. But at the beginning of the First Intermediate Period, thieves had tried unsuccessfully to enter the three big pyramids, but had succeeded in opening two of the small queen's pyramids. He did not remember which ones, but thought it was those of King Men-kaw-Ra.

I wanted to talk more, but he said, "Another time, Little One. Let us sleep. And we went and lay down on the bed. He woke me with kisses just before he left, and I decided to record this at once.

Shunet el Zebib

Omm Sety had told me that Bentreshyt was born in a nearby village a few hundred yards east of the massive, walled fortress-like structure called Shunet el Zebib. In 1997, 16 years after Omm Sety's death, Dr. David O'Connor and his team of Egyptologists unearthed an ancient village in the same location that Omm Sety had remembered from her past. She knew she had been the daughter of a very poor family there. She had small but vivid fragments of memory: walking barefooted to the village market with her mother, a vegetable seller; aching with loneliness after her mother died and her soldier father stayed away for long periods of time; then one day, going with her father to live at the temple. When I heard the news that the village had been discovered, my first thought was, if only Omm Sety were alive to see this most personal memory validated.

She had taken me many times to the spot where the village used to be and we had looked out from there to the brooding, silent shell of Shunet el Zebib, speculating about its purpose. Its name originally was Shuna pa hib, meaning the burial place of the ibis bird. The ibis was sacred to the god of wisdom, Thoth. It is one of the oldest mud-brick structures in the world and its purpose is still a mystery, though it is usually referred to as a funerary enclosure. Dr. O'Connor's team attributes it to the last king of the 2nd Dynasty, Khasekhemwy,* who built an immense desert tomb nearby.

In the 1990s, the team made an intriguing discovery when it opened 14 boat pits near the enclosure walls of Shunet and found ancient royal ceremonial vessels that could be linked to the pharaoh Aha of the 1st Dynasty – hundreds of years before Khasekhemwy. This would suggest that there was an even earlier important structure nearby, if not actually on the same site. Anyone who has seen the magnificent Solar Boat on display next to the Great Pyramid will be familiar with the type of boat found at Shunet el Zebib. The question of Shunet el Zebib's purpose – and true age – only becomes more puzzling.

Naturally, Omm Sety asked Sety about it. His explanation mentions a great religious festival called the *Heb-sed*, a jubilee that the kings of Egypt celebrated after 30 years of their reign and then every three or four years after that. From the earliest dynasties, the kings (and Hatshepsut as well) celebrated the Heb-sed as a sacred re-dedication to the service of the gods and the Black Land, a holy rite of religious devotion and offerings. In earlier times when the capital of Egypt was in Memphis, in the north, the kings performed the great ceremony in the Heb-

---

*circa 2686 BC

sed Court at Saqqara, which is part of the crenellated walled
enclosure than includes Zoser's Step Pyramid.

September 1, 1972

*H.M. came last night. We sat in the "garden," and he
remarked how the "hairs of Geb"* had grown! After the usual
preliminaries and silly names, I asked what was the original
use of the building called at one time "Shuna pa hib." He did
not know that name, but when I described the building, he
said, "Have you forgotten so much? Surely you remember the
great Heb-sed Palace built in the time of the Ancestors!" I
said that I had forgotten. He said, "Does it not resemble the
Heb-sed Palace of the Majesty of King Neter-khet** at Ro-
stau?" He meant the Step Pyramid complex at Sakkara. It
is true that Shuna, with its crenellated, whitewashed walls
and dodged entrances does seem to be a simpler form of Zoser's
Heb-sed Court.*

*H.M. continued. "There were four of these Palaces, two to the
north of the one that still stands, and one on the east, beside
the temple that I left unfinished. In the time of the Ancestors,
the kings made their Heb-sed in Upper and Lower Egypt, first
here, and then in the new northern capital, the White Wall.***
Later, to please the powerful priests and to show their glory to
the rekhyt, the kings made their Heb-seds in Thebes, Abydos,
the White Wall and Heliopolis. The Great Palace you speak
of was always kept in good order and was used. The last
king to use it before our time was the Majesty of King Neb-
Maat-Ra,**** and before him, the great Men-Kheper-Ra.*****
Ramesses tells me that he also used it six times, for he dearly
loved such ceremonies!"*

---

*grass (Geb is the earth god, and grass would be the hairs of Geb)
**Zoser
***Memphis. The royal necropolis of Memphis was nearby, at Saqqara.
****Amenhotep III, 1391-1353 BC
*****Thutmose III, 1479-1425 BC

"What happened to the other three palaces," I asked. He said, "One near the Great Palace was destroyed long, long ago. The Northern Palace, which was not so large and fine, had since very many years been used as a base for the Necropolis Guards. The one near my temple was also destroyed; only two of its walls were standing. Some of the Nomarchs of Abydos wanted to remove them, but the women of the town made a great outcry, saying that if a barren woman slept in their shelter, she would be visited by the god Min, and would surely conceive a child! You see, Little One, the rekhyt were ignorant, and thought that Min was a god, just as you did. They did not understand that he is only a manifestation of the Lord of All."

I told him that in later times the Great Palace was used as a necropolis for the sacred ibis, which were buried there in pottery jars. He said, "So that is why it was called Shuna pa hib! Perhaps in later times the custom of making the Heb-sed in Abydos fell into disuse, or perhaps a larger, finer one was built here."

Then I asked to whom the northern temple* was to be dedicated, and he replied, "I wished it to be for Our Lord Osiris, Lord of the Sacred Land, and for the souls of the ancient kings who lie in their tombs near the entrance to Pega." "So he [Ramesses] did," I said, "and your dear name remains in it, as well as his. But now it is nearly destroyed."

"But in Amenti it stands in all its beauty," he replied.

Beneath this long entry about the Heb-sed palaces I had written several questions of my own. One was, "Where exactly is the Heb-sed palace to the east of Sety's temple?" Omm Sety had squeezed her reply between the lines: "In the e. side of David's work" (referring to David O'Connor). "And the one N.

---

*the Sety Temple, which was finished by Ramesses

of Shunet el Zebib, where is that?" I wrote. Her written reply was, "the ruined walls at Deir Sitt Damiana" (a large enclosure near Shunet el Zebib).

26

a larger, finer one was built here". I asked to whom the northern Temple was to be dedicated, and he replied "I wished it to be for Our Lord Osiris, Lord of the Sacred Land, and for the souls of the ancient Kings who lie in their tombs near the entrance to Pega. Ramesses told me that he finished it for me." "So he did", I said, "And your dear name remains in it, as well as his. But now it is nearly all destroyed." "But in Amenti it stands in all its beauty" he replied. Then H.M. had an idea that we should lie on the grass and sleep! I got the pillows, but the ground was uneven and lumpy, so we went and slept in the bed.

*(1) Where exactly is the Heb. Sed palace to the east of Seti's temple (and the one N. of Shunet PHB?)
On the E side of Sadat's work. (2 ruining walls at Deir Sitt Damiana.)*

(2) Does H.M. know anything about repairs done by prince Khaemwese elder son of Ramses on the pyramids. what kind of repair exactly. Was this a hobby or a sense of duty?

(3) What was the exact construction of the Heb-Sed palace in the time of H.M. Was it well preserved. what part of Heb-Sed festivals it served... parades.., festivities, religious songs or folklore? Were there any rooms inside for the soldiers...etc. what were the exact construction and distribution of rooms inside the wall?

September 1, 1972 diary page showing my questions at the bottom and OS's jottings between the lines. In the previous pages Sety had spoken of a Heb-sed palace near his temple and described two others. Not all my questions to Sety were answered, but over time and during my years of conversations with Omm Sety, she was able to elaborate on many of them.

Looking again at Omm Sety's diary pages and our scribbled notations back and forth, I re-experience the joy we took in our pursuit of history's illusive truths. We were like two enthusiastic school chums passing notes to one another. Sety sometimes seemed bemused by our probings, but he was usually patient and forthcoming.

the secret of Sneferu's pyramids

Sneferu the Beneficent – father of Khufu and first king of the 4th Dynasty – built two large pyramids at Dahshur, a bleak desert promontory just south of Saqqara. He built a third pyramid some miles away at Meidum, an even more remote desert site. The natural assumption is that at least one of them would have been used as his tomb, yet no traces of Sneferu's burial have ever been found in any of his pyramids.

In the years since Omm Sety worked with Ahmed Fakhri's Pyramid Research Project at Dhashur, more questions have arisen about Sneferu's pyramids and purpose than there are answers. To start with, why did Sneferu build so many, when one pyramid should be adequate to house one king for all eternity? These were the early years of the magnificent Pyramid Age, a time of grand experimentation in architecture and stone. Perhaps Sneferu had reasons that we will never discover. Kings in those days didn't write autobiographies; their lives were godlike, not to be known or even thought about in their more mundane aspects.

Sneferu's two pyramids at Dahshur were positioned within walking distance of each other, overlooking the serene beauty of the Nile Valley below. The northernmost pyramid is known as the Red Pyramid, for its rosy-hued Tura limestone casings. The other, the Bent Pyramid, has caused the most speculation because, halfway up, the angle of its sides suddenly changes to a gentler slope. Did the builders attempt too steep an angle and run into problems, forcing them to reduce their slope by ten degrees, or had its odd profile been intentional?

Other things are peculiar about the Bent Pyramid as well: It has two entrances, the customary northern one, and a second one on its western face. No other Old Kingdom pyramid has two entrances. Its 230-foot long descending passage is the longest of any pyramid. The arrangement and placement of the inner chambers is unusual, and there has been speculation that there are hidden passages yet to be found. Nothing about the Bent Pyramid is easily explained.

Omm Sety never stopped wondering about the two pyramids at Dahshur, even years after Ahmed Fakhry's work there ended. She put her question to Sety:

September 14, 1973
H.M. has just left, it is nearly dawn, and I have lit the lamp to record this. I asked if he knew why Sneferu built two large pyramids so near to each other. He said, "Tradition of the time of the ancestors says that first the Majesty of King Sneferu built the southern pyramid, which has such a strange shape, but while it was being built a heavy and great stone fell from its place and crushed four men to death. Therefore, it was said to be impure and accursed. The remains of the crushed men were buried in a secret chamber within the pyramid, which was afterwards hastily finished.

"Then the Majesty of King Sneferu ordered the northern pyramid to be built. This is the story known in our time, but I do not think that it is true because the cult of the King was celebrated at both places, and there remained records of men who held office as priests of both the southern and northern Pyramids. Perhaps the true story was written and kept in the Hall of Records at Memphis, and was among those records that were destroyed in the revolt of the rekhyt.*

---

*at the end of the 6th Dynasty (circa 2100 BC)

"Now, my Little One, your poor old, bad Hyksos* wants to sleep, so come." He picked me up and carried me to bed. It was cold, so he spread his cloak over the blanket, and got in beside me. In no time at all he was fast asleep, but I lay awake for some time thinking about the story of the Dahshur Pyramids.*

September 15, 1973 (the next night)
I was awakened last night by H.M. sitting on the bed and patting my face. He said, "Wake up, Little Sleeping One! I have something to tell you!" After I had greeted him properly I asked what was his news.

He said, "Your questions set me thinking of matters which I had long since ceased to contemplate. You roused my thoughts concerning the two great pyramids of the Majesty of King Sneferu, and I asked a learned man named Ptah-em-wia, who was High Priest of Ptah in our time, what he knew about this matter. He told me a very strange story.

"He told me that the august mother of the King, the King's Great Wife Ni-maat-hapi, gave birth to twin boys. But the children were joined together at the hips by a thick piece of flesh. After they had lived thus for some time, a skilled doctor separated them. After a few days, one of the brothers died, and the survivor grew up to ascend the throne of the Black Land, and attached to his hip was a small lump of flesh, all that remained of his twin brother.

"As a young child, he was told the story of his twin, and it became fixed in his mind that his brother was part of him and

---

232

still lived, for the dead child had also been named Sneferu. When he ascended the throne and commenced to build his pyramid, the northern one, he declared that his dead brother, whom he believed to be still living in him, commanded that he should have that pyramid. Accordingly, the Majesty of King Sneferu completed the pyramid, and had the sahu of his brother brought from its tomb at Per-Itm* and interred there.

"He then built the southern pyramid for himself, with the opening high in its western face, which is not found in any other pyramid. It was made so that the two kas could easily go forth and re-enter whenever they wished to visit the sahu of the brother in the northern pyramid. It is a strange story, is it not, and yet I think it may be true."

I was very interested. I asked H.M. if he knew of other cases of joined twins. He replied, "Yes, I have heard of them. My mother told me of a woman known to her who bore a son and daughter who were joined at the breast by a bridge of flesh. The parents refused to have them separated, as they were sure that only one would survive. And so the children lived, and grew up; they loved each other and married and had many children." Then he laughed and said, "It would be good if we were so joined, Little One."

I said, "No, the bond between us is stronger than a bridge of flesh." He agreed, and after a lot of kissing, said that he must leave me, so it must have been near to the dawn. He promised to return soon. What a strange story that is, about the two pyramids, but perhaps there is some truth in it.

In His Majesty's second version of the story there is no mention of why Sneferu decided to design his own pyramid with two different angles to it. The ancient Egyptians wouldn't inten-

---

*Meidum

tionally create such a structure unless its design contained some symbolic meaning. Every great monument was meant to tell a story, even if only the privileged few were meant to understand it. If Sneferu, then, actually planned the Bent Pyramid to be bent – and it wasn't simply because of an accident – then there must be some further aspect to its design. John Anthony West, an American Egyptologist and symbolist, describes the Bent Pyramid's numerous "inexplicable features" in his book, *A Traveler's Key to Ancient Egypt*, and concludes that the pyramid was deliberately bent in order to reflect a *dual symbolism*. "This duality," he writes, "is unmistakably and emphatically underlined by its system of internal chambers,"* which he goes on to describe.

In light of Sety's tale of the conjoined royal twins, and West's observations about the Bent Pyramid's recurring symbols of duality, the question might now be: Did Sneferu commemorate his unshakable sense of twin-ship – of being a dual person – with a pyramid that was itself a symbol of duality?

The story gives an explanation for the two pyramids at Dahshur; but there was a third pyramid, the one Sneferu built at Meidum, several miles away. What was its purpose? Sety doesn't say, except that it was at Meidum that the sahu, or mummified body, of the infant twin had first been entombed (such a tomb would most likely have been a traditional flat-roofed stone *mastaba*).

As to Meidum, anyone who has visited that desolate place will immediately sense the sadness, even loneliness, around the crumbled remains of Sneferu's pyramid there. If Sety's tale represents what actually happened, then perhaps the pyramid at Meidum had been Sneferu's first attempt to place himself near to the sahu of his beloved brother, and only later did he built the pyramids at Dahshur as a final resting place for them both – their twin Houses of Eternity.

---

*West, p. 197

The beauty of Sety's narrative is that it offers a provocative, and even plausible, explanation for a vexing historical puzzle. And because so little is known about Sneferu the man, the tale also allows us to imagine that we have glimpsed the heart of a touchingly human king.

Royal Family Secrets: Two Queens

*"Sety said to me, 'Haven't you ever wondered
how Neb-Maat-Ra could raise a woman
of the people to be the Great Royal Wife?'" OS*

*"Tell me about Queen Hatshepsut,"
Omm Sety said one night to His Majesty.*

O mm Sety and Sety often spoke together about "family matters," meaning the royals who peopled the 18th and 19th
Dynasties.

Now, anyone who studies that period of Egyptian history
soon realizes that there is a big problem in assigning correct royal
family relationships. There are enough gaps and ambiguities in
the historical records to fuel endless speculation. Brothers may
not be brothers at all, but uncle and nephew or father and son;
a shadowy king may actually be Queen Nefertiti under another
name; Akhenaten may not have been physically capable of siring
his six daughters. And so on.

But Sety had a more personal perspective. In his conversations with Omm Sety he detailed for her the all-too-human private lives of the 18th and 19th Dynasty royals – which in some

cases explained who really *was* who in the palaces of Memphis and Thebes.

One of his stories calls into question a long-accepted part of the dynastic charts, and has to do with a beautiful and famous queen named Tiy.

shaking the family tree

Who was Queen Tiy?

She was one of the most influential women of ancient Egypt. As chief wife of Amenhotep III she was an active partner in the business of the far-flung Egyptian empire. She was also the mother of Akhenaten, the mother-in-law of Nefertiti, and the grandmother (or possibly mother) of Tutankhamun – making her a pivotal figure in 18th Dynasty affairs.

Existing records tell us that she was chosen by the young king Amenhotep himself to be the Great Royal Wife when both were still children, and that theirs was a true love match. What was unusual, but not unheard of, was that she was the daughter of commoners. Their wedding proclamation stated, *"the name of her father is Yuya, and the name of her mother is Tuya..."*

Tiy grew up on her father Yuya's estate in Middle Egypt near the city of Akhmim, the center for the worship of the god Min. Yuya was King's Master of the Horse and Overseer of the Cattle of Min. Tiy's mother, Tuya, was a woman with honorable positions in the temples of Min and Amun of Thebes. Though they were not royals, they were held in high esteem by the court. At their deaths, Yuya and Tuya were given a fine tomb together in the Valley of the Kings.

Based on what is known, there would be no reason to doubt that Yuya and Tuya were the true parents of Queen Tiy. Yet, according to Omm Sety, there was an ancient royal cover-up that was kept secret from all but a few.

the story

In a conversation recorded June 29, 1971, Omm Sety said something about Queen Tiy that took me by surprise. "But Omm Sety," I replied, "all the documents say that Tiy is the daughter of Yuya and Tuya, and now you tell me that Sety says she *isn't* their daughter? What exactly did he tell you?" The rest of our conversation went like this:

OS: First Sety said to me, "Haven't you ever wondered how Neb-Maat-Ra* could raise a woman of the people to be the Great Royal Wife?" I said I had wondered, but I thought perhaps he was so powerful that he was able to sway the priesthood to his thinking. And then Sety said that Tiy was actually the daughter of a girl called Thiy – Thiy being a daughter of king Amenhotep II and his concubine, Meryt-Ptah.

Now, apparently this girl Thiy wasn't very beautiful and she wasn't married – but she became pregnant. And then her brother, Thotmes IV, who by that time was king, asked her who was the father. He said, "With whom have you been eating the uncooked goose?" She refused to reply and he got into a violent temper.

And so he sent the wretched girl and her mother to a royal estate near Akhmim. This estate was called Djarukha and it was very popular with the younger members of the royal family because there they were free to amuse themselves away from the court and all its ceremonies. It happened that Djarukha adjoined the estate belonging to Yuya, who was a very wealthy man, though not of the nobility.

---

*Amenhotep III

Well, this girl Thiy was sent off to Djarukha with her mother Meryt-Ptah. When the time came for her to give birth she apparently went crazy and wouldn't let anybody come near her, not even her mother. But Tuya, the wife of Yuya, had made a friendship with Meryt-Ptah, and she was there and delivered the baby.

When the baby was born, Tuya showed it to the young mother, but the girl went quite mad and tried to strangle it. So Tuya, who had a child of her own that she was suckling, said she would take the baby and look after it until the priests and the doctor had driven out the evil spirit which was in the body of Thiy. She thought, as they all did, that any illness was caused by evil spirits.

They brought a *heri heb* priest* from the temple of Min to try and drive out this evil spirit, but he didn't have any luck. And then a dreadful thing happened. The girl crashed two oil lamps together over her head and set herself on fire and died. Meryt-Ptah, her mother, was beside herself with grief.

Thiy's body was prepared and mummified by the priests in Akhmim. She was going to be taken back to Memphis to be buried in the tombs of her mother's family, and so when Meryt-Ptah was ready to leave with the body of her daughter, Tuya brought out the little baby to give it to its grandmother. But Meryt-Ptah refused to even see it. "Take it away and do with it what you wish," she cried. "This child has cost my daughter her life."

---

*a priest adept in magic

Tuya was secretly glad because she'd grown fond of this baby, whom she'd named Tiy, and she was very happy to keep it. Her husband Yuya, who by all accounts was a wise and decent man, sent a letter to the king telling him what had happened and asked permission to adopt the child legally. The royal permission was given and the child was theirs, to be known always as the daughter of Yuya and Tuya.

Because Yuya didn't know if at any time it would be necessary to prove that this child was of royal birth, he wrote a report giving this girl's history and sent it, together with the letter of permission from Thotmes IV, to the Hall of Records at Luxor.

HZ: It's quite a story. Of course, the Hall of Records no longer exists at Luxor. If there were that report and that letter, it would be lost. Did Sety tell you more about Queen Tiy?

OS: I did ask Sety how it was that Amenhotep III got to know her – how he came to marry her. Sety said that it was on the Djarukha estate, where the children of the royal family used to spend their holidays. When Amenhotep became king he was still just a boy, and naturally much of his time was spent at play, since regents ran the country for him.

At Djarukha his constant companion was this little girl, Tiy – his little neighbor. He used to say that one day he would marry her and make her his Great Royal Wife, and people used to laugh at his childish idea. But Yuya and Tuya knew that this might become a reality, because they could prove that the child was of royal birth. And so it happened.

Omm Sety and I both thought the story was an interesting piece of royal gossip, whether or not it was true. At that time, in 1971, it seemed unlikely that it would ever be confirmed or disproved, or that the question of Tiy's parentage would even be raised.

But Tiy's story is not quite finished.

the Elder Lady in Tomb 35

We know that Queen Tiy outlived her husband and probably spent her last years in Amarna* near her son, Akhenaten. Her tomb has never been found, though fragments of her sarcophagus were unearthed in the Royal Tombs area of Amarna. It was assumed that her tomb was there – until the great excitement of 1907, when a wooden burial shrine bearing Tiy's name showed up in the Valley of the Kings, amid the jumbled wreckage of Tomb 55.

Strangely, the mummy found with it wasn't Tiy's; it belonged to a young man. So, where was Queen Tiy?

There was already controversy over an unnamed female mummy that had been discovered a few years before by Victor Loret, in 1898. That winter Loret, then director of the Egyptian Antiquities Service, had discovered and mapped 16 tombs in the Valley of the Kings, a prodigious effort in itself. Yet it was one tomb in particular that made him a world celebrity: Tomb 35.

The main burial chamber contained Amenhotep II's sarcophagus and mummy. After further clearing of the tomb, Loret entered two side chambers and beheld something almost unbelievable: an enormous cache of mummies and coffins – 17 in all. Loret blew the thick, gray dust from one coffin and then another, reading the names of the occupants within. He quickly realized that he was in the presence of some of the greatest pharaohs of all time.

---

*Tell el-Amarna, Akhenaten's royal city. Its ancient name was Akhetaten.

In one chamber, arranged in neat rows, were nine simple coffins containing the bodies of Queen Tiy's husband Amenhotep III, his brother Thotmes IV, Sety II, Ramesses IV, V, and VI, and three other royals – all of them stripped of their royal adornments.

In the other chamber three mummified bodies lay side by side without coffins, exposed to view and unnamed – one of them a regal-looking older woman with thick dark hair. Her face was arresting and proud, her left hand clenched across her chest as if it had once held a scepter. It was the traditional embalmment pose for Egyptian queens. For lack of any identification she was given the name "Elder Lady," but many believed her to be none other than Queen Tiy.

Why was she here? Why were any of them here? It is now known that the cache had been brought to this location around the time of the Pharaoh Smendes in the 21st Dynasty, most likely after the original royal tombs had been sacked by ancient grave robbers. It would have been the duty of the administrative officials of the Valley of the Kings to see that the desecrated royal remains were respectfully dealt with, placed in a secure situation, and the mass tomb resealed – the same thing that was done for that other famous cache of royal mummies, discovered in 1881 by Emile Brugsch.

in search of an identity

The Elder Lady in Tomb 35 kept that name for many years, despite speculation that she could be Tiy. And then in 1922, Howard Carter opened Tutankhamun's tomb. Among the dazzling golden treasures there was a small wooden box containing a locket, which held a delicate coil of hair. The box was inscribed with the royal cartouche of Queen Tiy.

It was a while before science was advanced enough to allow that lock of hair to tell its story. Not long ago an electron probe analysis was done, comparing a strand of hair from the box with a hair sample taken from the Elder Lady. It produced a match.

This was enough to convince almost everyone that Tiy was the Elder Lady, even though a few skeptics still want stronger proof.

Fortunately, that might soon be possible.

For several years a microbiologist from Brigham Young University, Scott Woodward, has been collecting ancient DNA, attempting to track genetic traits, and health and family relationships in many parts of the world, including Egypt. He was the first scientist to be given permission to extract DNA from a number of Egyptian royal mummies – including Thotmes IV, the supposed uncle in Sety's story.

DNA technology is able to trace close family relationships with some accuracy if viable tissue samples can be provided. In Tiy's case there seem to be potential tissue donors from several quarters. The mummies of Yuya and Tuya exist in good condition, as well as those of Thotmes IV and Amenhotep II (Tiy's supposed grandfather, according to Sety).

Of course, no one in the scholarly community has reason to even question whether Tiy was the natural daughter of Yuya and Tuya; the records seem quite clear that she was. But Woodward's and others' work with ancient DNA leaves open the possibility that one day the royal family tree will be filled in with scientific certainty.

As for Queen Tiy, her place in history is already assured, and it is undoubtedly of little consequence to her now what the world knows or doesn't know about her origins – the important thing is that we remember her name, and in so doing, ensure her eternal existence with the gods in Amenti.

death on the Nile

"Tell me about Queen Hatshepsut," Omm Sety said one night to His Majesty. And then, speaking of what he knew, Sety proceeded to lay out a grisly tale about the great queen who became a king.

But first, some background: In the 18th Dynasty there
were four kings who bore the name Thotmes (or Thutmose). It
is generally thought that all the Thutmosid kings died naturally,
without help from ambitious relatives or the palace guard. But
there was one king whose death in 1479 BC still has historians
wondering – Thotmes II. His queen was his powerful half-sister
Hatshepsut, who had always considered herself to be the rightful
ruler of Egypt.

Life in the Theban palace of Thotmes II was anything but
harmonious, with deeply divided political factions; the queen's
faction was led by a brilliant commoner named Sen-en-mut.

Now, 3500 years later, Sety has a tale to tell about all of
them. On a warm August evening in Abydos he revealed to
Omm Sety how everyone in this royal drama had his or her
revenge – except for the poor king – and how no one died
in peace.

Aug. 20, 1972
*His Majesty came last night – and set Ahmed's new dog howl-
ing. It was after midnight, but I was still awake. We took
chairs and went and sat in the "garden," which had sprouted
a few blades of grass since Ahmed watered it. Then we sat
quietly, holding hands.*

*Presently, he said, "To please you, I came tonight through
Pega-the-Gap. Are you happy?" "Of course," I replied, "I
am happy that you come to me by any road."*

He said, "I do not like those tall bones of Set that are stand-
ing in the Kheret-nouteri.** Why are they there?"*

*I told him that they, the electricity pylons, extended from Aswan
to Rakhoti, and were to carry the power that would bring light*

---

*The "bones of Set" refers to anything made of iron.
**the ancient burial grounds at Abydos

to all the towns and villages, like the light I had when I lived in the shadow of Akhet-Khufu. He was very fascinated by the electric light I had at the Pyramids! He said, "I do not like them, but if they are for the good of the rekhyt, I must endure them!" and he laughed.

Then, wanting him to talk about Queen Hatshepsut, I asked, "In the list of Kings' names in your House-of-Men-Maat-Ra, why did you leave out the name of Her Majesty the Great Lady, Hatshepsut?"

"O, Bentreshy," he replied, "I omitted her because I considered her to be a very bad woman. Perhaps you know that she loved her Overseer-of-All-Works, Sen-en-Mut, and that she bore him a daughter. She was quite shameless and did not try to hide her passion, even from her husband. As for Sen-en-Mut, he was of a low character, and used to boast of her love for him, and how he could have her body how and when he desired her. Hatshepsut's husband, Thotmes Aa'-kheper-en-Ra, a good and gentle man, could not endure this, and determined to have Sen-en-Mut killed secretly. But Hatshepsut seems to have known of his intention, and before he could act, with her own hand she put poison in his wine, and while he lay in agony she and Sen-en-Mut lay naked together before his dying eyes.

"Yet in spite of her evil nature, Hatshepsut proved to be a wise and good Ruler of the Black Land. I used to loathe the mention of her name, but that was before I had known the power of love, and how it can lead one into sin! Perhaps if Hatshepsut had married a lustful goat like Sen-en-Mut she would have been satisfied and the evil in her nature would not have burst forth."

"What was the end of the matter?" I asked.

He replied, "Thotmes had a concubine named Isis who bore him a son, also named Thotmes. He was later to become the *great warrior Men-Kheper-Ra.* Having no son, Hatshepsut married the boy-king to her eldest daughter. But Hatshepsut humiliated him in every way, and would give him no chance to gain power. At last, when he reached full manhood he could endure no more, and like the ancient son of Isis, he rose and avenged his father's murder. First, he arranged that a great stone should fall upon Sen-en-Mut when he was inspecting some quarries. Later, he secretly had Hatshepsut poisoned. He dared not act openly against her, as the people loved her in spite of – or because of – the earlier scandal of her passion for Sen-en-Mut. It was only after she had been dead for some years that he dared to vent his wrath on her monuments, and replace her name with that of his father.*

"Ah, Beloved, men envy kings, but well I know that the office is one of bitterness! The great Men-Kheper-Ra had very little happiness, save perhaps in his many victories. I had no happiness at all, save in your love, and even that was taken from me."

"But you have regained it, Beloved," I reminded him. "For which I thank the Gods with all my heart," he replied. "O Bentreshy, if you ceased to love me, I think I would become a fiend, more evil than the Great of Strength!"

"Do not fear that," I said, "I am yours for all Eternity, and nothing shall part us." He held me so tightly that I could feel his heart beating as though it would burst. I said, "Beloved, what is the matter? Be calm, rejoice that we are able to sit here together, to talk and laugh, to exchange kisses and caresses. Come and sleep beside me, and forget all those bad thoughts." We lay down side by side and I held him in my arms until he slept. But I did not sleep, and was still awake when he left.

---

*Thotmes III

He was calm and happy again. He kissed me tenderly when he left, and promised to return very soon.

I could not sleep after he left, thinking about the terrible story of Hatshepsut, who is a woman I had always admired. But I don't know how the details of the murder of Thotmes II came to be known. Perhaps that awful Sen-en-Mut boasted of what they had done? I must ask about this.

Aug. 21, 1972

H.M. came again last night, and how happy I am! I woke at 12.20 midnight, and found him sleeping peacefully beside me. I did not wake him, and soon I also fell asleep. It was shortly before dawn that he awakened me with kisses. He said, "I have passed a wonderful night beside you, Bentreshy, and I feel so happy."

I replied that I was glad, and hoped that he would continue to come often. Then I said that something in the story of Hatshepsut was troubling me. "How did it become known that she had poisoned her husband, and how was it known what she and Sen-en-Mut did while the King was dying?"

H.M. replied, "I do not know how this story got about. Some say that when Sen-en-Mut was drunk – which was often! – he used to boast about it. But I do not think this is true. Another story, which seems to be the real truth, is that Hatshepsut and Sen-en-Mut thought that H. M. Thotmes was dead when they finally left his room. But he was not, and soon his concubine Isis found him, and raised a great outcry. A doctor came and revived him, but warned Isis that he could not live. She turned everyone out of the room, and as he lay dying in her arms, he gasped out the terrible story. Hatshepsut gave out the news that her husband had died naturally, and Isis, who knew, as well as the doctor, and the embalmers also, that he had died of poison, kept silent through fear of Hatshepsut.

"It was only after his son, H.M. Men-Kheper-Ra, grew to manhood, that Isis dared to tell him the story, and urge him to vengeance. I believe this is the true way in which the crime became known. Is it not strange, Bentreshy, that a man as vile as Sen-en-Mut could make such a beautiful monument as the Djser-djseru?"* [Omm Sety added a note here: *Actually, he pronounced it Djoser-Djoseru.*]

After that, there were more kisses and silly names, and at last he said, "Now, Beloved, I have to leave, and again to please you, I will go back through Pega!" He walked to the center of the west side of the "garden," and just disappeared.

Hatshepsut as history knows her

When Sety was building his temple at Abydos he ordered that a list of kings' names be inscribed on one wall of the Corridor of Kings. The procession of royal names is still there today, carefully enumerated in chronological order. Hatshepsut's name is not among them, or the names of several other Egyptian kings and queens, including Akhenaten. The list was not meant to be a historical document, but to bring to the attention of the gods the names of those who had brought honor to the Black Land and to the holy city of Abydos.

Setting aside Sety's personal disapproval of her, how worthy a ruler was Hatshepsut? Based on what little is known today, she was an extraordinary woman.

She was born early in the 15th century BC, the daughter of Thotmes I. It was she who built the breathtaking architectural wonder known as Deir el Bahri, a temple cut into the sheer

---

*Deir el Bahri

sandstone cliffs of Upper Egypt, with its broad, columned terraces that still glow golden in the brilliant Theban sunlight. Just on the other side of the cliffs, in the Valley of the Kings, lies the tomb she prepared for her own eternity.

In her two decades of power she set a tone of great artistic achievement and, above all, peace. She did not enlarge on her father's earlier military expansions in Nubia and Asia, but she did lead the famous Expedition to Punt, a bold exploration into Africa that returned with botanical specimens and exotic creatures and opened important trade routes in ebony, gold and myrrh. One would imagine that such a queen – or king – would be remembered with pride by those who came after, but that didn't happen; instead, after her death, her name and likeness were erased from monuments all over Egypt. The mystery of Hatshepsut's reign seems to have more to do with what kind of woman she was than with her admirable accomplishments.

It couldn't have been easy to be the Princess Royal of a powerful king and his chief queen. From birth, Hatshepsut understood that the course of her life would be decided by political necessities. Not having a son by his principal wife, Thotmes raised young Hatshepsut to think of herself as a prince, training her in the duties of kingship. She is even depicted wearing boy's clothing and is variously referred to as "he" *and* "she." When her mother died, her aging father proclaimed Hatshepsut his chief queen, giving her great power and influence. She was only about 15 years old. And then, not long after, Thotmes died.

For a while Hatshepsut ruled Egypt alone, surrounded by a powerful circle of advisors. But it must have been a tenuous situation for her, which may be why she married her half-brother, Thotmes II, son of one of the late king's minor wives. The marriage could be seen as one of those political necessities to help solidify her power in a palace full of conspiring factions. They were both still in their teens. Apparently the new king was not an ambitious or vibrant sort, but he did have his own clique of supporters who would not have been pleased with the queen's dominance on the throne. She had plans for restoring Egypt to the grandeur of the early kings and she looked to her hand-picked advisors to make her dreams a reality.

One of those men was the commoner, Sen-en-mut, a talented politician and gifted architect. Among his titles was Over-seer-of-All-Works and tutor to Their Majesties' daughter, Nefrure. Such an elevation of a commoner was highly unusual and would have been the subject of speculation and gossip. There were rumors of intimacy and more between Hatshepsut and Sen-en-mut. Which may explain why, when the king suddenly fell ill and died, there were whispers of foul play.

No one has ever known exactly what killed Thotmes II, but a recent examination and x-rays of his mummy show a frail body, probably not yet 30, with an abnormally pale face mottled with scabs. The scabrous skin could be a result of mummification and not disease, and there have been no soft tissue studies that might determine the cause of death.

Since he had no male heirs by Hatshepsut, the crown went to Thutmose III, his infant son by his secondary wife, Isis. Hatshepsut immediately took power as the boy's regent, and for the next 19 years was acting sovereign of Egypt. Not only that, two years into her regency she declared herself to be king. In the spectacular art that decorated her mortuary temple at Deir el Bahri, she depicted her own sacred birth as a male, and continued to represent herself in an ambiguous manner in the thousands of statues that she commissioned. There was the beautiful feminine face, but there was also the symbolic beard of kingship. There is no doubt that she believed herself called by the great god Amun-Ra to be both king and queen. Blessed with a driving energy and vision – and with Sen-en-mut by her side – she built grand monuments that echoed the sublime architectural heritage of her ancestors.

But in those 19 years of her regency, the boy Thotmes III was growing up, showing his own brilliance and ambition, restless to rule in his own right. He was a natural-born warrior. The tensions on the shared throne must have been extreme.

At some point Hatshepsut's name ceased being mentioned anywhere and Thotmes declared himself sole ruler, embarking on the first of many great military excursions to the edges of the empire. It is likely that Hatshepsut did not go quietly into retirement, after such a life of power and with such a passionate nature. She lived – or was allowed to live – only at her stepson's pleasure, and probably not for long. Sen-en-mut may have been disposed of earlier, since his name ceased to be seen on any new structures as well

After the death of Hatshepsut, Thutmose III went on to become Egypt's most powerful king and empire builder, remembered to this day as the Napoleon of Egypt, while Hatshepsut's memory has remained under a cloud of rumor and unanswered questions. Sety's speculations were not the first, nor would they be the last, to deny this extraordinary woman an honored place in Egypt's history.

Earlier in this chapter, there was mention of a Hall of Records that once existed at Luxor. The next chapter considers the possibility that its location might one day be known.

SEVENTEEN

The Lost Per-Medjat

"If there is a house full of ancient records...
maybe it's in this mound..." HZ

E ver since Edgar Cayce spoke from his trance state about the
existence of a great Hall of Records in Egypt, the idea of
finding a treasure trove of manuscripts about the unknown origins of Egypt – going back even to Atlantis, as he believed – has
teased the public imagination. The Hall of Records was to be
found near the Sphinx, Cayce said. The ancient name for such
a library would have been *Per-Medjat*, and its discovery would
rival the importance of the Dead Sea Scrolls. It would be like
finding the lost archives of the Library of Alexandria.

Since Cayce's death in 1945 there have been repeated
attempts to find the Per-Medjat at the Sphinx, using a combination of psychic guidance and state-of-the-art scientific techniques,
but the Hall of Records has remained elusive.

In one of our conversations, Omm Sety and I discussed
Cayce's prediction, and we also talked about the possible existence of another Hall of Records – this one in Luxor. Our
discussion was recorded on a balmy May evening in May 1973,
just outside the Sety Temple, in the ruins of the Osirion. When
I first started to record our conversations, I chose the most serene
and quiet place in Abydos. There is a long stone staircase leading down into the interior of the Osirion, and part way along is

a kind of platform. That was where we sat when our conversations were to be about abstract, religious and spiritual subjects.

I recorded this particular session on May 26, 1973. For the record, I began with some introductory remarks:

HZ: It has been ages since I've come to Abydos to see Omm Sety. I have been ill since we met last on the 4th of April, and then I have been to Cairo twice. I'm not feeling very well with the heat and I found that Omm Sety is not at her best either, but fortunately, tonight is getting cooler and I think the awful heat wave is subsiding. Omm Sety, about that last encounter with His Majesty – when was it?

OS: It was on April 13th.

HZ: I would like you to talk to me about it because I remember having read your notes about it, and there was a declaration from Sety that there is some sort of hidden library in the vicinity of Luxor. I am very curious to know about this.

OS: Yes. I asked him if he knew anything about a building which Cayce, in his book, *There is a River*, mentioned as a Hall of Records that shall be rediscovered before the end of the 20th century. And Sety replied, "He must be speaking of the Per-Medjat."

He went on to explain that in every temple there was a place where books were kept. But in the great Temple of Amun-Ra in Ipt-sut, which is now Luxor, there was also a great Per-Medjat attached to the House of Life,* and here were kept all the important documents from the time of the Ancestors: records of wars, of

---

*The House of Life *(Per-Ankh)* housed the sacred and ritual texts.

the building of temples, of the digging of canals, of years of famine and years of plenty, of land endow-ments, of all new discoveries made by learned men – of every matter of importance that had ever occurred in the Black Land.

I asked him if this building was a part of the tem-ple and he replied, "No, it and the House of Life lie to the northwest of the House of Amun-Ra, but its approach opens out of the street of the Sacred Rams." There was also a great Per-Medjat by the Temple of Ptah in Memphis, he said, but some of its documents were destroyed during a revolt at the end of the Sixth Dynasty. What documents remained were brought to the Per-Medjat at Luxor.

I asked if anyone was allowed to see these records. He said any responsible person was allowed to con-sult them and many were copied and sent to differ-ent temples at the request of the chief priest or the nomarch. There were some copies here in Abydos on matters concerning the Ta-wer nome.* I wanted to talk more, but he said, "All this recalling has made me sleepy, so put your arms around me and be quiet." [laughter on the tape]

Luxor Temple is part of the vast temple complex of ancient Thebes. The temple, known as the Southern Harem of Amun, was dedicated to his consort Mut and their son Khons, the moon god. It was built by Amenhotep III on top of an older, smaller temple, and has a delicate, haunting beauty – unlike the more masculine drama of the Karnak Temple two miles to the north. Its central purpose was the celebration of the Opet Festival. Once a year, for several weeks, the people of Thebes went on

---

*the administrative district of Abydos

extended holiday to rejoice in the presence of the gods and ask for favors from them.   Only at the "Beautiful Feast of Opet" did the gods came out of their hidden temple rooms to be among the people.   Small statues of the gods were carried along the avenue that ran between the two temples (in later times the statues were carried on sacred boats along the Nile).

For most of the way the processional avenue is flanked by hundreds of ram-headed sphinxes, but for the final segment of the journey to the Luxor Temple the sphinxes are human-headed, bearing the likeness of the 30th Dynasty pharaoh, Nectanebo II. The most important moment of the great festival was the king's journey from Karnak to Luxor, where, in the holy of holies inside the temple, he symbolically reunited with his divine ka and became a god himself. It was a powerful declaration to the people of Egypt that their king had been annointed once again by Amun and was in truth a god on earth.

I have made particular mention of the processional avenue of ram-headed sphinxes because when Sety described the location of the lost hall of records as being to the northwest of the entrance to Luxor Temple, he used the "Street of Sacred Rams" as a reference point. Extending north from Luxor Temple for about the first 100 meters are the (newer) human-headed sphinxes, and then for the rest of the way north to the Karnak Temple they have the heads of rams.

To return to my conversation with Omm Sety about all of this:

HZ: You told me that you met Miss Seton-Williams* and discussed the matter with her.

OS: I asked her if she remembered what the land was like immediately to the northwest of the Temple of Luxor, and she said it was very high ground.   Part of

---

*Dr. Veronica Seton-Williams, research fellow at University College, London, and friend of Omm Sety

Luxor. Photo taken from the third floor of the New Winter Palace Hotel looking north. Luxor Temple is in the center, with the house of Tewfik Andrawos to the left-center beyond. The white Andrawos house is on the Nile Corniche, opposite the Abdul Haggag Mosque, and is most probably built above the Per-Medjat, the Hall of Records of the Luxor Temple. (Hanny el Zeini)

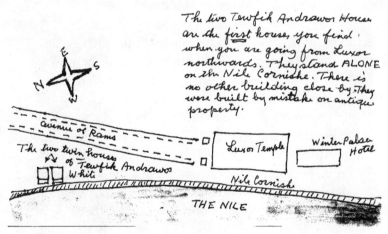

Author's (HZ) sketch of the area near the Luxor Temple where Sety said a great Hall of Records had once stood (showing the Andrawos House and the Avenue of Sphinxes).

it had been cleared away, but there is still remaining high ground. She said, "I think there must be some ancient remains underneath it." I asked if there was any chance of its ever being excavated and she said, "I doubt it, because the government owns houses on top of it."

H.Z.: It would be rather difficult because I think northwest of the Luxor Temple there is a series of houses, the biggest one built by the Andrawos family and now belonging to the Arab Socialist Union. And north of that there is what looks like government offices. I also remember that behind the Andrawos house there is a small mound which has not been cleared yet, and maybe it's in this mound that the Per-Medjat, the house of documents, might still be. If it is really northwest of the temple, then it should be underneath the office of the Arab Socialist Union. We have to look at a bifurcation of the Avenue of Rams, or at least something that looks like a crossroad, to be able to know exactly where that road would be that led to the Per-Medjat. What do you think?

OS: When I was in Luxor in 1952 the high ground came almost up to the Temple itself, and there were a lot of small houses on it. I think around 12 or 15 years ago they did clear part of it and they did find some more of these rams. The man who was doing the work, Abdul Kader, wrote to me and sent me some photographs and copies of the inscriptions on these rams to translate and make a report on them, which I did. I noticed that the inscriptions were on the two sides and the front – but on the back there was no inscription. And so I said to him in my letter, "As there are no inscriptions on the back, these rams must be close to some wall." And he replied, "Yes, there *is* the ruins of a wall at the back of them.

HZ: Then Miss Seton-Williams is correct; there is a possibility of a sort of small avenue or lane leading from the Avenue of the Rams. The Avenue of the Rams is practically cleared now, and I think there is a suggestion of a bifurcation at 100 meters or so to the north of the main entrance of the Luxor Temple. I think so, because there is a regularity of distance between each ram, and then there is a space where the rams look to me a little bit odd compared to the rest of the distances. Most probably that would be the lane that Sety talks about.

OS: Yes, that sounds like it. From what Abdul Kader told me, I took it that the Avenue of the Rams had a wall behind it – I mean, that you couldn't walk in from the town between the rams. And so if what Sety said is right, there must be also a space in that wall. And when you noticed that there is a difference in the distance between the rams, that sounds as if there *is* a sort of crossroads opening out of it.

HZ: As I remember, that odd space is exactly to the east of the Arab Socialists Union, and I think that most probably the eastern part of the Andrawos house would be the real place of this house of records. Didn't Sety give any specifics about its distance from the temple itself?

OS: He just said to the northwest. But it can't be so very far to the north because the land slopes down again. As far as I can remember, this high ground is fairly near to the temple itself.

Anyway, *he* said it's part of the House of Life. In that case, it must be a fairly big building, because the House of Life was where they used to copy all these sacred books. It was really sort of a publishing house. The scribes all sat facing the reader, the reader read out from the books in dictation and then they copied them. This is how they made all these Books of the Dead, and how so many mistakes came in too!

I shouldn't think it would be far from the Temple, but definitely not *part* of the Temple, because of this business of purification and all that. I'm sure all these scribes and the students and others were not ceremonially pure!

HZ: *If* there is a house full of ancient records it must be very worthwhile, don't you think?

OS: Definitely. And especially, you see, because it would contain not only documents from the Middle Kingdom, but also documents from the Old Kingdom – the remains of the Per-Medjat of Memphis! I mean, that's probably how they have all this information for the king lists. A pity about those documents that were lost in the revolution at the end of the 6th Dynasty. But it would be a *marvelous* thing if the Per-Medjat of Luxor could be found.

The prospect of a trove of records from the earliest times of Egypt's history is the kind of thing that keeps Egyptologists awake at night. Now I would like to add one more tempting possibility to their wish list: the location of the lost tomb of Nefertiti.

EIGHTEEN

She Who Waits: Finding Nefertiti

"I know where Nefertiti's tomb exists. One day I will tell you before I die." OS

Shortly after Nasser's death, while Omm Sety was still in mourning, I paid her a visit. It worried me to see her this way, and I hoped that she could forget for a while her grief over the dead "pharaoh." I knew she would warm up to a good controversial topic, so I suggested that we take a stroll out to the Osirion and spend some time together in conversation. The Osirion is a place of unusual serenity, far from the noisy village center.

Now, I knew very well that Omm Sety had strong opinions about Akhenaten and Nefertiti, which is exactly why my subject for debate that day was Akhenaten and everything related to his person, family reign and philosophy. First, I raised the question of Akhenaten's burial place, since the mummy found in his presumed tomb in the Valley of the Kings proved to be that of his younger brother Smenkhara.

"Why are you so interested in the burial place of this insignificant ruler?" she asked dismissively.

"I am interested also in the burial place of Nefertiti," I added. "Since I visited the royal tomb in Amarna I have become convinced that neither of them was ever buried there."

Omm Sety was silent, gazing at the immense pillars towering over our heads in the central island of the Osirion. Then quite suddenly she said, "I know where Nefertiti's tomb exists. It is in a most unlikely place. His Majesty told me about it. One day I will tell you before I die." I didn't press her for the information because she obviously wanted to choose her own time to speak of it.

Nefertiti is a name that has a lingering magic in it. Nefertiti: *the Beautiful One*...she of the long, slender neck and perfect profile. Who hasn't seen a copy of the Berlin Museum's famous sculptured head of Nefertiti, the very definition of regal beauty? Yet for almost 3000 years the world knew nothing of the existence of this great Egyptian queen – not her name, not her face. Nor was anything known of her husband, the heretic pharaoh Akhenaten.

This long time of forgetting was no accident. A deep and unforgiving hatred of the royal couple had caused their names and images to be wiped from the pages of Egyptian history.

Perhaps there would not have been such venom directed at them had Akhenaten not repudiated all the gods of Egypt except for one, shutting down their temples and shrines and stirring the wrath of the entrenched priesthoods – or had he not allowed much of the far-reaching Egyptian empire to be lost while he tended his dreams. Perhaps if he had been a different kind of man.

Early in his reign Akhenaten turned his back on all that had gone before and built a beautiful new city on the Nile, far from the traditional centers of Memphis and Thebes. He named the city Akhetaten, *Horizon-of-the-Sun-Disc*. It was a place of palaces and grand houses decorated with the breathtaking, sensual, naturalistic art so associated with his reign. The temples in this holy city were vast open courtyards where the sun-disc, the Aten, was worshipped as the one and only source of life, supplanting the old gods and their worship.

The construction of Akhetaten took no more than ten years. And then with the death of Akhenaten everything was gone, almost as quickly as it had been built – every edifice laid low, all mention of Akhenaten or Nefertiti erased, and anything connected with the old regime vandalized and scattered to the winds.

The heretic and his queen became nameless ones, denied eternal life, for without names they could have no existence in the heavenly realms. It was the ultimate revenge. And so this royal pair remained utterly and completely forgotten, while Egypt returned to its old gods.

Their ruined city slept too, its beauty unremembered. In time, villages sprang up where palaces had been, and people called the sandy plain along the edge of the river *el-Amarna*. The centuries rolled on, and then in the 19th century of our era the remains of the city were discovered by accident and archaeologists began to sift through the ruins.

But the story of the royal family of el-Amarna would be a long time unfolding because of the ancient, systematic obliteration of the site. No one even knew what the queen looked like, until one day in December 1911.

A German archaeological team had been working in the littered storehouse of the royal sculptor Thotmes, when one of them noticed something unusual lying half buried in the rubble. It appeared to be a painted portrait bust carved from limestone, but the face was not visible. With the utmost care he lifted it free of its long confinement and then, turning it towards him, he beheld the face of Nefertiti – so serenely lifelike he could only stare in wonder.

In the years since that moment, more has become known about the Amarna period and the family of the king who was called "the criminal." Yet, too much is still a mystery. No writings have ever been found that speak in depth of his short-lived new religion. We have only Akhenaten's own lyrical hymn to the Aten, which sounds so much like Psalm 104 of the Bible that people have thought one might have been the inspiration for the other.

Hymn to the Aten (excerpt): How manifold are all thy works! O thou sole God, whose powers no other possesseth....Thou shinest on the eastern horizon and fillest the whole earth with thy beauty...when thou shinest they live, when thou settest they die; in thee do they live....The world came forth from thy hand, inasmuch as thou madest them.

Psalm 104 (excerpt): O Lord, how manifold are thy works! In wisdom hast thou made them all: the earth is full of thy riches.... That thou givest them they gather: thou openest thine hand, they are filled with good. Thou hidest thy face, they are troubled: thou takest away their breath, they die, and return to their dust.... Thou sendest forth thy spirit, they are created: and thou renewest the face of the earth.

There *is* someone, however, who may hold the key to unlocking more Amarna-period secrets, and that would be Nefertiti herself. It is not known what happened to her after the death of her husband. Most scholars feel that she was buried in Akhenaten's tomb at Amarna, but the tomb was destroyed soon after Akhenaten's death (and hers, presumably), and there is no certainty that Nefertiti was ever there at all. Or perhaps her body and others in the family were spirited to safety by the faithful and put into unmarked tombs somewhere. Or perhaps, even, she later recanted the Aten religion and merited her own tomb near Thebes (as did young Tutankhamun, who changed his name from Tutankhaten).

Whatever actually happened, Nefertiti's tomb has never been found, and it can only be imagined what might have been buried with her – not only worldly treasure but scrolls and inscriptions that might illuminate a fascinating, important lost moment of Egyptian history.

Some months after telling me that she knew something about Nefertiti's tomb, Omm Sety re-opened the subject. We were again at the Osirion and had been speaking about the royal tomb complex that Akhenaten had built at Amarna. I wondered aloud what Sety might know about the burials of Akhenaten and his family – his six daughters and others.

"Sety should remember quite well," she said, "because he must have been a small boy at the time of Akhenaten's death. But he hates him – not so much from the religious point of view, but for his rotten administration and losing the empire. He hated him so much in his reign that people were not even allowed to mention his name. So far as anyone knows, the tomb of Akhenaten was completely destroyed – *and* the body. There isn't one fragment of his sarcophagus larger than a man's hand. It's absolutely wrecked. They have put it together as far as they can, and it was a very beautiful thing – but, like that golden shrine of Tutankhamun that has the four goddesses protecting the corners, in the sarcophagus of Akhenaten the four women are Nefertiti, not goddesses. Certainly Nefertiti wasn't buried there, because she had a row with him towards the end of his reign."

"But," I interjected, "suppose someone *can* find the tomb of Nefertiti. Since all the tombs of Amarna have been so badly damaged, one can hardly find anything to explain the real cult of Akhenaten. And there is such a great division among Egyptologists about the person of Akhenaten. If the tomb of Nefertiti could be found maybe it could show us something of Akhenaten's thought."

Omm Sety wasn't hopeful on that point. "Some Egyptologists think that at the end of his reign Akhenaten would have been willing to make friends with the priests of Amun, but Nefertiti stopped him. As far as I can see, it was the other way around: I think that Nefertiti saw the handwriting on the wall and said to her husband, 'Don't be a damn fool, make it up with the priests,' and he wouldn't. And with that, she got fed up with him and left him.

"Now, about the tomb of Nefertiti," she continued, sounding a bit hesitant. "I did once ask His Majesty where it was, and he told me. He said, 'Why do you want to know?' I said I would like to have it excavated, and he said, 'No, you must not. We don't want anything more of this family known.' But he *did* tell me where it was, and I can tell you this much: It's in the Valley of the Kings, and it's quite near to the Tutankhamun tomb. But it's in a place where nobody would ever think of looking for it," she laughed. "And apparently it is still intact."

"I'd like you to ask His Majesty for permission to open the tomb," I said, "for the sake of science and history, nothing else. I'm absolutely sure there are other documents written by Akhenaten. If Nefertiti was a loyal follower of her husband, I think we might find something to clarify his philosophy."

"I doubt very much that Nefertiti was faithful to the Aten religion," Omm Sety said, "because if so, she would not have left Akhetaten, and she would *not* be buried in Thebes. If Nefertiti *is* in the Valley of the Kings, as His Majesty says, I would think it's pretty sure that she must, at least on the face of it, have returned to the old religion. On the other hand," she said after a pause, "His Majesty got quite excited when I said I wanted it to be discovered. He didn't want it to be discovered at all. Whether it was just because he hated Akhenaten for losing the empire, I don't know – or if there was something special there that he didn't want known…"

That was more than 30 years ago. Even if Omm Sety or I had told someone in authority about Sety's revelation, no archaeologist would have paid serious attention to such a story – at least publicly. If anyone were to seek a concession to dig for Nefertiti's tomb in the Valley of the Kings it would have to be because of new information that came from more "normal" channels.

For a long time that didn't happen.

And then, in 1998 – for the first time in 75 years – archaeologists were granted permission to search for new tombs in the Valley of the Kings. That year The Amarna Royal Tombs Project (ARPT) began its work, anticipating a number of seasons of exploration and evaluation. Among other things, they were looking for missing members of the Amarna royal family, and early on they unearthed strong evidence of two previously unknown, unopened tombs. Where are they looking? Exactly where Sety said Nefertiti's tomb was to be found: *"in the Valley of the Kings, quite near to the Tutankhamun tomb."*

But why would they be looking there, when most scholars felt that Nefertiti, along with other close family members, would have been buried with her husband in the royal cemetery of faraway Amarna? The answer is a combination of science, practicality and serendipity.

The element of serendipity that started it all can be explained by British Egyptologist Nicholas Reeves, director of ARTP and widely respected authority on the Valley of the Kings. In a 2000 letter to my co-author, Dr. Reeves wrote:

> In 1976, Lambert Dolphin* and his team came to the area for the purpose of testing the accuracy of their sonar equipment on the ground. But first he wanted to test it by taking soundings in Tut's tomb. They took a reading vertically down from Ramesses VI to Tutankhamun, which of course they knew was there. The tomb of Tut showed up in the test, and so they decided to take a reading out from the annex,** which happened to be in the direction of KV56.*** I don't believe Lambert had any personal thoughts about that area before he sonar-ed it. That test produced two "anomalies," the significance of which we are still investigating.

The anomalies were two areas of empty space, which might or might not be new tombs. So why did it take between 1976 and 1998 before anyone investigated? Dr. Reeves offers an explanation: "[T]he general view was that after Tut there was

---

*a geophysicist with the former Stanford Research Institute (now SRI International)

**a part of Tut's tomb

***known as the "Gold Tomb." The notation "KV56" identifies it as a Valley of the Kings tomb.

nothing more to be found. My own feeling is that one or more further Amarna period caches remain to be found – or at least identified. This was obviously a factor in my deciding to take a closer look."

Even *before* Tut there had been those who doubted the usefulness of further exploration in the Valley. In 1912 British archaeologist Harry Burton famously said, "I fear that the Valley of the Tombs is now exhausted."

An ARPT report may help explain why Sety was so sure no one would succeed in finding Nefertiti's tomb:

> The technique of the early explorers was to excavate along the line of the exposed cliff face and through the overlying scree down to the bedrock into which, it was hoped, tombs had been sunk. Several tombs were found in this manner.

> The work of The Amarna Royal Tombs Project, however, reveals that this bedrock at the base of the cliffs is merely a ledge, and that what has been systematically explored to date in the Valley is merely the uppermost of a series of tiers. This is why the tomb of Tutankhamun evaded detection until 1922; it had been cut into the second of these tiers, some distance from the cliffs that previous excavators had been guided by. Unlike the uppermost ledge, this secondary tier has never been systematically explored.*

And there are more tiers beneath that. When Dr. Reeves' team began digging they soon found themselves deep in a pile of ancient debris left over from the digging of Ramesses VI's** tomb next door. Clearing the area and getting down to the earlier layers was not going to be a simple task because every bit

---

*www.valleyofthekings.org
**Ramesses VI lived in the 20th Dynasty, nearly 200 years after Nefertiti.

of that debris needed to be sifted with painstaking care. By the end of the first season of the dig, fragments of gold foil had been uncovered, as well as the foundations of a living area for the workmen who built Ramesses VI's tomb. The foundations blocked any deeper exploration and would have to be thoroughly documented before going any further. Reeves' team of archaeologists and technicians practice state-of-the-art techniques not often found in Egyptian archaeology. If there were untouched tombs to be found, it was going to take time and extreme care every step of the way.

And then one day something fantastic came to light: On a newly cleared rock face could be seen the incised name of *Wennefer*. It couldn't have been more promising news. Wen-nefer was a 20th Dynasty scribe whose name has been found at the entrance to many of the tombs in the Valley of the Kings. As part of his official inventory duties he affixed his name to the outside of each tomb to record its presence.

And now here, halfway down to bedrock, was Wen-nefer's seal – not once, but twice! – indicating the existence of two tombs, apparently undisturbed at the time he set his name next to them. Dr. Reeves believes that Wen-nefer may have been "moving down the escarpment in the course of his official duties, marking the positions of those burials which were known to him from ancient archival sources. That the scribe wrote his name at two as-yet-unexplored points within our concession, where no burials have previously been noted, was intriguing in the extreme. Wen-nefer seemed to suggest that, beneath these Ramesside-period buildings, there might be further surprises in store."*

In a 1999 BBC/Learning Channel documentary about the search, *"Nefertiti: Egypt's Mysterious Queen,"* Prof. John Harris of the University of Copenhagen said, "If we could find Nefertiti buried *as* Nefertiti, that would be the Holy Grail." American Egyptologist James P. Allen added, "The big hope is the documents,

---

*ibid.

the history." The narrator ends the program with, "This ancient mystery is very close to being solved."

What waits behind the priest's seals in a difficult-to-reach location quite close to Tutankhamun's tomb, as Omm Sety described? The signs of an Amarna discovery were so significant that ARTP pressed forward with a growing sense of expectation. A new radar analysis of the area in 2000 had produced even more clear evidence of two unidentified empty chambers,* the second one very deep and almost straight down from Tut's tomb.

And then the next worst thing to a mummy's curse struck the Project: in 2002 an accusation of complicity in antiquities theft was made against Dr. Reeves. The Project's work was immediately suspended pending Dr. Reeves' reinstatement in 2005 and the dismissal of the false claim. But three years' work had been lost.

Meanwhile, Dr. Otto Schaden, Egyptologist with the University of Memphis, had been working on his own dig nearby at the tomb of Amenmesse (KV10). Completely by chance, in February 2006, his excavations stumbled upon a shaft that led to what appeared to be a tomb. Unbeknownst to Dr. Schaden, it was in fact one of the two anomaly chambers that ARTP had identified earlier and had been carefully preparing to approach and open. The discovery by Schaden – given the name KV63 – caused excited headlines all over the world. By July the tomb's contents had been examined: seven beautifully carved wooden coffins containing not mummies but mummification supplies – salts and linens, and numerous storage jars. This was not a royal tomb at all, but a preparation and storage facility for a royal interment close by – an Amarna interment, based on decorative fragments found with the other items.

That leaves open the possibility that ARTP's second radar anomaly is the true royal tomb. According to Dr. Reeves, it is situated in an area that was out of bounds to earlier excava-

*ibid.

tors and it is almost certain to be an undisturbed tomb. "From its location," Dr. Reeves said, "the feature revealed on our radar had the potential not only to be a tomb but to be intact." He continued:

> An intact tomb, whether royal or private, is an excep-
> tionally rare phenomenon in Egypt generally and in
> the Valley of the Kings in particular. The prospect
> of excavating such a find is − or ought to be − a
> daunting one.

> What an intact deposit of this sort has the potential
> to tell us about aspects of ancient Egyptian life, death
> and burial is considerable. Properly handled, such a
> find has the potential to revolutionize, on many lev-
> els, our understanding of the ancient past. In order
> to fully achieve this potential, however, the manner of
> excavation is crucial.*

Before ARTP's work was stopped, it had been proceeding meticulously with its interdisciplinary technical team to preserve the record of layers of the past. But if ARTP is not able to resume its work there, who would excavate and how careful would that excavation be? Would the ancient air and pollen inside the tomb have a chance to be studied, or would the tomb be simply opened wide, as Howard Carter had done with Tut, thereby losing precious information about the past? No doubt archeologists proceed now with much more care and knowledge than those in Carter's time, but care and patience are still often the first casualties in the rush to lay claim to great new discoveries.

Dr. Reeves writes, "If, like the burial of Tutankhamun, the new tomb proved to be hermetically sealed, the excavator would have before him not only a valuable collection of funerary objects

---

*ibid.

but a unique day-in-the-life of ancient Egypt. Air samples, smells, pollen, insects, microbes, dust – an entire ancient environment of inestimable scientific value. The rarest of all possible data, immensely difficult to gather – and in the case of Tutankhamun gone forever when Howard Carter and Lord Carnarvon clumsily broke through the sealed doorway to peer in."*

Unfortunately, the unexpected opening of KV63 happened in such a way that air and pollen samples could not be preserved. KV63 also alerted the world to the possibility of an important royal tomb in the immediate vicinity, since Tut's tomb had also had a mummification chamber next to it.

Fearing that high enthusiasm for opening a major tomb would cause a rush to find it, and a potentially dangerous "hunt and peck" eagerness for quick results, Reeves did something startling: He publicly revealed the location of the second tomb and offered to open his records and share his data, in the interests of assuring that the tomb – which he believes could contain the body of Nefertiti – will be given the highest level of scientific oversight. USA TODAY referred to the contents of the second tomb as "a potential scientific gold-mine."**

Dr. Reeves is currently writing a book titled, *The Lost Tomb of Nefertiti*. He has given the new, so-far-undiscovered tomb the name KV64. And where is KV64? Just a few feet from Tutankhamun's tomb, and at a deeper level than anyone would have thought to search.

And so we have the words and work of 21st century archaeologists addressing the possibility of finding Nefertiti's tomb where Sety said it would be found: *"quite near to the Tutankhamun tomb...in a place where nobody would ever think of looking for it."*

If Nefertiti's tomb *is* brought to light I pray that it will be because of careful, scientific work, and that we will finally learn more about the life and times of Akhenaten and Nefertiti.

---

*ibid.
**usatoday.com online science update, August 14, 2006

And maybe even feast our eyes on artistic treasures to rival the glories of Tutankhamun's. If that comes to pass, perhaps we will be able to say, "Omm Sety and His Majesty knew it all along."

Epilogue

Allegretto finale

One day in the late '70s, I paid Omm Sety an unexpected call. This was shortly after she had asked me to send her two painters to whitewash the outside walls of her bed-sitting room and paint the interior light blue. I found instead that the two men had just finished digging a grave in the small courtyard garden and had lined it with brick and plaster. I discovered Omm Sety down inside, painting the walls of the mud-brick "tomb."

"What in heaven's name are you doing?" I called to her.

"I am preparing myself for my last dream, to be buried in Abydos," she replied matter-of-factly. She had already covered the entire breadth of one wall with a winged disc of the sun.

"Don't you think it is a bit early to do all this?" I asked. "You know that what you are doing is not legal. You cannot be buried except in the cemetery, and not in the middle of occupied houses, among the living."

"But there is a technical difficulty there," she retorted with an edge to her voice. "I cannot be buried in the Coptic cemetery because I am not Christian, and I do not want to outrage dear Father Gregorios. I have no place in the Muslim cemetery because I am considered to be a heretic. So, where can I find a resting place? Have you any suggestions?"

I thought for a moment. "I think you will be more comfortable in the space between the two cemeteries, farther north."

"I'll keep that in mind," she tossed back, "in case the neighbors break their silence and make an official complaint to the health inspector." And she returned to her work. I watched for a while, bemused by the spectacle before me. The entrance to her tomb faced west, to Pega-the-Gap, which did not surprise me.

Some time later, after Omm Sety had decorated her tomb to her satisfaction, complete with inscriptions on the walls enumerating the offerings of food for the deceased, the local authorities learned of her project and ordered the tomb filled in. I had immense difficulty convincing her to put back all the earth and restore the ground to its original state, but eventually Omm Sety relented. While the workers shoveled dirt, a delegation of cats stood watch, headed by her favorite, Hassouna, an uncouth, ugly tomcat.

Undaunted by this setback, she asked me to assure that she would be buried as near to Sety's temple as possible, preferably between the Sety and Ramesses temples. She asked me to recite for her burial the *Hetep-Di-Nesout*, the ancient formula in which the deceased asks Osiris to grant her a beautiful burial with many offerings.

At that time we were working on a project dear to both our hearts, our book, *Abydos: Holy City of Ancient Egypt*. It would be illustrated with photographs I had taken using the ancient mirror method of capturing the light inside the Sety Temple and the Osirion. By the beginning of 1980 we were well along with the writing and the only thing that remained was for Omm Sety to compose the captions for the photographs, which numbered well over 100.

On January 16, 1980, I was with her when her friends at Chicago House in Luxor threw her a party to celebrate her 76th birthday.

A month later on February 19th, I awakened with a premonition that something unwelcome was about to happen. I was away from home on a consulting job with a University of Chicago archaeological team on the Red Sea, at the ancient trading port of Qusair. I was there to, among other things,

At Chicago House. Omm Sety with Dr. Labib Habashi, dean of Egyptian archaeologists. Here they are celebrating her birthday in Luxor. Born the same year, they were close friends who collaborated frequently on scientific issues. He always made a point of getting in touch with her whenever he came to Luxor for research and he generously contributed to the building of her last home in Abydos. (Hanny el Zeini)

help the team explore some of the ancient desert caravan trails that connected the old port to the cities on the Nile. That day, I received a message from the governor of the State of Kena, informing me that I was urgently needed at the Baliana Government Hospital. Something had happened to Omm Sety.

My driver, who was an expert in desert travel, knew what to do when I told him to "drive like hell." At the end of the five-hour, 400-kilometer ride to the hospital I found Omm Sety lying in her bed looking ten years older than when I had last seen her just a few weeks earlier. She had fallen and fractured her right femur. It was evident that she was trying hard to hide the excruciating pain. When she saw me she broke down and cried.

"Dr. Hani, please take me home. I can't stand this place anymore," she implored. Her physician was reluctant to let her leave, as was I. She would need hospital care for several weeks. Omm Sety was not a good patient. She wanted to get back to her uncouth band of cats.

When the time came that she could leave the hospital, I accompanied her back to her modest home in the village where she faced a noisy welcome from the cats, who jumped up on her to be kissed one by one. The next wave of welcomes was from the women of the village, dressed in long black galabeyas and crowding the door to come inside. I kissed Omm Sety goodbye and ordered her to take care of herself. I worried, as always, about her, but I was also sure that the women of the village for whom she had done so many favors would never leave her side. I stepped outside to let the women flow into the tiny room. Before I turned to go, I watched them kiss Omm Sety on both cheeks and say, *"Hamdillah Ala Salama,"* thank the Good Lord for your safe return.

The next day, on my way back to the Red Sea port once more, I passed by Abydos to bid Omm Sety a quick recovery. With the aid of crutches she was beginning to walk again. As I left her room I noticed four sets of cat eyes just peeping out from underneath the bedclothes. I have to admit that I never had any special love for cats, except for kittens. I have always considered cats to be born thieves, never obedient, and extremely self-indulgent. But as I witnessed their unwavering loyalty to my friend, I began to reconsider my old prejudice and take a softer attitude.

Shortly after finishing up with the Qusair Port expedition, I embarked on two missions to Somalia and Maghreb to inspect factories. On my return six months later I found a big package of photos waiting for me. Omm Sety had been busy with our Abydos book, arranging the pictures chronologically with extensive captions. We spent time together in November doing the final revisions. When we sent the book off to our publisher it was with a sense of real accomplishment. Omm Sety was still suffering terribly from the pain in her hip. I considered the book to be a testament to her determination.

I was quite concerned about what the future would bring for my dear, implacable old friend, yet since our last meeting in November I had been fully taken up with my business and consulting work and could not to go to Abydos to see her. The rest of Omm Sety's story had to be told to me by others.

Later that November, she went to the temple for the first time since her fall – with the gentle assistance of a film team from the BBC who were making a documentary about her life in Egypt.

A few months later, in mid-March 1981, producer Miriam Birch came to Abydos to complete a documentary for *National Geographic* on the life and times of Ramesses II, "Egypt: Quest for Eternity." One of the highlights of the documentary was an interview segment with Omm Sety, who was presented as a scholarly Egyptologist. The film team was thoughtful enough to bring her a walker. This would be the last time she ever went to the temple. The entire team of Chicago House was there too, and they used the occasion to wish Omm Sety a belated happy birthday, which they must have known was really a farewell to a beloved compatriot. On April 17 the National Geographic team returned to shoot a final day with Omm Sety. These were the last words she ever recorded.

She died 48 hours later and was buried soon after, before I could be notified. When I arrived in Abydos I found her modest tomb outside the Coptic cemetery, midway between the Sety and Ramesses temples. The villagers had decided on a place

A few days before her death in April 1981, Omm Sety spent time chatting with Egyptologist Ray Johnson at her tiny mud-brick house (which she named Heartsease-in-Abydos, the same name as Sety's small palace adjacent to the temple). Dr. Johnson said she was perfectly alert, and her usual self in spite of much pain from her broken hip. Ray Johnson is now Field Director at Chicago House in Luxor. (Hanny el Zeini)

that is frequently visited by tourists and Egyptologists. It can be seen on the left side of the road leading to the Ramesses temple – a simple, undecorated resting-place for a woman who had loved Egypt.

I think she must have known that she was about to join His Majesty, because her last visitor, just a day or two before her death, was Gamal el Abboudi, one of Egypt's finest tourist guides. She had handed him her unfinished diary for 1981 and told him to be sure that I received it. When I read her last entries I could see the increasing difficulty of each day. April 10: "Gave Ankhsi and Ahmes away [two of her favorite cats]. Hope they will be happy." April 11: "Woke up with a bad cold and sore throat. Feeling very ill." April 16: "Feel very bad. Hope to get my voice back before the TV people come tomorrow." April 17: "Miriam and the TV people came early. Put in a hard day work with them. Leg now aches like Hell, but I enjoyed their company."

On April 21 Omm Sety passed away in her sleep. The exact time of her death was never known. A group of tourists who knew her well knocked at the entrance door of her little garden but got no response. Then someone said, "Listen – the cats are crying!" They forced open the door to her garden and to her bedroom.

The scene inside was poignant. At least 20 cats were in the room, half of them on the bed with her body and the rest on the floor surrounding her bed. And indeed, they were crying. Her permanent guest cats were about seven, but the number of casual visitors could never be known. Omm Sety cared for even the filthiest vagabonds of the village, offering food and drink to any and all. My mental image of that scene spoke volumes about Omm Sety's relationship with the animal kingdom, and about simple devotion.

acceptance

I have frequently spoken about my work at the Sugar Company and the difficulties I experienced, especially in those early years when crises on the international level created enormous problems for our newly nationalized industry. Sometimes, when I was tired and generally fed-up with the situation around me, I sought solace in the desert. One day, thinking to go see my friend Omm Sety, I set out in a big, clumsy Russian-made Jeep with my half-mad driver, but instead of taking the civilized paved road, we aimed the car in the direction of the ancient camel caravan track west of the Nag-Hamadi factory, then out towards the village of Farshut, a principal camel market. To avoid scaring those untamed beasts we drove along west of their track, a bumpy, bone-jarring drive, until Abydos appeared in the far distance up ahead. This was very different from the approach one usually takes, but that day I badly needed the desert.

My driver skillfully navigated among the dunes and arrived in this most unlikely way at Abydos. I could discern the shape of Omm Sety sitting on the verandah of the Antiquities Department's rest house. She looked very happy to see us.

"What a blessing from Lady Isis to have such a pleasant surprise!" she exclaimed. "But why did you chose this abominable route? It stinks of camel smell all the way."

I had brought with me a thermos of tea, some biscuits and marmalade sandwiches. We ate in companionable silence, with the desert air moving gently around us. After a while, Omm Sety said in a low voice, "How lovely it would be if His Majesty could find time and come now. How much I want you to see him. You will be pleased."

She had said things like that before and I had tossed them off, yet there was something different about today. We passed a few more minutes in complete silence. Then Omm Sety looked at me and quite earnestly said, "I have made several allusions to this matter, but you have never shown any interest, so I preferred to keep my mouth shut. I once asked His Majesty if I could tell you our story. He said to me, 'If you trust him you can tell him our story.' Well, I do, and I would like to."

"And I would like to hear it," I said, feeling in that moment that an unspoken wall standing between Omm Sety and me had suddenly collapsed.

When Omm Sety decided to tell me her real story I was at last prepared to listen and believe. I came to be convinced that she truly did live in two different worlds separated by more than 3000 years, and that she could cross from one world to the other with ease and clarity. She made no point of it; it simply was.

In most ways our friendship was not exotic at all. We shared our love of Egypt and good books and the great master-works of classical music. When I bought a medium-size German Telefunken Radio for her in 1963 she was as happy and joyous as a kid receiving his first football. After a long day spent photo-graphing the temple or working on our Abydos book it was sim-ply heavenly to sit together on the stone stairs leading into the Osirion and give ourselves up to Beethoven's Pastoral Symphony, that poetic ode to nature's moods. I always felt it was an apt metaphor for Omm Sety's life. The fifth and final movement, the Allegretto, comes after the storm and troubles, bringing a promise of joyful awakening to a glorious new day.

adieu

I have only the deepest respect for the love that existed, and no doubt still exists, between Omm Sety and the king. I found it tender, fierce, beautiful and unwavering. There is one more entry from Omm Sety's diaries that belongs in this place at the end of our book. It needs no commentary on my part:

August 2, 1972
True to his promise H.M. came again last night, and we spent together one of the nicest of times. We took chairs into the garden, and I had the idea to arrange them like a Victorian love nest, one chair having its back to the north and one to the

south, but both close together side by side. This arrangement is very convenient for talking (also for kissing!) When we had finished our preliminary kisses etc., H.M. leaned back in his chair and said, "It is very good here, Little One. See, we have the Royal Fan-bearers to attend us!" and he pointed up to the palms, which were waving gently in a breeze, and the whole place was full of moonlight.

Presently he sighed and said, "Ah, Bentreshy, how many weary years have passed since that night when we sat together in the moonlight in the garden of the House-of-Men-Maat-Ra and I first knew of my love for you! Now again we sit in a moonlit garden in Abydos and our love is unchanged. Is it not strange that great monuments of imperishable stone have completely vanished, and yet our love remains unchanged?"

I replied, "Not only monuments, but great empires have risen and fallen, never to rise again, since we first knew of our love." I told him about the poetess Sappho of Lesbos, and the lines she wrote:

> *Love is so frail a thing: a look, a word may kill.*
> *O lovers, have a care how you do deal with love.*
> *Love is so strong a thing:*
> *When it is welded fast with the unflinching Truth,*
> *even the gods must yield.*

He liked it and asked for more. I recited all of the poems of Sappho that I could remember, and told him how in the end she jumped into the sea because a man she loved did not return her love. He said, "Poor woman, she deserved a better thing than that!"

He pulled me sideways towards him, with his arms around me. We stayed like that, quite quiet and satisfied. Later, he sighed contentedly, "I thank the gods for this moment in time,

Bentreshy. I dare to hope that this peacefulness is a sign that we are forgiven. Are you also happy, Little One?"

"More than happy," I said. We kept silence again, and I must have fallen asleep in his arms. I vaguely remember him carrying me to bed and covering me up and kissing me forever...

Looking back on my own life, I don't think I have ever known a more vivid personality than Omm Sety's, or a more passionate, honest heart. She had an incredible intellect and a disarming sense of humor. She was Dorothy Eady and Bulbul and Omm Sety. But she was also Bentreshyt, the beloved of Sety, and I believed her.

I did not recite the *Hetep-Di-Nesout* at her burial because I was not there, but I have done the other thing that she asked of me that day when she was preparing her tomb: She asked me to not let her name be forgotten. ▲

(Omm Sety, my dear friend, I have no idea how things are going in Amenti, but I thought you would like to present this poem to whom your heart knows best.)

To the Master

As a swimmer is borne onrushing
On the whitening crest of a wave,
Flying a-pace through the surging sea
Where the pounding breakers ceaseless rave
On the shelving beach;

So do I ride on the crest of Love,
Helplessly driven, I know not where,
On the wild, tumbled ocean of Life;
I know not whither; I hardly dare
To wonder or guess.

Will Love's wave bear me 'neath sunny skies,
Through sparkling water, through singing wind,
And lay me gently on rapture's beach
Where the joys of Heaven are mine to find
In your arm's strong clasp?

Will Love's wave sweep me through darkling storm,
Through biting wind and through stinging spray,
To bitter death on the cruel rocks
Like jagged spears that in ambush lay
For the reckless ones?

O Lord Beloved, if it be my fate
To sink in the waters dark and cold,
Wilt thou ever guess I loved but thee;
Wilt thou learn the truth my lips ne'er told,
Hear the song unsung?

by Dorothy Eady, Cairo, 1949

Appendix

Osirion and Temple of Sety I at Abydos

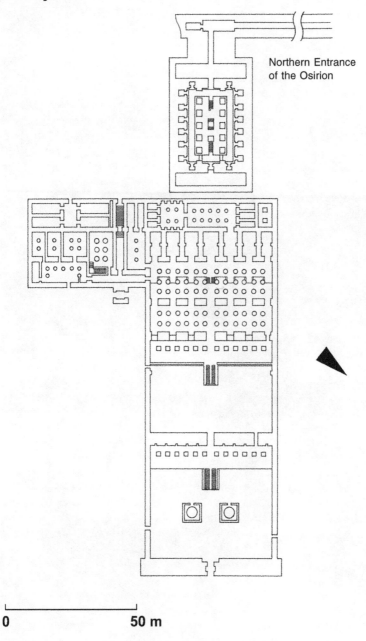

Northern Entrance of the Osirion

0   50 m

Temple of Sety I at Abydos

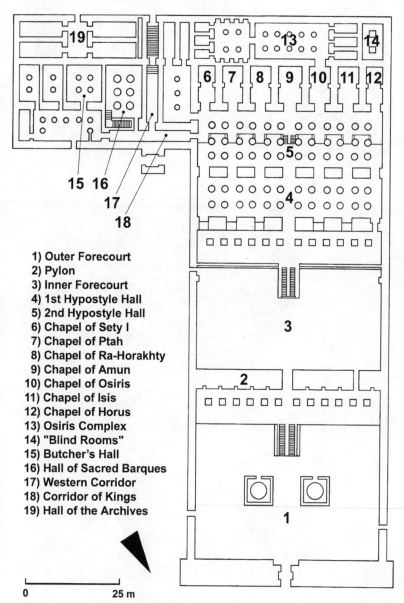

19

13

14

6 7 8 9 10 11 12

5

4

15 16

17

18

1) Outer Forecourt
2) Pylon
3) Inner Forecourt
4) 1st Hypostyle Hall
5) 2nd Hypostyle Hall
6) Chapel of Sety I
7) Chapel of Ptah
8) Chapel of Ra-Horakhty
9) Chapel of Amun
10) Chapel of Osiris
11) Chapel of Isis
12) Chapel of Horus
13) Osiris Complex
14) "Blind Rooms"
15) Butcher's Hall
16) Hall of Sacred Barques
17) Western Corridor
18) Corridor of Kings
19) Hall of the Archives

3

2

1

0   25 m

Osirion

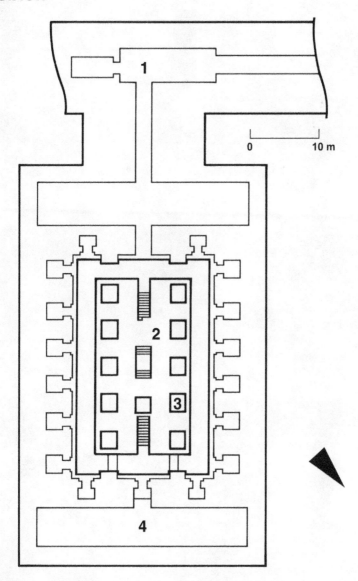

1) **Entrance Passage**
2) **The Great Hall**
3) **Seventeen small chambers or "cells" surround the Great Hall.**
4) **Sarcophagus Room (Eastern Transverse Hall)**

The Egyptian Dynasties

There are many ways of computing the dynasties and individual reigns, especially before the New Kingdom. Great gaps remain in our knowledge. This dynastic list draws from several authoritative sources and is not itself in any way the last word.

(Names mentioned in the text are shown in **bold**. All dates are BC.)

Archaic Period, Early Dynastic Period: circa 3150 – 2649
- Dynasty "0": circa 3150 – 3050; King Scorpion and Narmer
- 1st Dynasty: circa 3050 – 2890; includes the legendary **Menes, Aha, and Djer**
- 2nd Dynasty: circa 2890 – 2649; 5 kings, including **Khasekhemwy**

Old Kingdom (the Pyramid Age): circa 2649 – 2150
- 3rd Dynasty: circa 2649 – 257 5; 5 kings, including Zoser
  Zoser circa 2630 – 2611 (Step Pyramid at Saqqara)
- 4th Dynasty: 2575 – 2465
  Sneferu 2575 – 2551 (Pyramids at Dhashur and Meidum)
  Khufu (Cheops) 2551 – 2528 (The Great Pyramid)
  Djedefre 2528 – 2520
  Khafra (Chephren) 2520 – 2494
  Men-kau-Ra (Mycerinus) 2490 – 2472
  Shepses-ka-ef 2472 – 2467
- 5th Dynasty: circa 2465 – 2325; 9 kings; the last is Unas
  Unas circa 2355 – 2325 (pyramid at Saqqara; Pyramid Texts)
- 6th Dynasty: circa 2325 – 2150; 5 kings

First Intermediate Period: 2134 – 2040 (a time of disorganization)

- 7th – 10th Dynasties
  Khati (in latter part of the period)
  Mentuhotep I (last king; Thebes is new political center of Egypt)

Middle Kingdom: circa 2040 – 1783

- 11th Dynasty: 2040 – 1991
- 12th Dynasty: 1991 – 1783; a period of artistic heights and prosperity

Second Intermediate Period: 1783 – 1550 (a time of confusion and invasion)

- 13th – 17th Dynasties; the Hyksos conquer Egypt circa 1663, later overthrown

The New Kingdom: 1550 – 1070 (A time of empire building, prosperity, high art)

- 18th Dynasty: 1550 – 1307
  Ahmose   1550 – 1525
  Amenhotep I   1525 – 1504
  Thutmose I   1504 – 1492
  Thutmose II   1492 – 1479
  Thutmose III   1479 – 1425
  Hatshepsut   1473 – 1458 (as king and queen)
  Amenhotep II   1427 – 1401
  Thutmose IV   1401 – 1391
  Amenhotep III   1391 – 1353
  Akhenaten (Amenhotep IV)   1353 – 1335 (and Nefertiti)
  Smenkhara   1335 – 1333
  Tutankhamun   1333 – 1323
  Ay   1323 – 1319
  Horemheb   1319 – 1307

- 19th Dynasty: 1307 − 1196
    Ramesses I 1307 − 1306
    Sety I 1306 − 1290
    Ramesses II 1290 − 1224
    Merneptah 1224 − 1214
    Sety II 1214 − 1204
    Amenmesse 1202 − 1199
    Siptah 1204 − 1198
    Twosret 1197 − 1196 (ruling queen)

- 20th Dynasty: 1196 − 1070; 10 kings, including Ramesses III
    − XI

Third Intermediate Period: 1070 − 712
- 23rd − 25th Dynasties of Nubian kings ruling from several
    capitals

Late Kingdom: 712 − 332
- 25th − 30th Dynasties of Nubian, Greek and Persian rulers;
    then a return to Egyptian rule in the 30th Dynasty.
    Nectanebo II is the last of the Egyptian rulers of Egypt
    until the mid-20th century of the modern era.

Glossary

Ab: the heart or conscience; weighed against the feather of truth at judgment

Abdu: ancient name for Abydos

Akh: the shining, radiant, spiritualized form symbolized by the sacred ibis

Amenti: the realm of the dead

Architrave: a horizontal stone beam that rests atop two pillars or across a doorway

Ba: the animating spirit that gives life to the body; often shown as a human-headed bird hovering over the mummy

Black Land: the Egypt of the Nile (desert Egypt was called the Red Land)

Bulbul (Arabic): nightingale

Cenotaph: a ritual, symbolic tomb meant to receive offerings, but not to contain the body of the deceased; often erected at holy places like Abydos

Ghaffir (Arabic): watchman

Gods and Goddesses:

Osiris: god of the underworld, judge of the dead

Isis: sister-wife of Osiris, lady of magic, healing, compassion

Horus: son of Osiris and Isis, champion of good on earth

Nephthys: protectress; sister and companion of Isis, wife of Set

Set: the Great of Strength, god of the desert, brother of Osiris; represents the dark side of life, the opposing energies

Fellaheen: the people of the countryside and villages

Heka: magic

Heliopolis: ancient center of the worship of Ra (near modern Cairo)

Ka: the life force of the individual ego

Kesma (Arabic): Fate

Khaibet: the ghostly, lower form that still has earthly appetites

Khat: the physical, mortal body

Khawagaya (Arabic): European woman

Khem: Egypt

Men-Maat-Ra: Sety I

Men Nefer (Memphis): capital city of the early dynasties; also called "The White Wall" – near Saqqara and the Pyramids of Giza

Neteru: the gods (plural of *neter*)

Peak-of-the-West: the pyramid-shaped mountain above the Valley of the Kings; symbolically similar to Pega-the Gap at Abydos

Pega: (Pega-the-Gap) gateway to the land of the dead; the notched promontory at Abydos where the sunboat of Ra collects the souls of the dead for their journey to the underworld

Per-Ankh: the House of Life, a school for scribes associated with the major temples

Per-Medjat: the Hall of Records, containing the documents and chronicles of history

Ren: the name, which is magical and essential to perpetuating the memory (and thus the immortal existence) of the deceased

Sahu: the mummified, eternal body

Sekhem: vital force of the body

Shay: Fate

Sia: wisdom

Temenos: the wall enclosing the sacred precincts of a temple or shrine

Valley of the Kings: New Kingdom tomb area of ancient Thebes

Wasit: ancient Thebes, modern Luxor

Acknowledgments

We wish to extend our special thanks to two people who were essential to the creation of our book: to Paul Kelly, publisher of St. Lynn's Press, for believing in *Omm Sety's Egypt* and guiding it through its birth pangs with such great care and respect; and to Abby Dees, whose keen editor's eye and sensitivity to the story added immeasurably to the final outcome.

from Hanny el Zeini

For the final stages of this book I called on the assistance and good will of a number of people, many of them members of my extended family. For photography and computer work I am most grateful to Amr Hanafi, my daughter Randa el Zeini, Mohamed Wahby, Mohamed Khalifa and his wife Basma.

In the generation of grandchildren I want to thank Ahmed El Borollossy. To Randa El Borollossy I owe a very special debt. Randa undertook the impossible task of rearranging the awful mess of drafts and pictures, and with great efficiency and positive attitude handled the flood of e-mails that at times threatened to overwhelm me. I shall not forget her remarkable loyalty.

The photographs of the interior of the Sety Temple and the Osirion are only a few of thousands that I have taken of those two great monuments. Over the years, I have had an excellent team to help me with the task: my wife, Dr. Gowhara Sabry, and our daughter Zeinab (Kotkot), who made the long hours of hard work go smoothly. Together, Kotkot and I developed the technique of using mirrors and aluminum-framed reflectors to permit photography under seemingly impossible interior lighting conditions.

I want to thank my friend Jonathan Cott for giving me *Selected Poems*, written by Omm Sety. This was one of the most welcome surprises during the writing of this book. In our 25 years as friends, I never knew that Omm Sety was such a talented and sensitive poet. And finally, in spite of our occasional skirmishes, it was a real pleasure to have such a patient, creative and tolerant co-author and friend as Catherine.

from Catherine Dees

I am grateful beyond words to Hanny el Zeini, for giving me the opportunity to enter the life of one of the most amazing women I have ever known. He provided me with a treasure of material – both his own and Omm Sety's. I thank Gowhara for her kind and gracious hospitality on my visits to Egypt, and the two Randas (bless you both) who kept the process humming on the Cairo end of things while I worked on the manuscript in California. E-mail was a godsend for our long distance collaboration

I must also thank Dr. Nicholas Reeves, director of the Amarna Royal Tombs Project, for his willingness to answer the questions I had concerning his work in the Valley of the Kings; and Stephan Schwartz, director of research at the Rhine Institute, for sharing with me his personal thoughts about Omm Sety. Thanks to John Anthony West for his always-provocative observations about ancient Egypt and "the way it was." I am extra-grateful to Mark Stone for creating the map of Egypt and the temple plans (and the ancient symbols) under a looming publishing deadline. And I want to thank my wonderful writers group, who were fascinated by Omm Sety's story from the beginning and generously offered their constructive thoughts.

To my eternally supportive family (you know who you are), my deepest love and appreciation for always, in every way, going above and beyond.

About the Authors

Hanny el Zeini is the retired Director-General of the Egyptian Sugar Company, one of the largest such industries in the world. Although educated as a chemist, he was always a keen student of literature, languages and the long stream of human history. His love of Egypt runs deep, as does his knowledge of its archaeological sites. Over the years, he has acted as consultant-advisor for a number of archaeological projects, which at different times involved diving in the Red Sea for ancient ships and trekking into the great deserts of Egypt, tracing for the origins of the Egyptian people. An innovative photographer, Dr. el Zeini uses a mirrored light technique to capture the elusive moods inside some of Egypt's most beautiful monuments. His photographs illustrate the comprehensive study of Abydos that he and Omm Sety wrote together, *Abydos: Holy City of Ancient Egypt*. Dr. el Zeini lives with his wife, Gowhara, in the Cairo suburb of Maadi, where he devotes himself to investigating and writing about the unsolved chapters of Egyptian history.

Catherine Dees is a California writer and editor with an abiding love for Egypt and its brilliant, still-unfolding legacy. Two of her lifelong interests come together in the story of Omm Sety: the enigma of human consciousness, and the lost history and wisdom of the ancient world. Catherine was co-producer of the exhibit, *Continuum: the Immortality Principle*, and historian for The Alexandria Project, a search for the tomb of Alexander the Great and the lost Alexandrian Library. She is currently developing an exhibit that explores the human capacity for compassion. Catherine is a member of the American Research Center in Egypt and the Egyptian Exploration Organization, and is a sponsor of the Amarna Royal Tombs Project in the Valley of the Kings.